THEY'RE GOING
TO KILL
MY SON

THEY'RE GOING TO KILL MY SON

Shirley Dicks

NEW HORIZON PRESS
Far Hills, New Jersey

Library of Congress Catalog Card Number: 92-060563

Dicks, Shirley
  They're Going to Kill My Son

ISBN: 0-88282-112-1
New Horizon Press

1996   1995   1994   1993   1992   /   5   4   3   2   1
Manufactured in the U.S.A.

"But now lying between the two guns, as nipped in the vise of fate, Billy's agony, mainly proceeding from a generous young heart's virgin experience of the diabolical incarnate and effective in some men—the tension of that agony was over now."

—Herman Melville

BILLY BUDD

For my son, Jeff Dicks
and my loving father, Ernest Mathews

ACKNOWLEDGMENTS

I would like to thank my mother for her love and unending support. My daughters, Tina and Laurie, and my youngest son, Trevor, for all the love and devotion they gave me throughout the years. I would like to thank my sister, Brenda, my brothers, Mike, David and Roger, who stood behind me no matter what I did and continued to love me. To my granddaughter, Maria, for all her love to her daddy and me that has kept me strong through the years. Also, I would like to thank Gary Cone of Tennessee's death row for his information about Jeff and life on the row. I would like to thank other men of Tennessee's death row who have helped me by providing an inside glance into their daily lives, but prefer to be left nameless. And so many thanks for the support and friendships I have made here in Tennessee, both on the outside and with the men on death row.

And most especially thanks to Elaine Neel, who has been my best friend the past few years, who helped edit this book, and is always there when I need a friend.

AUTHOR'S NOTE

These are my actual experiences. The personalities, events, actions, and conversations portrayed within the story have been reconstructed from memory and notes kept. In addition, I have used court transcripts, letters, personal papers, and the memories of participants. In an effort to safeguard the privacy of certain individuals, I have changed their names and, in some cases, altered otherwise identifying characteristics and chronology. Events involving the characters happened as described; only minor details have been altered.

PROLOGUE

"Open up." They heard Chief's thunderous voice through the thick oak door. Jeff stood up and began walking toward it. He had known Chief, whose real name was Donald Strouth, and who claimed among other dubious things that his father, a full-blooded Apache, had given him the nickname, for only a few weeks. Nevertheless, helping him out with food and a place to sleep had become a habit. It was a habit of which Jeff's fiancée, who had been sitting beside him at the worn kitchen table sipping early morning coffee, didn't approve.

"I wish he'd hang out somewhere else," Cindy said, her piquant face frowning. "He's not like the other stray people and animals you're always picking up. He scares me."

"Shush," Jeff, who had almost reached the door, called back. "He'll hear you."

The pounding began again.

Jeff reached his hand out to turn the door knob, and as he did, Chief, who had obviously been heaving his shoulder against the door, crashed into the room.

"What's the matter, you playin' hide and seek with me?" Chief said, grabbing Jeff in a half-bear, half-choke hold. "I thought you said we were friends."

"We are, we are," Jeff sputtered.

"Well then," Chief replied, and his ice blue eyes pierced Jeff, cutting through him like a knife. "Open the door when I tell you." Abruptly he let Jeff go, and the boy, caught off balance, tumbled back. Chief caught him by the wrist.

"Here, let me help you, man."

Chief's voice softened, "Didn't hurt you, did I?"

"It's okay," Jeff said, flashing that warm lopsided grin that his mother and women in general loved. He moved away, walking toward Cindy, who was still seated at the tiny table.

Chief flopped on the faded chintz couch.

"What are you doing today?"

"Looking for a job, what else," Jeff sighed. "It's tough finding something when you're eighteen and haven't much experience."

He glanced at Cindy and she smiled back. "But we don't want my mom supporting us forever. Cindy and I want to make it on our own." Shy, embarrassed that he had revealed more than he wanted to, Jeff turned back to Chief. "What are you going to do?"

Chief lit a cigarette and blew a chain of smoke rings in the air.

"Pretty good, huh? How about applause?" he said, making a half bow from his reclining position. Then he paused, his upper torso in mid-air. "Maybe I'll just go out and rob someone," a slight smile flickered at the corners of his mouth, "or maybe I'll do something worse." He stubbed out the cigarette on the scarred coffee table.

Jeff cut him off. "Why do you talk stupid like that, Chief? You know you don't mean it."

"I don't," Chief said softly, brushing his stringy black hair from his eyes with long tapered fingers.

"No, you don't. It's just a lot of talk like always. You're probably just hungry again." Jeff said frowning. "You always talk dumb like that when you don't have no food in your belly. How long has it been since you had something to eat?"

Chief shrugged. "I don't know, I don't remember."

Jeff nodded knowingly, "See, what did I tell you. Now you come over here and sit beside me." He patted the empty seat next to him. "Cindy's gonna fix you something. Aren't you, honey? Then you'll feel better."

Cindy grimaced, but she rose from her chair dutifully, went over to the tiny fridge, pulled out a carton of eggs, some sugar, cured ham, and butter. Walking over to the cast iron stove she grabbed a skillet, popped it on a burner and began cooking some breakfast for Chief. As soon as she had put the food in front of Chief, he wolfed it down.

"Thanks," he said, acknowledging Cindy's presence for the first time.

She nodded but was silent.

He turned to Jeff. "How 'bout going for a ride? Sharon," he gestured in Jeff's direction, "my girlfriend, loaned me her car while she's at work. We don't have to give it back until she needs to be picked up."

Jeff started to shake his head no.

But Chief began to plead. "Please, I really need company today bad."

"Alright," Jeff said slowly.

The two men left the apartment, went outside and began walking down the street. Suddenly, Chief started talking about robbing someone again. "You known that second-hand clothing store around the corner? It would be easy. There's only one old man in there. We could run in, grab the money, and run back out before the old man knows what's happened."

"Chief, you're talking stupid again." Jeff shook his head. "This is like all those stories you tell of being in the Mafia and making big hits. It don't amount to a hill of beans. Anyway, I don't want to get involved in any robbery with you or anyone else. And as far as the old man's store goes, I've sold some clothes in there. That old guy only had a few dollars. You want to rob someone and go to jail to get that?"

Turning the corner, Chief stopped in front of the store and peered in. "Hey," he called to Jeff, who was already a few paces ahead.

"Now what?" Jeff said.

Chief caught up with him. "There are too many people in there now anyway."

"Yeah, right," Jeff said, and could not help smiling as they walked back to the apartment and Chief talked non-stop of other things. By the time they got upstairs Jeff noted happily that Chief seemed to have forgotten all about robbing anyone, just as he usually forgot the other nutty things he sometimes said.

They sat around, shooting the breeze for a while, and then, when Cindy left, Chief turned to Jeff. "Hey, let's go for a ride," he said. "Come on, put on that army coat I gave you. It's cold and we'll have to walk a bit. I had to park a few blocks away. Let's go right now, alright?"

Jeff, glad that Chief's bad mood had dissipated, agreed. It was a fateful decision.

When they reached the car, Chief tossed Jeff the keys. "You drive, amigo," he said smiling.

As soon as the car started, Chief began complaining. "Look at my clothes, they're threadbare. No wonder Cindy keeps looking at me so funny. I look like a bum."

Jeff sighed, "We can go to the Salvation Army and get you some food and clothes, maybe even some money to tide you over."

Chief's voice rose, "I may look like a bum, but I ain't no beggar."

Abruptly Chief's angry tirade passed. "Heck, maybe I will take your advice, Jeff," he said. Then he turned and stared out the window. "We'll both get dressed in Salvation Army duds and party." A few minutes later he called out, "Stop the car." It wasn't until Chief hopped out that Jeff noticed they were only a few feet from the old man's store. Even so, he was sure this was another of Chief's practical jokes. Chief was going to walk in the store, stay there a few minutes, and then walk out mugging and laughing that it had all been a joke. Jeff was getting tired of Chief's pranks. He was of a mind to tell him so as soon as this one ended.

Jeff waited there double parked for a long time. People walked up and down the street, in and out of the stores. An old man in a pickup truck stopped and looked hard at him, then back up the street. Jeff craned his neck to stare in that same direction. His heart stopped. There was Chief, running toward the car, his arms full of clothing. "Oh my God," Jeff said when Chief swung open the car door. "Are you crazy?" He started up the car, ready to leave the place, to get away from Chief.

"You'd better drive around to the alley, boy," Chief said, getting in. His voice had a steel edge to it. "Drop me off near the back door and wait."

More frightened than he'd ever been in his life, Jeff obeyed.

Pulling up the car where Chief indicated, Jeff watched wide-eyed while Chief got out. He strained his ears to listen as Chief walked through the back door into the store. There was nothing, no sound, only dead silence.

Some time passed.

"Chief must have tied the old man up," Jeff muttered to himself. "What have I gotten myself into?"

Just at that moment Chief came running out the door and jumped into the car. "Move," he ordered. Paralyzed, Jeff stared at him. Chief had a rock in his hand; he threw it out the window. Then Jeff noticed the blood splattered on the bottom of Chief's jeans.

"What's that?" he pointed to the stains.

"I had to hurt the old man," Chief said matter-of-factly. "Now, you'd better get us out of here and back to the apartment to grab a few things."

Jeff just sat there.

"Are you deaf? Get going."

Jeff couldn't speak. Words froze in his throat. Mechanically, he reached over and turned the key in the ignition.

Somehow he drove. Cindy was waiting inside the apartment. As soon as she saw Jeff's face she knew something was wrong.

"What happened?"

Jeff just shook his head and began frantically gathering up some things. Cindy followed him downstairs to the car and got in. Immediately she noticed the blood on Chief's hands.

"What have you done?" She stared at Chief.

"I had to hurt an old man in a robbery," he said quietly.

She looked over at Jeff. "Jeff wouldn't hurt anyone."

Jeff didn't say a word. He just sat in the driver's seat, looking like he was in shock.

"Drive me to Johnson City," Chief demanded.

Jeff drove as if his life depended on it.

Chief directed them to a used car lot he knew. While Jeff and Cindy sat in Chief's girlfriend's car, Chief bought an old white Cougar. Then he walked back to Sharon's car.

"You want some of this money?" he asked Jeff.

Jeff shook his head. "We don't want any part of it. I just wanted to find a room in some motel so I can call my mom."

"Okay, sonny boy," Chief said. A slight smile played at the corners of his mouth. "But we have to give Sharon's car back first. Follow me."

They drove to Elizabethton where Sharon was at work. Chief called to her and she came out.

As Sharon walked over to the Cougar, she yelled at Chief. "Where did you get this car? This morning you didn't have the money to buy a pack of cigarettes. And why are Jeff and Cindy sitting in my car?" She waited for Chief's answer. He got out of the car, pulled her to him and began to kiss her. She pulled away. "No, Chief, not now. Now I want answers."

"Oh, all right. If you must know, I did what I know how to best. I robbed an old man and bought this car. Are you satisfied?" Chief tried to kiss Sharon again, but she pulled back.

Noticing the blood on his jeans for the first time, she cried out, "Tell me you didn't hurt anyone! Where did the blood come from?"

"I had to quiet the old man."

"What part did Jeff have in it?" she asked Chief.

"Are you stupid? He chickened out and waited in the car. He didn't believe I was going to do that. You should have seen his face when I told him I hurt the old guy. It was comical."

Sharon walked away, yelling at Chief. "Go away and don't ever come back here again!"

"Go ahead," Chief waved her off angrily.

"Come on, Jeff, you two get in this car; let's go to a motel. I can't believe you all are making such a big deal out of this."

They drove to a ramshackle motel and took a room. As soon as they were safely inside, Jeff flipped on the T.V. to the news. "What are you doing?" Chief asked. "The news is always rotten."

"I want to know how badly the old guy was hurt," Jeff said, quietly staring at the screen.

The shapely blond newscaster's voice was grim: "On this otherwise quiet February day an elderly businessman who never did anyone any harm was brutally attacked, his throat slashed, and left to die in a pool of his own blood. His name was James Keegan, and he lived in Kingsport."

"Oh my God," Jeff cried out. "You killed that old man while I sat outside waiting."

Jeff Dicks' hand would not stop shaking as he fumbled with the telephone and haltingly dialed his mother's number.

ONE

By five the mid-February day was dark as a moonless night. Shirley Dicks had begun switching on lights about the shadow filled room when the telephone rang.

"Mom, I need you," her son Jeff said, as soon as she answered. From his quivering voice she knew immediately he was scared. An icy involuntary shiver passed through her body.

"Cindy and I are at the motel in Johnson City with Chief. He's leaving; can you come and get us?"

"What's wrong?" Shirley asked slowly, trying not to panic.

"I can't say over the phone. Will you please come?"

Shirley took a deep breath. She knew something terrible had occurred. Nervously she moistened her dry lips. "I can't come right this minute, but as soon as I let my boss know I won't be in, and borrow some money for the trip, I'll be on the road." She waited for her son's reply.

"Okay. But, please, hurry." Jeff's voice trembled and she felt his fear. She could picture her son's face as he spoke. She knew her son. Whatever had scared him had to be pretty bad for him to ask her to come. Hanging up the phone, Shirley hurried out of the house and over to the Holiday Inn where she had worked for the past year. Luckily her boss was in. He could see how upset Shirley was. Without asking questions, he loaned her some money and said she could have the night off.

An hour later she began her drive over the winding, dark, mountain road to Johnson City. Her thoughts darted to and fro trying to figure out why Jeff had called. She was afraid of what lay ahead of her, and even more afraid of not knowing what was wrong. The drive seemed to take forever. The road was completely deserted. She did not see another car. As she drew near her destination, her mouth grew dry and she could feel tears well up just behind her eyes, threatening to fall. Shirley didn't know why she felt like crying. She didn't know yet what was wrong. She just felt an unexplained dread in the pit of her stomach.

As Shirley pulled into the parking lot of the motel she spotted Cindy, Jeff's fiancée, pacing in front of the rooms. Her long brown hair framed a face taut and pale under the artificial lights.

Cindy spotted her, waved and slowly walked toward the car as Shirley parked. They walked to the room without speaking. Once inside Shirley saw Jeff sitting motionless on the bed. His face was pale, and terror was in his eyes. Shirley looked at her shaking son, all six feet three of him, and knew he was still a child at eighteen. He might look like a man, but he was still a very young boy—a scared boy at this moment.

Shirley broke the silence. "What happened?" She wasn't sure she wanted to hear what he was going to tell her, but she had to know. Jeff looked up at her and tears glistened in his green eyes. They were silently pleading with her to understand what he was about to tell her. He sighed heavily, but no words came out. Shirley sat down on the hard-backed chair that was beside the bed and waited. Silence filled the room.

Shirley started to grow impatient as she watched her son trying to get his thoughts together . . . how to best explain to his mother what was still a bad dream to him.

His eyes glazed over as he began reliving the events of his day in a trembling voice.

Every few minutes Jeff paused and took a deep breath. His face grew even whiter as he talked, and the knuckles of his hands now folded in his lap reddened as they gripped each other. Shirley watched silently. As each word came out she felt worse. Her stomach began clenching like it had a rock in it.

Then Jeff began crying. Shirley wanted to comfort him, but she sat very still listening, trying to make sense of what she was hearing.

She remembered the time Jeff had written some checks to buy clothing for some neglected children he was babysitting. Then, when he couldn't get the money into the account fast enough, he was charged with passing bad checks. Until Shirley and her husband, Nelson, could raise the money to replace the amount he owed, Jeff had left town and used a different name. Until this night, it was the only trouble he'd ever gotten into. He had never given her any other problems in his eighteen years.

"I would never hurt anyone, Mom, you know I wouldn't," he cried out. Then he broke down and Shirley held him in her arms as she had when he was a child. Now he was in deep trouble because he trusted a friend.

"You were right all along about Chief. I wish I'd never met him. And now—now a man is dead. What am I going to do?" he sobbed. "Maybe I should go to the police."

Shirley shook her head. She didn't trust these southern small town police. From all she had seen in the movies and on television they were often prejudiced against outsiders, especially if they were poor and from the north.

"They'll never listen to what you have to say. They'll never believe you," she protested.

"God, I wish I'd gone in that store with Chief. I'd have stopped him from doing what he did."

Shirley said in an agonized voice she hardly recognized as her own, "Don't say that, Jeff. You couldn't have stopped him. It would have made you an accomplice to it. You'd just be in a lot more trouble than you are now."

"Well, Mom," Jeff finally ended with a huge sigh. "I guess that is all there is to tell. What should we do?"

Shirley was agonizing about it also. She couldn't let him call the police; they might say he did it. She couldn't let him stay here; Chief might come back.

"I don't know," she said wearily. Her head was swimming and she bit her lip to hold her tears in check.

"This has all happened so fast. Time. We need time to think it through. I'll help you find a place to stay until we can figure out what to do. Did you bring anything with you from the apartment?" she asked.

"Very little. We just left everything there and got out. We were so scared, Mom." He looked at his mother hoping she would have an immediate solution. A mother was supposed to know everything, and his always had. Jeff had always obeyed her even as a young child. Hanging around with Chief was the first time he had gone against his mother's wishes, and what a tragic mistake he had made.

Shirley was thinking the same thing. Shaking her head, she remembered the first time she had laid eyes on Chief.

Her husband, Nelson, and she had driven to Elizabethton, where Jeff and Cindy were living. As they walked inside the building and up the stairs to Jeff's apartment, they saw Jeff and another husky guy standing there talking. Shirley glanced at the young man and the first thing she noticed was his eyes. They sent a chill up and down her back. They were steel blue and had an intense, hypnotic quality. He smiled a mocking smile as Jeff introduced him. Almost instinctively Shirley could feel evil coming from him and wanted to get away. He stared at her as if reading her mind; so she quickly turned away and hurried inside the apartment.

"What are you doing hanging around with someone like that?" she asked Jeff as soon as he came inside. He looked at her for a moment without saying anything. She raced on, "I don't think you should hang around with him. There is something about him that I don't like. I feel something awful will happen if you remain friends with him." Shirley walked over to the little kitchen table and sat down. Cindy didn't say anything, just sat there drinking a coke.

"Oh, Mom, he's all right. He just looks like a bum because he's so poor. He's had a hard life and no one likes him. I just feel sorry for him so we talk once in awhile. We don't do anything wrong, just sit and listen to tapes and maybe have a beer or two." Jeff sat down next to her and gave a little boy smile that could melt her heart. "And besides, remember it was you who told me to love everyone. You said to help those less fortunate, and Chief is surely less fortunate than we are. I feed him because he's not working and would go hungry if I didn't."

She smiled at Jeff and knew he had her there. She was proud that he had such compassion for others. She had tried to teach the kids to help anyone who needed it.

Still, she had an eerie feeling when she looked at Jeff's friend. And now it had come to this. Her worst nightmares had come true.

Standing up and looking around the motel room, Shirley quickly made up her mind. "We'd better leave before the police find you," she said. "We'll take my car and just start driving."

"Where?" Jeff asked.

"Anywhere . . . ," Shirley said hoarsely, "as long as it is away from here."

TWO

Shirley looked at the map in the car and spotted a town called Greenville, South Carolina. By taking the long way around, they could get there in a few hours.

As they rode, every car that passed them became, in their minds, a police car. It was a silent trip. Each one was lost in his or her own thoughts. Shirley kept shaking her head unbelievingly as if to snap herself back to reality. She was beginning to blame herself for what had happened. She had planned to help find Jeff another apartment the weekend before, but put it off one more week. Perhaps she thought to herself, if she had, things would have been different. Why, she thought to herself, why had she waited?

It was close to midnight by the time they reached Greenville, so they got a motel room for the night. "Morning will be soon enough to start looking for a place to live," Shirley said.

Wearily, Cindy and Jeff nodded. It was a long and sleepless night for all of them. Pretending sleep Shirley tried to stifle her sobs, but Jeff heard. He hated causing such pain to his mother, but he was in deep pain himself. He cried softly to himself like a little boy again. Why had all this occurred? Such things only happened in the movies, not in real life. But it had happened, a man was dead, and now they were on the run.

"We'll get the paper and see what apartments are for rent," Shirley said as the three of them sat sipping coffee the next morning. She looked searchingly at her son. She knew Jeff hadn't slept. She had heard him crying in the night and had wanted to comfort him but knew he'd be embarrassed if he knew she had heard. He had Cindy now, and she would do the comforting.

"Okay," Jeff said. None of them were hungry. They were still too upset over the day before to eat anything. Cindy sat silently watching mother and son, then took Jeff's hand.

Later that morning they found a small apartment, and Shirley paid a month's rent on it. Jeff and Cindy didn't have a car, so she took them around trying to find work. Jeff finally found a job with Manpower, and Cindy got a waitressing job in a small restaurant within walking distance of their apartment.

As they walked back to Shirley's car Jeff said, "Thanks, Mom, for all you've done for us. I'm sorry to cause you this pain, but I swear I never meant for anything to happen that day." Jeff hugged his mother tightly, fighting back the tears. "Don't worry, Mom. We'll be fine now."

"I'll be back next week to see how you're doing," Shirley said. "Here's some money to tide you over until you get paid. We'll get through this thing. Don't tell anyone anything about what happened. I'll let you know if I hear anything." She looked at Cindy warningly. She knew Cindy had a mouth that ran all the time.

"Are you sure I shouldn't call the police, Mom?" Jeff asked. "I didn't take part in the murder, and I'm willing to take my punishment for being there in the first place. I should have listened to you about Chief. You usually know people, and when you said you felt evil about him, I just should have listened." Jeff looked at her searchingly.

"No! I don't want you to do that. I'm afraid. I don't

know why, but I just don't want you to do that." She gave
Jeff a hug, blinking back the tears.

"All right, Mom. You've always told me right so I'll do
as you say. I love you, Mom. Always know that." With that,
Jeff bent down and kissed his mother. He stood watching
as she drove away and the car was completely out of sight.

"Come on, honey," Cindy said to Jeff taking his hand,
"let's go inside. Everything is going to be all right."

"I hope so," he said putting his arm around her. He
loved Cindy completely. She was the first girl Jeff had ever
gone out with and she had stolen his heart. He knew his
mother didn't really like her, but believed she would in
time.

As soon as Shirley got home, she woke her husband,
Nelson. Only a few weeks before, Shirley and Nelson had
decided to split up. Despite her deep feeling for him and his
for her, Shirley couldn't any longer handle the aftermath of
his memories of Vietnam, mirrored in his heavier and
heavier drinking. Still they were friends. And because they
couldn't afford two places, they still lived in the same
house. Now she told him the whole story. Although Jeff was
her son from a previous marriage, Nelson loved him as his
own and offered to help in any way possible. She thought
of going back to Jeff's apartment in Kingsport, Tennessee,
emptying it out and obliterating any traces of Jeff's being
there. Back and forth her ideas went. She didn't know
what to do. Never had she imagined being in a situation
like this. Never had she felt so overwhelmed. The only thing
she felt sure of was that she had to protect Jeff as much as
possible from whatever harm might come.

Telephoning her mother, Shirley told her the story.
They decided not to tell her dad because of his bad heart.
He knew about the bad check charges; so they left it at that,
letting him believe Jeff was still hiding from those charges.
Again Shirley felt guilty. If only she had encouraged Jeff to

stay in Asheville and face those charges none of this would have happened.

Shirley had been the one to decide Jeff should move to Knoxville until they could pay the checks off. Just as he always had, he did whatever she told him to do without question. This may have been the biggest mistake she had ever made.

The next weekend Shirley and two of her younger children, Laurie and Trevor, headed back to Greenville. It was then Jeff and Cindy told her Cindy was two months pregnant. "We want to get married, " Jeff said. "Cindy didn't want the baby but I've convinced her to have it." Cindy smiled warmly in agreement. An exhaustive search turned up a Seventh Day Adventist minister. He talked to them for a long time and finally agreed to marry them in his small church. Then came the problem of getting a marriage license. "What if they can tell he's wanted?" Cindy asked.

"Maybe we can find someone else to go into the license bureau and say he is Jeff," Shirley said. Things were already such a mess, all she could think of was finding a way to help the kids and not let anyone know Jeff's cover and get him caught. "That way, if the police catch up with the name, they won't have a true description of him." "How can we find someone that will do that without telling him why we need a stand-in?" Cindy asked in her childlike way.

"We'll do it somehow," Shirley said, not really sure how.

Finally Shirley came up with a half-baked idea that the other two in their naiveté grabbed onto.

"I guess we could go downtown and just ask any man walking if he wants to earn some money. We could try to find those who looked like they could use a few extra dollars and wouldn't question the reason why." Since neither Jeff nor Cindy had any other ideas, Shirley and Cindy drove downtown and parked on the main street. There were a lot of people walking around, and she thought it would be very simple.

Cindy approached a shabbily dressed man. "Mister, you want to earn some money?" she asked.

The man looked at her in disbelief. "You must be crazy," he muttered as he hurried on down the street.

She came back to where Shirley was sitting laughing and asked, "What did I do wrong?" Shirley couldn't stop giggling. "Did you see the look he gave you?" she said struggling to be serious.

"He hurried off like someone was after him. It sounded like you were propositioning him. We'd better try a different approach," Shirley continued. After an hour with no luck, they drove to the other end of the street.

Cindy got out, and Shirley joined her. Because of the sunny, unseasonably warm weather, the streets were still pretty crowded at the late afternoon hour. They searched up and down for possible surrogates. Suddenly she spotted the same man Cindy had "propositioned" earlier walking toward her. As soon as he saw Cindy he ran to the other side of the street, shaking his head. "This isn't going to be as easy as I thought," Shirley chuckled. "They must think we're crazy and are afraid to even find out what we need from them."

Finally, a young man from New York agreed to help them. He refused to take any money for doing it, and they went into the courthouse for the license. The young stranger played his part to perfection. "I don't even re- member my name, lady, much less hers, he stammered out to the clerk. They had forgotten to tell him Jeff's name, or Cindy's, in their haste to get the license. Everyone laughed it off, the clerks passing it by as pre-marital nervousness. The license issued, Shirley felt a sense of dishonesty and shame in what they had done, but the thought of having protected her son's safety and welfare dispelled her bad feelings.

The ceremony was to take place that Friday in the

church in Greenville. Shirley's parents, Nelson, and her daughter Tina were expecting to come out for the wedding. The next day Shirley's mother, whom she called Teeny, telephoned. "Maybe we'd better not come. The police came here looking for Jeff," she said. "They found out his real name, Shirley. They said he was wanted for questioning in a murder case over in Tennessee. They'll surely track him down and God knows what will happen then," Teeny said in an anguished tone. "I'm afraid for Jeff, and for you. If Jeff doesn't give himself up the police will charge you with hiding him out," her mother raced on. "But I don't want to see Jeff in prison for something he didn't do. What are you going to do?"

"I don't know, Mom," Shirley said wearily. "But one thing I know for certain, I can't let him turn himself in. They'll railroad him for the murder." She paused and took a deep breath. "Better not come for the wedding; they might follow you. I'm sure they think you know where we are." Shirley passed a hand across her aching head. How much more could she take? It was a nightmare and getting worse each day.

"All right, " Teeny said, her voice breaking. "Your father and I will go for a drive and spend the night in a motel somewhere. That way if the police are following us, they'll be led in a different direction. I'm so worried. I don't know where this will lead, and your father isn't well. What will all this do to him?" She was crying now.

"Mom, please tell Pop not to worry. Tell him that we'll be fine. Does he know what the charge is now?"

"Yes. He was here when the police came to question me about Jeff and you. He seems to be alright outwardly, but I know it's eating at him. Be careful whatever you do." Shirley turned to Jeff and Cindy, who were standing by the phone. She could see fear on their faces; so she put up a front for their sakes.

"It's better that they don't come for the wedding. Don't worry, everything will be all right. I'll think of something. This is supposed to be a happy time, remember. You're getting married, so smile."

Despite Cindy being pregnant Shirley had gotten her a long, white dress for the wedding. She didn't think it would hurt anyone if Cindy wore white. It was every girl's dream to be married in a wedding gown, and Shirley wanted Jeff and Cindy to be as happy as possible in spite of all that might happen.

"I want to thank you, Mom," Cindy said with tears in her eyes. "No one ever did anything for me before, and I want you to know how much I appreciate it." Cindy had grown up in an orphanage with no one to love her. Cindy felt deserted because her parents hadn't wanted her and had given her away. It showed in the distrust she had of everyone. Shirley wanted to be a good mother-in-law and tried to be Cindy's friend. Sometimes it was hard. Cindy didn't seem to want to be close to anyone but Jeff.

The morning of the wedding dawned hazy and cloud-filled. Shirley tried to shake off the feeling of foreboding which had constantly been with her since Jeff had first told her about the robbery.

As the minister said the words of the ceremony, Shirley's heart ached. She had always been close to Jeff, her first born. Now he might be accused of a horrible crime, and here he was getting married. Never had she felt so utterly bereft. Tears slid down her face; secretly Jeff glanced over at his mother and she managed a weak smile.

Back at the apartment, Shirley snapped picture after picture of the couple. Shirley was a photo addict. She had dozens of albums of pictures. Mostly of her children. Pictures of everything that had ever happened in their lives.

When they had all changed from their wedding clothes, Shirley asked Jeff to clean her car before she headed back to North Carolina. Surprised, he found the pistol she kept in the glove compartment and brought it to her.

"What are you carrying this thing for, Mom?"

"Safety," Shirley said.

"Did you know it has chocolate melted all over the barrel?" Jeff laughed. "Are you going to load it with M&Ms?" Jeff held the gun up as if he were a gangster on television, "I'm the chocolate bandit," Jeff said, mugging.

Struck by how funny he looked, Shirley snapped a quick picture. "Well, I know it doesn't shoot. I don't even have any bullets for it. But you know if anyone tried anything or if I broke down with the kids in the car, I'd feel safer. Just letting someone see that I have one might make them go away. Not that I'm planning on breaking down, but you never know."

Afterward she put the camera away. She never gave a second thought to the picture she had just taken. Over the years, she had snapped thousands of such shots for her books; memories to be relived when she got old and grey. This picture, however, would turn out to be another fatal mistake Shirley had made.

"Well, guess I'd better be going, you two," she said. "You both be careful and try to be happy. Don't call me at home. They might have the telephone tapped. I'll be back in a few days."

She looked at Jeff and Cindy and could not stop her tears as she thought of them starting their marriage with such an ominous cloud hanging over their heads.

"Mom, it's all right. Please don't worry about Cindy and me. We're going to be fine. Now that we have jobs, no one will know who we really are. Take care of yourself. I love you."

Shirley slowly drove back to Asheville, her mind a jumble of fears for Jeff. She thought of one wild scheme after another to help him and then discarded each one. "Nelson will know what to do," she murmured. "I'll talk it over with him and we'll work it out together."

She felt tears blinding her eyes as she ran in the house. She began rambling to Nelson as soon as she saw him. "Shirley," Nelson said, "I'm afraid you're going to get sick. Look at you, you've already lost so much weight." He wrapped her tightly, protectively in his arms, and her body

slackened against him. She didn't even care that he
smelled of liquor. She knew he couldn't stop the cycle of
drinking, the nightmares about Vietnam, the bad dreams
that went on and on, but at that moment, she forgot how he
was making her life and his own miserable. All she could
think of was Jeff.

"I think he should turn himself in, but if you want to
hide him out, let's take the two of them up north somewhere," Nelson said as he sat Shirley down on the couch,
his arms still around her.

"But where up north?" she asked plaintively. She had
been strong for Jeff; now she needed someone to lean on,
someone to tell her what to do.

"Maybe Pennsylvania. That's close to Canada, and
perhaps we can get them over there when we figure out
how he could get work and live." He looked at Shirley.
"You're so precious," he said. "Even with your face
streaked with tears, you're the prettiest woman I've ever
seen." Shirley smiled. Nelson could be so understanding,
even drunk as he was now. And he loved the children. They
had two of their own, Laurie and Trevor, and he had
adopted the other two, Jeff and Tina. They had been three
and five when he fell in love with Shirley, and he loved both
as his own.

"I don't think we should use our own car to take them
up there. Let's ask Donald if we can use his without saying
why. I trust him, but it's best to be safe." Shirley had met
Donald, Nelson's friend, a few years back when Nelson
brought him home for supper one night. They worked together and over the years the three of them had become
close.

Donald had even been counseling Shirley on her mari-
tal problems. He always listened and tried to help her.
Donald knew she still loved Nelson, but he understood why
she felt she had to leave Nelson. After each bout of drinking, she would plead with Nelson to seek help. His denial
and refusal had eventually forced her to seek a divorce.

The next night, with the borrowed car, Nelson and

Shirley headed to Greenville to pick Jeff and Cindy up for the long trip north. Then they stopped at the small apartment, where they loaded the kids' belongings onto the roof of the small Vega. When everything that would fit was finally tied on, there were two boxes left.

"Why don't we leave these things here and I'll come back for them later," Shirley said to Jeff. "Is there anything in either box that you'd need right off?"

Jeff looked through the boxes and said most of it was baby clothes the church had given to them. "I don't think we'll need most of this for a few months anyway, Mom. The only thing I want is my army coat. It's sure to be cold so I'd better wear it." He took the coat out of the box and put it on.

"I hate that coat," Shirley said miserably. "It belonged to Chief. I can't figure out why you love that thing so much. I bought you a new jacket just last month and you still like this one better."

Jeff shrugged, "Oh, Mom, just because it was Chief's doesn't mean it's tainted; it's plenty warm. The one you gave me looks good but I'll freeze in it."

Shirley shook her head. "It looks terrible on you and it's probably in the description the police have of you. That's the same coat you wore on the day of the murder, isn't it?" Jeff nodded. "I think it's best to just leave it here and wear the one I bought for you." Shirley hoped he'd agree. She hated anything that reminded her of Chief. She didn't want her son to even touch a thing that belonged to that man. Slowly he took the coat off without a word of complaint and put it back in the box. This was another deadly mistake.

The Vega was small and uncomfortable. Jeff and Cindy were squeezed in the back seat, and Jeff's knees almost pushed into his face. No one talked much. They all thought of the separation hovering above them. Shirley swallowed her tears trying to be strong for Jeff's sake. But she knew the thousand mile drive to see them could not be done very often, and this upset her.

Even a phone call would be difficult. Jeff would have to get a phone for himself, and Shirley's calls would have to be from a phone booth. She knew her phone would probably be tapped, if not now, then surely at some point in the future. The long, tedious trip seemed to go on and on. When they entered Pennsylvania the Vega's shocks could not handle the potholes. The car bounced from one to another. Shirley looked over at Cindy, worrying about the baby, and then at Jeff, whose face looked agonized, and began worrying about him. Nelson reached over to grab Shirley's hand. He squeezed it so she'd know he was there for her. She could feel more tears welling up and her throat tightened.

They drove straight through until they reached Erie, stopping only for gas. "We must be a sight, rolling into town at this time of year with almost all of Jeff's and Cindy's belongings strapped to the roof," Nelson said. "Let's drive around and look for a place to rent."

The one room efficiency apartment they found was on the second floor of an old red brick building at the top of long and narrow stairs. The door opened up into the kitchen. It had a small living room and just one bedroom, but it was clean and at least it was on a quiet street in what seemed to be a nice neighborhood.

"Well, guess this is our new home," Jeff said to Cindy. He put his arms around her for a moment, quickly kissing her on the tip of her nose. Then moving away he looked searchingly at Shirley and Nelson. The thought of them leaving in the morning made his stomach ache. It was a scary feeling to think about being so far from his family. He turned back to Cindy and sighed. At least she seemed happy. She was humming and said she was hungry.

They went to the small grocery store on the corner and bought food to last a couple of weeks. Shirley had given her son money to tide them over until she could send more. Back at the apartment, Shirley fixed dinner. It was strangely quiet during the meal. Jeff, noticing his mother's red rimmed eyes, said, "Mom, I know how hard this is for you." His own tears glistened. "Mom, I love you. You know I never wanted to hurt you."

Shirley couldn't trust herself to speak. Nelson tried to divert the conversation to keep his wife's mind off the separation. He knew it was going to be a hard parting. Looking at Jeff, he saw the uncertainty in his hazel eyes. Jeff hadn't ever been on his own; he'd always lived at home and hadn't had much freedom to run around like other boys his age. Shirley had been strict about the kids being home at night. He wondered if Jeff was mature enough to make it on his own, especially now.

The night was another long one. Shirley tossed and turned all night long. When she dozed off, she would moan long and eerily. Jeff, who had been pacing back and forth until one or two A.M., hadn't gotten much sleep either.

The next morning Shirley went to the telephone company and put a deposit on a telephone in a phony name. It would be installed in a few days.

They'd have to walk to any job interviews, but they were in the center of town. Hopefully, they could find something close to their apartment.

"Don't worry about us, Mom. We'll be all right. I love you," Jeff said as he gave her a big hug and kiss. She could see the hint of tears in his eyes and knew he would break out crying if she started to cry. But despite herself the tears ran down her pale, heart-shaped face, ruining the makeup she had so painstakingly put on that morning. She no longer cared what she looked like. Her oldest son was going to be thousands of miles away from her hiding from the police, who wanted to prosecute him for a crime he hadn't committed and for which he might spend years in jail if they found him. The well of pain was beyond tears. Grief and despair tore at her. Shirley's teeth began chattering, and suddenly her whole body was shaking.

"Please don't be so upset, Mom. I love you so much,

and I really appreciate all you've done to help me." He
turned to Nelson. Shirley stood staring at her son, and for
an instant a hint of a smile played about her lips. It was
almost comical to see the two of them together. Nelson was
5'8" and Jeff towered above him at 6'3". It looked like Jeff
was the father, except for his baby face for which they all
teased him. He had tried hard to grow a mustache, but to
no avail. He had peach fuzz but no real whiskers. She saw
a tear roll down his face and knew they had to leave
quickly. It was just too hard to say goodbye.

"Just be careful," Shirley choked on the words. "Don't
write to me or call. I'll call you when your phone's hooked
up. I'll call collect from a phone booth; that way no one can
trace it. I'll send some money as soon as I can." She turned
to Nelson. "Let's get going, please." She watched in the
rear mirror as her son became smaller and smaller. She
was all out of tears. She closed her eyes, her heart aching.

"He'll be fine," Nelson said putting his hand over
hers. "Try not to worry about him." He gave her hand a
squeeze and turned his attention back to the road. Shirley
didn't answer because she couldn't. Talk was beyond her at
the moment. She began to take deep breaths to control the
panic she felt.

The morning after she and Nelson arrived home, Shirley headed back to Jeff's Greenville apartment to pick up
the boxes of clothes that had been left behind. As she put
them into the back seat of the car, the green army coat
dropped out. How she hated that coat. It seemed like Chief
was still in it. She could sense his evil; she shuddered and
stuffed it back in.

"What's the matter, Mom?" her other son, Trevor,
asked as he helped with the boxes. "Don't you feel good?
I'll take care of you now that Jeff isn't here." He put his
arm around his mother and hugged her tight. He was only
eleven years old, but he knew a little of what was going on.
And now he knew his mother was suffering because Jeff
was gone.

Shirley burst into tears again. Where were they all

coming from, she wondered. She turned to Trevor and clasped him to her. She loved all her children. They were such good kids. They loved their big brother, who had always been so gentle and good-hearted with them. How could she explain what was happening and what might happen to Jeff? Shirley tried not to think of it—to concentrate only on the task at hand and to reassure the small boy whose clear eyes met hers. "I'm all right, Trevor. I'm just sad that Jeff has moved so far away from us. I'm going to miss him. You have to be careful when you're talking about your brother and Cindy. No one must know where they are living." She gave him a hug and smiled through her tears. "Come on, let's get an ice cream cone."

"Okay. That sounds good." Trevor got inside the car and was quiet. They drove to the Dairy Queen. Each ordered a hot fudge sundae, and in the car as they sat eating them, Trevor said in a small voice, "I heard you and Dad talking and I know the police are looking for him. I know he didn't do it. Jeff wouldn't hurt anyone. Not ever!"

Shirley looked in surprise at her youngest child. She put her arm around Trevor to comfort him. His big brother was gone, and he needed some reassurance too. She realized that all that was happening to their family had made Trevor grow up in the past few weeks. She smiled at him, watching his face turn chocolate covered as he spooned in mouthful after mouthful of the ice cream non-stop. She smiled at his appetite and handed him her sundae. He grinned taking it, "Don't worry, Mom. Everything will be fine. I'll help you. I'm a big boy now."

"Yes, son, you're a big boy and I know you'll be a help to me," she said. Her heart felt like it was breaking.

Nelson was already home when she and Trevor got there. Donald was there, too.

"How come you're not at work?" she asked Nelson, collapsing in the lawn chair. She was so tired. The past couple of weeks had been harder on her than she realized. The lack of sleep was catching up with her.

"Well, it seems as if I don't have a job anymore. I was

fired. They didn't take kindly to my being gone without calling in and asking to be gone for a few days." He took a long drink from the beer mug he'd been hiding behind him. Shirley could tell he was on his way to being drunk again. She sighed and asked him to get the boxes out of the car and put them in the attic.

"No sense putting that junk in the attic. They'll never come back here to get it, and I know you, you'll buy the baby all new things anyway. I'll just burn it all here with the rest of the trash." He headed for the car to get the boxes with Donald tagging along.

Her lip tightened, quivering. There was no use arguing with Nelson once he was drinking. Moreover, she had no energy for a fight.

Shirley watched as he and Donald put the junk on the pile and added new fuel. Red and yellow flames leapt up. Then as dark smoke curled above the pile she realized the hated army coat was being consumed with the rest and was almost glad.

"How are you doing?" Donald asked looking worriedly at Shirley, who was staring almost as if hypnotized at the glowing embers. Deep shadows lined her green eyes. Her swollen face made it obvious she had been crying for days.

She managed a weak smile as she glanced at him. "I'm fine," she whispered. The three of them sat silently for a long time. She snuck a look at her husband, who was drinking yet another beer. Nelson was supposed to have gone to New York to live with his mother but decided against it when Jeff's trouble had begun. Looking at him swilling the beer down, Shirley wished suddenly he had already gone. But she couldn't kick him out, especially now. Another emotional confrontation was beyond her. Anyway, seventeen years counted for something. She turned away and stared again into the now charred embers.

"Are you going to see if one member of the family still has a job?" Nelson broke the tension. "You didn't call or tell your boss anything either. Maybe we're both out of work. Good thing we still sell Fuller Brush products. At least we won't go hungry." He grabbed another beer and began talking to Donald, not waiting for an answer.

Shirley left the yard and went inside to get dressed for work. Jimmy Delworth, her kindly white-haired Santa Claus-looking boss at the Holiday Inn where she worked at night as a cocktail waitress, had been very understanding. She made good tip money and really needed the night job. During the day she sold Fuller Brush products, taking Trevor and Laurie with her. The customers didn't seem to mind, and that way she didn't have to trust a baby sitter.

"Is everything all right with the family?" Delworth asked Shirley as soon as she hung her coat up. "Shirley, I don't like to pry, but your eyes are swollen and you have circles underneath. I can't help knowing something is terribly wrong." He paused. "Look, if you don't want to talk about it, that's all right."

Shirley nodded. "Thanks for asking, Jimmy, but I think we got everything straightened out," she slowly answered. "I'm real sorry I didn't call to tell you I was going out of town again. I know I should have, but it all happened so fast and I wasn't thinking straight." She hoped Jimmy would understand. He had told her more than once that she did a good job and that all the customers liked her. She didn't want to lose this job. It took all she made at both her jobs to pay the bills and support four children.

"That's all right. I know it must have been an emergency for you not to have called." Jimmy waited, but she didn't say anything more. So he turned and went back to the bar.

A few days later Shirley arrived at work at five as usual. As she stepped into the dimly lit lounge, Jimmy walked over. "There are a bunch of men over there who want to see you," he said quietly. He nodded over his shoulder. "I'll stay nearby."

Shirley looked over in that direction. Five men in dark suits sat clustered around a table. The empty table and their quiet demeanor made it apparent that they were not waiting to be served. Somehow she knew before meeting them that they were police officers. Slowly she walked over.

"Mrs. Dicks?" the tallest of the group stood up. "I'm Detective Gregory Wilcox. We're here to ask you some questions about your son, Jeff. Is there a quiet place where we can talk?"

"I'll ask my boss," she said somberly. "Jimmy," she called, "can we use the room behind the bar?" It was the manager's room, a combination office/meeting room.

"Sure, why not," Jimmy called back.

Shirley's legs felt like a Gumby doll. She was afraid if she took a single step, she'd fall. Goosebumps ran up and down her arms. She wondered if she had to talk to them and decided she did. Summoning every ounce of courage she possessed, she put one leg in front of the other and led them into the small room.

"Please have a seat, Mrs. Dicks," Wilcox began. "Allow me to introduce these other gentlemen. Mr. Calvin Birch and Frank Rollins are from Buncombe County Sheriff's Department here in North Carolina. Mr. Robert Paterson and myself are from Tennessee." As each man was introduced, he took a seat at the long table. Shirley sat down, conscious of her short skirt that was the uniform at the Holiday Inn. She smoothed it down. The room was cold and she shivered. "We're just going to ask you a few questions," Wilcox said. He stood well over six feet tall. His hair was dark, but he wasn't what she'd call "tall, dark and handsome." Maybe it was his grim face and his deep, brusque voice which made her feel that he looked down at her even when he was seated.

Shirley, determined not to tell where her son was, felt a sudden, intense fear of these men. They sat so solemn, never smiling, just staring at her. Then they began to question her.

For the next three hours, Shirley felt more uncomfortable than she ever had in her life. Over and over they asked

Shirley about Jeff. Over and over she repeated that he had not been involved in the murder. Many times they reduced her to tears. When she asked for an attorney, they repeated she didn't need one. They weren't charging her with anything. "We're only asking questions, Mrs. Dicks," shouted an angry Wilcox, whose voice rose as he lost his temper.

"Look," Wilcox said in a quieter voice as he once again regained his composure, "we only want to question Jeff about Donald Strouth, who calls himself Chief. We know that Strouth committed the murder. We only need Jeff to fill in a few pieces of the puzzle."

"What would the charges be against Jeff if he did come in?" Shirley asked, her voice trembling. Her legs were cold. She ached all over from the stress and from sitting so long in the same position. She didn't like Wilcox. He along with Sgt. Rollins did most of the talking. Mr. Paterson from North Carolina looked at her with soft brown eyes and instinctively Shirley felt this man could be trusted. But he hardly spoke, letting the three officers from Tennessee do the questioning.

"He'll be charged with being an accessory to robbery. I promise you that's all we want him for. We already have Strouth in custody." Silence filled the room.

Shirley shook her head, "I don't know."

"You're not an easy woman to crack," he said smiling. "Now are you going to tell us what we need to know?"

More silence.

Shirley got up.

Wilcox's smile failed.

"We're not playing games here!" He was shouting now. "You'd better tell us where we can find him. If we have to look for him, we'll shoot to kill. Both of them—him and his wife. You'd better speak up right now if you don't want something like that on your conscience." He paced back and forth at his end of the table, glaring at her. She felt like he would hit her if he dared.

She shook her head, tears falling on her blouse, but he wouldn't relent.

"Tell us!" he shouted.

"I'm not going to tell you where he is. But I will tell him what you said," she replied.

She started to leave, but Wilcox held up his hand, "Sit down." The anger in Wilcox's voice made her quickly obey. She felt cold and pain filled her entire body. Why won't these men leave me alone, she thought. She was tired. Her head was throbbing. Looking first into one man's eyes and then the next, she saw some sympathy, but it was clear that Wilcox was in control. She saw no sympathy there, only anger and frustration.

"I'm tired and cold," Shirley whimpered. "I want to go home. I want to talk to Nelson. I'm not going to say anymore. I know Jeff didn't hurt anyone. I also don't know if I believe you or not that you just want to question him."

Wilcox's face got redder as if he were going to explode. Shirley's lips quivered.

"You will tell us where you're hiding him out if you know what's good for you," he said in a very quiet yet menacing voice.

One of the North Carolina detectives interrupted, "I know you love your son, Mrs. Dicks. But we need to question him about the murder. We know Strouth did the crime; his own girlfriend gave a statement to that. But we need to fill in the missing pieces. Only Jeff can tell us the rest." She felt this man was trying to be kind, but still she couldn't bring herself to tell him where Jeff was hiding.

For a while no one spoke.

"You can leave," Wilcox finally said with a sigh. He knew he wouldn't get any further with this woman. He would let her leave and follow her home in the hopes that Jeff would be there. "Don't forget, you're only hurting Jeff and Cindy by not telling where they are. I guess you are aware that you can be arrested for harboring a fugitive. We may just do that." He stared at Shirley. As she stood to leave her legs began buckling from the cold and cramps, but she caught herself before falling.

"I don't care what you do to me. I'm not going to let

you get hold of my son." She turned and walked out into the cold, dark bar. Jimmy Delworth was still there.

"Shirley, are you alright?" he said staring at her. He knew this was serious business for those detectives to be talking to her for so long. He knew also from the agonized look on her face that it had been a grueling five hours.

By the time she reached home, Shirley was not only exhausted but near hysterics. She shook Nelson awake. "They know who Jeff is!" she cried. Her makeup was smeared all over her face, and her eyes were swollen from crying.

"Those detectives have been questioning me all night about Jeff. They said they only wanted him for an accessory to robbery. What are we going to do?" The words seemed to rush out of her. She took a quick, shallow breath and tried to stop.

Nelson put his arms around her and held her tight against him. "I hate the thought of you going through so much. I'd like to punch those detectives, but there's so little I can do but be here for you."

"We'll call Jeff in the morning and tell him to come back and turn himself in," he said. "That's the only thing to do."

"But what if it's a trap?" she said, bursting into tears again. She felt trapped herself. She couldn't think. "What if it's all a lie and they just want to get their hands on Jeff. I don't trust the Tennessee detective, Mr. Wilcox. He kept yelling at me all the time. I think if the others hadn't been there, he might have roughed me up. I think Jeff should stay where he is. At least I know he's safe." Shirley collapsed on the couch.

Nelson shook his head. "Look, I don't think they would lie. Policemen don't lie," he said definitively, "so Jeff has nothing to worry about. Let's go in the kitchen and I'll fix you a cup of coffee. Just try to relax a little." He took Shirley's hands and guided her to the kitchen. She sat at the kitchen table and watched silently as Nelson put the coffee on. He opened the window so the smoke from his cigarette would not bother Shirley, who had emphysema. Then he took the chair next to hers.

Suddenly Shirley realized how exhausted she was. "Thank you for everything, Nelson, but never mind the coffee," she said stumbling to her feet. "I really need to lie down."

The next morning she went to the Buncombe County Police Station and talked with Detective Dalton there. He seemed nicer and was more patient with her than the other detectives had been.

"Were those men telling me the truth last night?" she asked, glancing around his office. A picture of his wife and child stood on the desk. Looking at the picture, the protective way he had his arm around his wife and the smiling child in his lap, she thought maybe he would understand. He had a child he loved. She sighed heavily. Maybe he was someone she could trust.

He assured Shirley that the detectives from Tennessee were telling the truth and that it would be best if Jeff were to come on back and turn himself in. She left the office feeling a little better.

That afternoon Nelson called Jeff from a pay phone. He told Jeff what had happened. "I think you should turn yourself in," Nelson said.

When Shirley got on the telephone, Jeff asked her what she thought about it. "I really don't know. I want you to be safe. I just don't know if I believe what we're being told or not," Shirley said. Then she started crying. She missed Jeff. She feared for his future and didn't know which way to turn.

"Well, I'm going to come on in," Jeff said with determination. "I didn't hurt anyone and I didn't go in the store. I know I was wrong to even be there, but I can't change that any." Shirley told Jeff that they'd start out the next day to pick him up.

After hanging up the telephone she felt a sadness come over her. "I don't feel right about this," she said to Nelson. "I don't know that we can trust those men. I'm afraid for Jeff. Maybe he should just stay where he is until he can get to Canada."

"Come on, Shirley," Nelson said impatiently. "Jeff has to grow up. If you hadn't taken him over to Knoxville in the first place, he wouldn't have met Chief. He should have stood trial for those checks. Now he should come in and tell the truth. Cops don't lie. It's going to be alright."

Shirley felt guilty at Nelson's words. She shouldn't have had Jeff run because of the checks. But it was only until they could pay them off. Then he was going to come back. Now she didn't know what to do. Trust her instincts or trust Nelson and his belief in the system?

They went back to the police station a second time and talked to Mr. Birch. Detective Birch told them he believed everyone was telling the truth. He said Jeff would probably get a few years for being an accessory to robbery, but he felt sure that would be the extent of it.

"Mr. Birch," Shirley finally said, her voice shaking, "we're going to pick Jeff up, and he is going to turn himself in."

On Sunday, March 19, 1978, the whole family gathered at Shirley's home to visit with Jeff before he went to the police station. They were supposed to bring him in at noon but called and asked if they could bring him in at 4:00 P.M. instead so they could spend just a few hours more with him before he left. It was so hard, knowing that he could be in prison for several years. Shirley felt anxious, but Nelson was sure that Jeff should give himself up. After all, the police had assured them that all he was going to be charged with was robbery. It was bad, but not as bad as it could be.

"You will take care of Cindy for me," Jeff pleaded with his mother.

"Of course I will, Jeff. You know I will," Shirley promised.

"I love Cindy so much and I have to know that she will always be taken care of," Jeff said, wrapping his arms around his mother. Her tears were wet on his face. They would not stop.

"She will stay with us as long as need be, and we'll take care of the baby once it is born," Shirley said hoarsely. "Don't worry about anything right now; time is too short." She tightened her arms about Jeff. Trevor was staying close to his big brother. Tina and Laurie were, too.

At 4:00 P.M. Jeff, Cindy, Nelson and Shirley went to the police station. Inside the office, they sat on the cold, blue plastic couch silently huddled together as one of the detectives brought out a warrant. As he began reading it to Jeff, their eyes widened in horror. The charge was "murder one."

THREE

Shirley felt fear as she looked at Wilcox. He was smiling a faint sardonic smile; she felt faint. She had been tricked, she knew it.

"What does that mean?" she cried. "You said it would be accessory to robbery when we talked before."

"This doesn't mean anything," Wilcox said, serious faced now, all business. "It'll be changed before the trial." Wilcox seemed to hurry, "Jeff won't need an attorney since he turned himself in. We just need to get a statement from him."

Wilcox led Jeff away to a room through a side door. Silently, Shirley followed them down the hall. The room where they had taken Jeff was all enclosed by glass. She could see in, but she couldn't hear what they were saying. She watched Wilcox writing something down on a pad of paper. Fear clutched at her.

An hour later Wilcox brought Jeff back. "You can talk for awhile, but let's not get carried away." Wilcox seemed to be back in only a minute and led Jeff into the prison. Shirley watched in silence as her son walked through the doors that led to his cell and an uncertain future. Tears rose in her eyes again, and Shirley tried to hide them from the officers. This was just a nightmare that wouldn't end.

Nelson drove them back home. Shirley was tired, as tired as she ever remembered being. But, as only a mother can do, she held on to the hope that things would turn out for the best in the end. Her mother and other children were waiting for them when they arrived. They were full of questions. She tried to be reassuring, but one especially unnerved her.

"Did you get an attorney?" her mother asked.

"No," she said. "Were we supposed to?"

"You ought to know you can't say anything without talking to an attorney. Lord, I hope he didn't go giving a statement to them," Teeny said. She had a frown on her face and Shirley could see the dark circles under her eyes. This had been almost as hard on her mother as it had been on her.

"Yes, he did. They told us that we didn't need to get a lawyer because he turned himself in." Shirley felt fear in the pit of her stomach and wished her mother had gone along with them that day.

"I knew I should have gone down there with you. They lied if they said he didn't need an attorney. You never give a statement without one," Teeny shook her head.

Shirley slowly sat down. Her initial instincts were the right ones. Too late. There was no turning back.

That night Shirley lay awake, unable to erase the horror of the past few hours from her mind. She couldn't believe the police had arrested Jeff for murder, but then she couldn't believe other things that had happened in her life either. The room grew dim and scenes of her past crowded in.

Growing up, Shirley lived in a small white house with green shutters—not much different from the others on a quiet tree lined street in Concord, New Hampshire. Two large maple trees shaded the front yard. Winters she would help her mother make maple syrup from the sap out of those trees and candy, which they made by pouring the syrup on the snow. Nothing again ever tasted so sweet and pure. The park right across the street was always a beehive of activities. Summer evenings Shirley's entire family would sit in the wicker chairs on their front porch watching baseball games and eating homemade popcorn. They were far from wealthy but considered themselves rich in love, if nothing else.

The summer Shirley turned thirteen years old she met Joe Murray. She remembered the day as if it were yesterday. Her mother had taken Shirley and her younger brother, Mike, to the park to swim. She watched Joe as he swam, and seemed unable to pay much attention to anything else. She liked his strong, athletic strokes in the water and the way he flipped his black, curly hair out of his eyes every time he came up for more air. It was the first time Shirley had that strange quivery kind of feeling when she looked at a boy. She liked it.

"Do you come here often?" Joe asked as he pulled himself up to sit on the side of the pool where Shirley was sitting.

"No. We usually go to White's Park swimming pool. That's where we live. Not in the pool, but across the street," she stammered, her face flushed. She noticed her mother watching from the bench, and she didn't want to appear to be interested in Joe.

"Maybe I could come over there to see you sometime. That is, if you would like me to." He smiled at her.

"I'd like that," she said, and the funny feeling came back. Getting up, she walked back to where her brother Mike was playing.

"Shirley's got a boyfriend, Shirley's got a boyfriend," he sang at the top of his voice.

"Shut up! He'll hear you." Shirley reddened; she felt

like everyone was looking at her, and she didn't like to be the center of attention.

"Shirley's got a boyfriend," Mike started again when his mother yelled at him to be quiet. He soon found someone else to tease and left her alone—alone with her daydreams of the wonderful boy she had found.

From that time on Joe and she were practically inseparable. Her parents wouldn't let her date at thirteen, of course, but she and Joe spent as much time as they could together walking to and from school and going to the ice cream parlor.

After a while Shirley's parents commented that they were together a little too much. "Shirley, your father and I have been talking about you and Joe," Teeny began. "Both of you need to spend some time with other kids your age. It's not healthy to be together so much."

"But I love Joe," Shirley said defiantly. "We're going to get married someday."

Teeny stiffened. "You're only a child, Shirley. You're too young to know what love is all about. Joe isn't a good influence on you, and it will be best if you don't see so much of him."

When Shirley still insisted on seeing Joe, Teeny's commands grew sterner: "Your father and I don't want Joe here anymore."

Shirley cried until her eyes were red and swollen and did not speak to her mother or father for two weeks. "I won't give up Joe!" she swore. "I'll wait until I'm old enough and then get married."

"Shirley, your father and I are not trying to hurt you. Joe is not the kind of boy we want you to get seriously involved with when you start dating. He quit school; he doesn't even work. All he does is run around the streets and hang out. We want better for you." Teeny looked at her daughter and saw the determined look in her tear-filled eyes. "Don't have him over here no more, Shirley!"

But when you're determined about something, you

find a way to make it work. You learn to avoid the obstacles, and Shirley did. Her father worked during the day and would get home around five thirty. Her mother left for work at four so it gave them an hour and a half each day to be alone. She was responsible for taking care of her younger brother, Mike, but sometimes they'd walk downtown to sit in front of the courthouse with the other kids. This was a good place to spend time with Joe.

Several times more Shirley's parents tried to break the couple up. But by the time Shirley was sixteen she was sure she wanted to marry Joe. She needed parental consent, and her parents, saying she and Joe were too young, refused to give it.

The following year Shirley discovered she was pregnant. She and Joe were married at the same church Shirley attended each Sunday, and on December 6, 1957, little Jeff Stuart Murray made his entrance into the world. He had Joe's dark curly hair and weighed in at a healthy eight pounds plus.

That year, Teeny also had a son, Roger Wade Mathews. He was eight months older than Jeff. He was the fifth and last child Teeny would have. David and Brenda were in the middle, with Roger at the tail end of the family. Shirley and Joe moved in with her parents. It was crowded, but there was plenty of love and life went smoothly for awhile. When Shirley got a job working as an aide in a hospital they moved into their own apartment. Joe would stay home and watch Jeff while she worked.

By the time Jeff was one year old, Shirley was pregnant again. She pleaded with Joe to find work, but nothing seemed to do any good. He was simply too young to accept the responsibility of providing for a family. Her parents' words now echoed inside her head, as she saw for herself that Joe wasn't ready to settle down.

Shirley moved back in with her parents, this time without Joe. She tried to find work and care for Jeff, but she had no training, jobs were scarce and she couldn't seem to make ends meet. It was then she decided to give the new baby up for adoption upon its birth. Her parents begged her to think it over and told her that things would work out somehow.

"Please don't give away your flesh and blood," Pop said with tears in his eyes. Shirley felt shame. She loved her dad and would do anything he wanted, but this time she felt she had no choice. All he had he gave to his family. There just wasn't much, and money was always very tight.

"I know you'd help me if you could, Pop, but I got myself in this mess and I have to get myself out of it. You've done the best you could, but you all have so little, I can't let you take from the others. It wouldn't be fair to them."

When Shirley felt her labor pains beginning, she went to the hospital. As she fought her way out of the darkness, she could see a nurse leaning over her bed. "How are you feeling?" the nurse asked. Shirley wasn't sure how she felt —she was still woozy from the anesthetic. She slid her hand under the covers and felt her stomach. It was flat again . . . Her baby had been born.

Curtains had been pulled around her bed, cutting her off from the other two young mothers in the ward. Then she remembered: She had told the doctors she would give her baby up for adoption.

"I'm all right," Shirley said, trying not to cry. Without a word the nurse turned and walked out of the room.

Shirley thought to herself, Why am I feeling so awful? I knew it had to be this way . . . I just can't keep my baby.

She could hear voices coming from the other side of the curtain. "What happened to her baby?" one of the young mothers whispered.

"Nothing. She just didn't want to keep it," the other one said.

Shirley wanted to shout through the curtain that it

wasn't true. She did want to keep her baby. She just couldn't afford to keep it. Being eighteen and having a year-and-a-half-old son at home was all she could handle right now. She thought of Joe and wondered what he was doing. She still loved him but knew they couldn't make it together. Why did life have to be so difficult?

Shirley's thoughts were interrupted by a small stern-faced woman who strode around the curtain and sat down ceremoniously smoothing her dark gray suit. The woman's gray hair pulled back into a bun added to her harsh appearance.

"Are you ready to sign these papers now?" she asked. Shirley could tell the woman didn't approve of her by the way she kept her eyes focused on the papers on her lap and spoke in a clipped, cold manner. "I hope you realize that you are doing the right thing for your child. After all, we both know you could never provide the things it will need."

Shirley didn't answer the woman. She couldn't. Tears welled up in her throat. She tried not to let them come.

"Did I have a boy or a girl?" she asked hoarsely.

"You know the rules," the woman snapped. "I can't tell you that. It would be much harder on you if you knew. There might also be a chance that at some future time you would want to see the child, and that wouldn't be good for either of you."

She handed Shirley the papers and a pen. "Sign at the bottom on the right," she said impatiently. "Right over there." She pointed with a well buffed nail, in Shirley's direction. What was her hurry anyway, Shirley thought. I'll be here for seven days. What difference would a few more hours make?

"I wanted a girl so badly," Shirley said softly. "Just tell me if I had a girl."

The woman shot Shirley a look of disgust, "You girls! Get yourself in trouble and then don't want to pay the consequences." Quickly she got to her feet, "I'll be back to see you the first thing in the morning. Please be ready to sign the paper, I won't have much time. I'm sure you want to do what's right for the baby."

Shirley lay there. "How can I possibly give up my baby? Do I have to? I'm trying to do what is best," Shirley said aloud to the walls. "Everything inside me tells me I'm doing the wrong thing." Morning came finally, and she could hear the bustle of the nurses as they brought in the babies to be fed. The curtain still hung around Shirley's bed. She could hear other women cooing over their newborns.

Shirley buried her head in the pillow. She cried until there were no tears left.

It isn't fair, she thought. I want my baby, but I just can't make ends meet. As these thoughts raced through her mind, she heard a noise in the doorway. It was Joe. He came in and kissed her. "I love you, Shirley. I don't know why I can't seem to find a job I can stick to, but I love you and always will." Pain overcame her. She looked at him forlornly.

"I love you, Joe, and I probably always will, but I have to think about Jeff. I can't go on supporting us and you too. My heart is breaking right now. I don't want to give up my baby. I don't even know if I had a girl or a boy." The tears came now in great gulping sobs. "Joe, please, leave." He hesitated for a moment and she saw tears in his eyes too; he left the room.

Slowly Shirley crept out of bed and walked down the hall to the nursery, where fathers and mothers laughed and tapped on the plate glass window as if their babies knew who they were.

A lone crib stood way in the back. She could see little hands and feet moving above the top, but she couldn't make out the name printed on the card. Still somehow she knew this was her baby.

She brushed away the tears and hurried back to bed. A young nurse was watching her. "Bring me my baby," Shirley demanded, crossing her fingers that the nurse would ignore the rules just this one time.

She looked at Shirley for a moment and then, with a smile, turned and headed for the nursery. She was back within minutes, cradling a small bundle. She placed it gently in Shirley's arms.

"It's a girl," the nurse said softly and left them alone. Shirley felt that the baby looked up at her as if she knew her mother. She knew in that moment that she loved this child and that, no matter what, she could never give her up. Maybe she would not have all the material things in life, but was that really so important? She would always have love. Together, Shirley, little Jeff, and the new baby would make it somehow.

When the nurse came to take the baby back to the nursery, Shirley told her she had changed her mind—that she was going to keep her. "You're doing the right thing," the nurse said smiling.

Later that day the grim lady in gray returned. "Are you ready to sign these papers now?" she asked curtly.

"I'm not ready now, and I never will be," Shirley told her fiercely. "I'm going to keep my baby. I've given her a name already. It's Tina. She's my baby and you'll never get your hands on her." The woman left muttering about teen-age mothers, but Shirley didn't care. She felt a great weight had been lifted from her mind.

Her parents were overjoyed at the news that Shirley was going to keep Tina. "We'll make it just fine," Teeny said to Shirley, giving her a hug and kiss. I knew in the end you would keep the baby. I'm so happy she's a girl. She's so pretty with those green eyes."

Shirley filed for a divorce. She took two full-time jobs and worked hard to keep the children in clothing and food. It was hard, but well worth it to see her beautiful babies happy.

One weekend her brother Mike, knowing she needed some relaxation, suggested she go roller skating. It was on that outing that she met a handsome young Marine named

Nelson Dicks. Their courtship lasted only three months before he asked Shirley to marry him. He got along great with Jeff and Tina, and he loved Shirley even though she told him candidly that she still loved Joe.

"I know you'll grow to love me one day," Nelson said to Shirley the evening he asked her to marry him. "I'll take the chance. With my pay and benefits, you can quit working and spend time with the kids. They need a full-time mother and father. I'm willing to wait for your love." He took her in his arms and kissed her gently. "You're so beautiful," he whispered, "for as long as it takes, Shirley, that's how long I'll wait."

"I hate to do that to you, Nelson. It seems like I'm using you just to have a place to live and to be able to stay home with the kids. And I don't want to do that. I want to be honest with you. I do care a great deal about you, but the fact is, I'm still in love with Joe. I can't help it." She took Nelson's hand in hers as she spoke.

"I don't care, Shirley. I love the kids, and I love you. I can't give you diamonds or furs, but I can give you all the love you'll ever need. And I know in time you'll love me too. Please say yes. Make me the happiest man on earth." Nelson kissed her passionately. Shirley hesitated for a few more minutes, then answered.

"All right, Nelson. I'll marry you. But don't say I didn't warn you ahead of time."

"Thank you!" Nelson shouted. "I love you and I'll make you happy. Just wait and see. Shall we go and tell the kids?" Nelson was bursting with happiness. "I want to tell the world. I'm going to marry the girl of my dreams." Shirley laughed and said that was fine with her. She knew her family would be happy. They all loved Nelson.

Their wedding was held at Shirley's grandmother's house with just family and a few friends present. Nelson and the best man were in their dress blues. Shirley wore a pale blue silk dress. Everyone in her family marveled at how attractive a couple they made. They took Jeff and Tina on their honeymoon trip to visit Nelson's family in New York.

As soon as they returned, Nelson announced, "I want to legally adopt Tina and Jeff and be the father they've never had." Joe agreed. He wouldn't have to pay any child support, but he lost all visitation rights to them.

In 1963, Shirley and Nelson's daughter, Laurie Jean, was born. Her birth cemented their love, and this time that love was not one-sided. It was mutual.

They moved to Maine and found a house on the base. The tiny house had a yard for the children. It seemed Shirley's dream for a secure place for her family had come true.

But Shirley's happiness was short-lived. Nelson received orders for Vietnam. The days and weeks of Nelson's tour crept by. Working all the time did not help. Even the children couldn't keep her mind off the fear that something was going to happen to Nelson in the jungles of Vietnam.

Shirley became even more frightened when Nelson wrote about a couple of their friends who had been killed, their bodies sent home in body bags. She became afraid that one day she would see the Marine Corps general bringing the news that Nelson had become another casualty of the war. By this time she had fallen in love with him, and being separated was taking a heavy toll on her.

So it was with relief Shirley learned that Nelson was finally returning from Vietnam. Rather than it being an occasion for celebration, however, it was marked by a family crisis. Shirley's father suffered a nervous breakdown and was put on disability. He had been working two full-time jobs for a long time, and it finally proved to be too much for him. Her parents called the family together to talk about the future of the entire family.

"I think we should move to the south," Teeny said. "We don't have anything left here. We're losing our home, and the warmer weather might be better for Ernest than the cold winters. How do the rest of you feel?"

"As long as we're all together," Shirley said, "I don't care where we move to." So the decision was made to move south. While waiting for Teeny and Ernest's house to sell, Shirley delivered her fourth child, a son. She and Nelson decided to name him Trevor Richard. As soon as she was able to travel, Shirley, Nelson and the kids piled everything they owned into the travel trailer her parents owned, got in their car, and headed south. Her parents and brother David, along with his new wife, were packed and ready to go also.

They settled down in Clinton, Tennessee. Nelson worked as a mechanic in Knoxville, which was twenty miles away. Teeny and Ernest found a small apartment nearby and settled in.

It wasn't long before her brother Mike and his wife, Karen, moved to Clinton, too. Shirley's sister Brenda had just gotten married and they also moved to Clinton. Brenda was pregnant with her first child, and a short while after her arrival there gave birth to a daughter.

They were all together again, except for David, who had gone back to New Hampshire. For Shirley, having almost all the people she loved nearby was a dream come true. For the first time in what seemed so long, Shirley felt secure and, finally, happy.

FOUR

When the Fuller Brush Company offered Shirley's brother Mike a job as manager in Asheville, North Carolina, where he would be making more money, he took the position.

Nelson wasn't making much money at his job as a mechanic, and when Mike offered him a job working for Fuller Brush they decided to take him up on it. Asheville was about a hundred miles away from Knoxville, over the mountains. It was a beautiful little town, and the people there seemed so friendly they took an immediate liking to it.

Shirley worked part time at first. Money was tight, but they even managed to scrape together the down payment on a tiny brick home on the outskirts of Asheville in Swannanoa. They all worked putting the finishing touches on the house; then they moved in.

Jeff was fifteen years old then. Because both his parents had to work, he helped take care of the other three children and did the dishes and housework. Tina, his younger sister, also helped him out when she could. He never complained and seemed tolerant and compassionate for someone as young as he. His mother was very proud of him. Jeff was almost as tall as his mother already, and she

knew that by the time he reached adulthood he would
stand over six feet like his father. She hadn't heard from
Jeff's real father in over fifteen years and didn't know if he
lived in Concord anymore. She'd heard he'd remarried and
had other children.

When Jeff was sixteen, knowing how the family had to
struggle to make ends meet, he decided he would help with
the family finances. Shirley tried to talk him out of it, telling him he needed time to be young, but Jeff insisted. Since
both his parents were selling Fuller Brush, he decided to do
that too. He was very successful as a salesman, and it
wasn't long before he outsold both Nelson and Shirley.

Jeff only kept a little of the money he made for himself.
He insisted on giving his mother the bulk of it.

His one luxury was an old car he managed to buy. It
was always breaking down, but he wouldn't give up on it.

Things seemed to be going well. Perhaps too well.
Then they found out Nelson had started drinking—a lot.
Night after night he came home and drank until he passed
out. It wasn't the environment Shirley wanted for her children. She and Nelson argued about it constantly. He would
promise to straighten out, and Shirley would take him back
only to find him drinking again.

"I'm sorry, honey, I really am. I do want to stop drinking, but I dream about the things I did in Vietnam and I feel
like I'm going to explode. You don't know what it was like
over there in the jungle." He put his hands across his face
and cried like a baby. Shirley tried to soothe him, but his
tears wouldn't stop. The sobs of grief and anger and frus-
trations wracked his entire body.

"Tell me about it, Nelson. Maybe it'll help if you talk to
someone about what went on over there. I know you lost
good friends, but you must go on with life. You can't keep
on thinking about what went on twenty years ago." Shirley
couldn't understand why the dreams kept on and on
through the years, and Nelson couldn't explain.

"You would hate me if I told you about what went on
in the jungle. I did what I was ordered to do. I was ordered

to fight, to kill, and I did my duty. I didn't do the things because I wanted to. I didn't run away to Canada like some of the guys. I fought for my country and it's tearing me apart. Where is the help the government promised us? No-where! They don't give a damn about us."

"Please, Nelson, just talk to me. I won't judge you for anything that happened over there. I know you were a good Marine and followed orders. I wasn't there Nelson. I don't know what went on, but I want to understand. I can't understand if you don't tell me." She waited for his an-swer, holding his hands in hers. It seemed like forever, but he finally began to talk.

"We were in the jungle on patrol. We came upon this camp of Vietnamese people. They were screaming and cry-ing and blood was everywhere. I saw a little girl, about nine years old, screaming for help. The gooks had stuck a bamboo pole up her rectum, and she was just stuck like a pig waiting for slaughter. I didn't know what to do, we couldn't save her. I couldn't help her and her screams were tearing right through me. She seemed to know she was dying and her eyes were pleading with me. I didn't have any choice. I pointed my rifle at that little girl and pulled the trigger.

"Then I ran. I ran until I couldn't run. I fell to the ground and got sick. I lost everything on the ground of that stinking jungle, including my self-respect. Oh God, Shirley, she was Tina's age; a baby, and I killed her. Every time I look at Tina I'm reminded of that little girl."

The haunted look in Nelson's eyes was something Shirley would never forget. She held out her arms as she would to one of her children and he clung to her.

In desperation Shirley took a second job. She worked nights as a cocktail waitress at the Holiday Inn from five in the evening till one or two in the morning. It was hard, but she had to do it if they wanted to keep their home. Nelson was spending more and more time drinking and less and less working.

Shirley's father, Ernest, became seriously ill the following summer. Teeny was in Massachusetts with her sick mother when Roger called Shirley one morning and said Pop was holding his chest and saying it hurt. Roger was petrified.

"What should I do, Shirley. Pop is lying back in the chair, clutching his chest, moaning and yelling."

"Get him to the hospital quick!" Shirley shouted. "I'll be there as soon as I can!"

When she got to the hospital, Shirley's sister, Brenda, met her at the emergency room. She had her two little girls with her and was crying.

"Where's Pop!" Shirley yelled with tears running down her face. She was so afraid her father was dead that fear had begun to consume her. She could hardly breathe as she waited for the answer and began to hyperventilate. Then they saw Roger walking toward them with Pop's clothes in his hands.

"No!" Shirley screamed, afraid he was really gone. Roger came running over. "Pop is all right. Really, Shirley. I was just taking his clothes home." Brenda turned and put her arms around Shirley.

"He's upstairs. He's had a heart attack." Roger answered and they could see he had been crying also. "Come on, I'll show you." They turned and started walking to the elevator. Brenda's daughters were following. A nurse hollered after them to stop, for children weren't allowed in that part of the hospital; but they kept on going. They knew the one thing that would cheer Pop was seeing some of his grandchildren.

By the time Teeny got there Ernest was out of the coronary unit and in a regular room. He was out of danger, but still very sick. He had diabetes as well as the heart condition.

After that Ernest would never let Teeny go anywhere without him. He was afraid to be without her. It was about this time, the summer of 1977, when Jeff, then seventeen, met and became friends with a couple named Buddy and Lisa. Buddy was gone most of the week truck driving while

Lisa worked in a factory. They had five children. In addition to his job and helping with his sisters at home, Jeff babysat for them, never accepting any payment for it.

They were having a tough time making ends meet, and Jeff liked the kids a lot. He'd stay there every afternoon that Shirley didn't need him while Lisa worked. At night he would go out and sell Fuller Brush products. Shirley suggested to him that it was all too much and he shouldn't spend so much time with them. "I can't stop helping them," Jeff said. "They don't have anything, Mom, and they can't afford to pay a sitter. They both have to work. They're not taking advantage of me. I don't mind doing what I'm doing. I really don't. I just want to help them until they get on their feet." He gave Shirley that irresistible smile he knew she couldn't resist and she dropped the subject.

About a week after that, a sheriff came to the house and asked for Jeff. "Jeff," Shirley said shocked. "Why in the world would you want Jeff. He's never in his life done anything wrong."

"I'm afraid he's written some bad checks, ma'm," the sheriff said.

"Bad checks, Jeff?" Shirley said shocked.

Jeff wasn't home at the time, and the sheriff said to bring him down to the station when he came home.

For practically the first time in Jeff's life, Shirley yelled at him. "Why did you write those checks when you didn't have money in the bank to cover them?"

He looked at her sheepishly and said, "I bought Lisa's kids some clothes and food."

"Are you crazy? They can take care of themselves! They're both working. Now how are you going to get the money to pay for those checks, plus the court costs?" She knew they didn't have any spare money and she was afraid for him.

"I don't know," he said giving his mother a pleading look. "I just know I had to do something. They didn't have any decent school clothes and with winter coming they didn't have any warm coats."

"Well, it's done now," she snapped. "We'll see about what they say at the station, then we'll get you an attorney." Shirley was frustrated. It was hard to yell at Jeff, especially after hearing what the checks had gone for. But he was wrong and she remained firm with him as they drove down to see the sheriff.

They went to see an attorney that day, one of the best in Asheville. He told them that the judge would decide how long or how short of a jail sentence Jeff would get. He said it could be a year, or it could be five years on each check Jeff had written. There was no way to foresee what would happen.

Nelson and Shirley talked it over that night. He wasn't drunk at that point and she wanted him to tell her that everything would be fine. "You know," she said, "the judge could give Jeff thirty years for writing those checks."

"That's right," Nelson said as he opened a can of beer. "He has to face up to what he did. No matter if he thought he had a good reason for doing it." He flipped on the television and turned away looking at the screen and guzzling the beer. Shirley became angry.

"That would ruin his whole life. If we could raise the money to pay for those checks, I'm sure the charges would be dropped."

"There's no way we can come up with that money before his court date, we haven't got an extra cent right now and no savings. It'll teach him a lesson," Nelson said calmly. "He'll have to face up to what he's done like a man."

"What kind of father are you?" she shouted. "You'd let Jeff go to prison because of money? I can't believe you can be so calm, you and your damn beer. I'm going to help him even if you don't." With that Shirley threw the beer can on the floor and snapped off the television.

"There's not much you can do about it, Shirley. It's up to the judge." He got up shaking his head and picked the can of beer off the floor. "Now I'm going out to the kitchen and open another can," he said, slurring the last few words.

Angrily, Shirley followed him, "I'm not going to sit back and let them put Jeff in jail because he tried to help someone in the wrong way."

"And so? It kind of stops there, doesn't it?"

"I've been thinking, Nelson. I want to take him over to Knoxville until we can get the money to pay off the checks and the charges," she said adamantly.

Nelson sighed, "Go ahead and do what you think is best. I know I can't change your mind once it's made up." He sat back down and became involved in the television again.

When the weekend came, Shirley drove Jeff over the mountain to Knoxville to look for a small, furnished room he could stay in. Roger planned to live with Jeff in Knoxville. Roger was only a year older than Jeff; they shared the same playpen when they were babies, but Roger was not as naive as Jeff was in the ways of the world. Jeff still depended on his mother; she was always there. Now it was doubly hard to let him go and face his responsibilities on his own.

Shirley looked all day for a place they could afford. At the end of a long and weary search, they found a dingy white stone hotel that looked to be a hundred years old. It was a tall building set in the middle of downtown Knoxville with a high set of stairs. Inside, the smell of mold and stale cigarette smoke made her gag.

"Come on, Mom," Jeff urged. "We'll find something else later. It's getting late and you have to get back to Asheville. This'll be okay for a little while. It is in the middle of town. I have to find work, and if we get anything further away, I might not be able to get around."

They walked up five flights of stairs to the room. It was even worse than she had expected. A double sized bed stood in the middle of the room. The heat made the stench worse when the door was closed. Off to the side was an-

other small room that had a tiny refrigerator and a table in
it.

"No, let's keep looking for something better than
this," Shirley said. "This place is just too awful. I can't
leave you here to live like this." She wrinkled her nose in
disgust. "It probably has roaches crawling around, too,"
she murmured.

"Don't worry, Mom. It's all right. I'll get by until I can
find a job. Then I'll move." Shirley stifled a flow of nausea
as Jeff continued. "I'll get used to the smell. Now you'd
better get going. It'll be dark soon, and I don't like to think
of you driving over the mountain at night." He gave his
mother a hug and a kiss walking her outside. Then he stood
on the sidewalk watching her leave.

Shirley cried as soon as she drove out of sight of the
old hotel. This was the first time she and her son had ever
been separated. She worried about someone hurting Jeff in
the rundown section he was living in. He was six foot three
inches tall, but to Shirley, he was her little boy and always
would be.

Jeff got a job at Manpower. He and Roger worked
there all day, came home, watched television and once in a
while they would go out in the evening for a beer. One
night a young girl with long, silky brown hair and a piquant face was sitting at a nearby table. Roger and Jeff
asked her to join them and learned that her name was
Cindy. She lived in Knoxville and worked at a little eatery
called Shoney's.

She was accompanied by her brother. As they talked,
the four became fast friends. Jeff made a date to see Cindy
the next evening, and soon their dates were a nightly occurrence. He fell in love for the first time in his life.

Shirley first met Cindy in Jeff's apartment the next
weekend when she had driven over to bring Jeff food and
make sure he was all right. She told him a warrant had
been issued for his arrest for not appearing in court, but
Shirley was confident that they would soon have the money

needed to pay the checks off. Then he could come home where he belonged.

Shirley didn't particularly like Cindy, who seemed to her to giggle at everything and ask insipid questions. But if Cindy was what Jeff wanted, then Shirley wasn't about to interfere.

A short while later Cindy moved in with Jeff, and Roger came back to Asheville. When Roger told Shirley that Cindy was telling people about Jeff's being wanted in North Carolina on the check charges, Shirley was furious.

The next time Shirley visited she confronted Jeff. "Why did you tell her that?" Shirley asked Jeff. "You shouldn't be telling anyone that stuff. Do you want to land yourself in jail? You can't trust everyone. I know you think that people won't tell on you, especially people you really care for, but that's not the way it goes." Then the bomb hit.

"I love her, Mom. I'm going to marry her." He looked at his mother nervously, hoping she'd understand. Shirley saw happiness in his eyes and knew he really did love Cindy; why, she didn't know. She sighed, realizing she'd have to trust his instincts.

"All right," Shirley finally said.

"I love you, Mom." He could always find his way into her heart.

They found another apartment in Elizabethton, Tennessee, about one hundred miles away. It wasn't much better than the hotel room he'd just left in Knoxville, but at least the neighborhood didn't look like there was much crime there. Shirley took Cindy aside and told her that she must never tell anyone about Jeff being wanted. Cindy promised.

On their next visit Shirley and Nelson and the rest of the kids drove over. As they walked into the apartment building Shirley saw a man with Jeff. He stared at her, smiling, as Jeff introduced them. Shirley shivered. His smile didn't reach his intense icy blue eyes. Shirley stood still for a minute and then walked by them as quickly as she could up the stairs to the apartment. Jeff called to her, "I'll be right there."

"Who was that?" Shirley asked Jeff as soon as he opened the door.

"Oh, he's just a guy I met here."

"Is he a friend of yours?" she asked, hoping that he wasn't.

"Yes, why? Is something wrong with him?" Jeff looked at his mother.

"I don't think you should be hanging around him, Jeff. There's something about him—something I don't like. He's scary and the way he looked at me made my skin crawl."

Jeff laughed. "Oh, Mom. He's all right. Nobody likes him because he doesn't have very good clothes but he doesn't have money to buy any. He goes around telling all these stories about how 'bad' he is. It gets to some people, but I just don't pay much attention. He's had a real hard life. He doesn't have a family like I do. I feel sorry for him; he's hungry and has nowhere to sleep so I let him come here."

"I just have this feeling. Like something bad's going to happen to you if you hang around him. What's his name?"

"His name is Donald Strouth, but we call him Chief. He likes to be called that. He says his father was full-blooded Apache and used to live on a reservation in New Mexico."

After they left, Shirley got to thinking more and more about "Chief." He reeked of trouble. Shirley knew Jeff had been sheltered and would be easy pickings for someone who pretended to be needy but had bad motives.

"We've got to move Jeff again," she told Nelson that night.

"What now?" he asked with a resigned look on his face.

"I've got to get him away from that guy he's hanging around with."

"Shirley," Nelson sighed, "Jeff's a big boy now. Let

him grow up, will ya? You can't always be around to fight his battles, you know."

But Shirley felt strongly about her intuition. Finally Nelson gave in to her pleas. In January Jeff and Cindy moved to a small town about twenty miles from Elizabethton, to Kingsport.

Shirley and Nelson rode over one weekend to see Jeff. It was such a gorgeous day, and they were singing dumb little songs as they drove over the mountain, temporarily forgetting why they were headed this way.

Jeff answered the door and stammered a little, "Hi, Mom. Uh, I didn't expect you here so early."

She knew Jeff's 'I've got my hand in the cookie jar' look and walked around him to see what he was hiding. There was Chief.

"Why did you tell him where you lived?" she asked Jeff. He looked nervously at her.

"I went back to get my last check at the grocery store and I ran into him. I couldn't just walk past him. We started talking. What else could I have done? It would have been rude to just not say anything. I slipped and told him where I lived. I'm sorry, Mom. I didn't mean to make you mad."

"You should have walked right on past him, that's what you should have done! He's trouble Jeff, I can feel it." Shirley looked out the window. "What am I going to do with you? I know you feel sorry for everyone, but you have to start looking after yourself and your family now. You've got to start getting tough. He's only using you because you feed him and let him hang around here."

"Mom, I gave him some food and a place to sleep. That's all." He looked at Cindy and then back at Shirley, pleading for understanding.

She shook her head. "No, you're just going to have to move again," she said adamantly.

"Okay," said Jeff. "I won't see him again. I promise."

Shirley frowned. "Jeff, you can't feel sorry for the whole world. You and Cindy have to look out for each other. That guy'll get along okay. He has so far without your help.''

The next weekend Trevor was sick. Shirley called and told Jeff she would be there the following weekend to move them. In the meantime she promised to send a little money to tide them over until she did get there. Little did she know that the next time she saw Jeff, he would be wanted for murder.

FIVE

The day after Jeff turned himself into the authorities, he waived extradition to go to Tennessee. The family was allowed to see him for a few precious moments. He said he had been questioned about the old army coat—the one Chief had given him.

"What happened to it?" Jeff asked. "They wanted to know, and I had to tell them that I didn't have any idea. I left it back at the apartment in Greenville when we left for Pennsylvania."

"I burned it," Nelson said. "It was with all the other junk your mother brought back home with her. Why on earth do they want to know about the coat?"

"They said they wanted to know if there was any blood on it."

A coldness came over Shirley. "Don't tell them that it was burned," she quickly said. In that instant, she knew there was going to be more trouble than they had anticipated. "It'll just look bad for you, and they'd never believe your story now. Just forget about it." She knew Nelson shouldn't have burned all that stuff. They could just as easily have put it all up in the attic, but Nelson was too drunk to do it. She felt fear now. The detectives had told them they knew Chief committed the murder. Why would they think there was blood on the coat that Jeff had worn, when he never went inside the store? Later she talked to Nelson about the coat.

"I think we should tell them I burned the coat," Nelson said. "There wasn't any blood on it, and I didn't have any ulterior motives for burning it. It was in the pile with all the rest of the junk. I burned it all."

Shirley shook her head vehemently, "No! Don't tell them that. I don't feel good about it. For some reason that coat is going to be a big thing in this whole mess. Otherwise, they wouldn't have brought it up."

"All right. I won't say anything, but I think we should tell the truth. Jeff isn't guilty, and he will only get probation."

Nelson was drinking again that night. Without anyone else's knowledge, he found his way down to the police station and proclaimed his act of destroying the coat to the detectives there. He told them there was no blood on it, and he would do anything to help the police prove that. He offered to dig up the place he'd put the burned trash in to see if he could find some pieces of the coat that were not damaged. Detective Wilcox said that they could analyze the coat for blood stains and that the ashes of the burned coat also could be examined.

When Nelson got home and told Shirley what he had done, she told him to leave and never come back. "Do you realize what you've done?" she screamed at him. "You had to be a big shot—out on a drunken toot confessing all to anybody who'd listen! Why did you do such an idiotic thing? Don't you know they will use that information against Jeff and not for him?"

"Don't worry," he said. "It's going to be fine. They're going to dig up what they can of the coat and do some kind of tests on it to prove there wasn't any blood on it. It'll really help Jeff." He staggered into the kitchen for another beer and came back gulping it down.

"Wilcox told me that they could really tell by sending the coat to the lab. I wouldn't do anything to hurt Jeff."

"Since when is Wilcox on our side?" Shirley had been near the breaking point for weeks; now all the frustration building in her exploded. "You can just go back to New York and live with your mother!" She stormed out of the room.

The following day she visited the police station and talked to Wilcox.

"If you had a picture of Jeff wearing the coat, couldn't we blow the picture up and tell if there was blood on the coat or not?" he asked. Shirley didn't like the man, but he was a detective and should know about things like that. She gave him the only photograph she had of Jeff wearing the army coat. It was taken after the murder on his wedding day when he was cleaning out her car. It was another mistake.

Jeff was taken to Kingsport the next day, and Shirley and Nelson rushed over there to see him but were told that they could not. They could see him the following Sunday in Blountville, where he would be taken.

As soon as she returned home, Shirley got out a telephone book and began a frantic search for an attorney who would take Jeff's case. Call after call brought no results or encouragement. She finally found a lawyer who said that he would represent Jeff, but it would cost at least $20,000, and that sum had to be paid to him before the trial. Beside herself, Shirley went begging to her parents, who loaned her $500. She brought it to the lawyer, telling herself that somehow, someway she would come up with the rest of the money.

Nelson didn't want to leave for New York; so Shirley let him stay in one of the rooms in the house. He cried and said he was sorry, but he still continued to drink at home in front of the kids. Even during his apologies his words were slurred, and his red eyes were a dead giveaway to his lack of sobriety. He stuck by her and Jeff, though, and she badly needed someone to lean on, even if the support they could offer was minimal. His friend Donald would come over quite often, and the three of them would talk and try to figure out how they were going to raise the money. As time went on she began to lean on Donald's quiet strength.

When Sunday came, they all went to Blountville to see Jeff. Jeff was imprisoned in a brick building behind the courthouse. Once inside, they were searched, as were all visitors, before guards led them to the visiting area.

The long dark visiting room of the jail had four small windows inside it that you visited through. They stood anxiously at one of the windows and waited for Jeff to come in.

Shirley wasn't prepared for what she saw when Jeff was finally led in. She stared at the dark circles under his eyes and his ghostly white skin and began to cry. She just knew they must be mistreating him, but of course Jeff wouldn't admit it. "I'm fine, Mom, really," he said hollowly. She didn't believe him. He wouldn't say anything to make them worry more about him.

It was hard to hear him as people stood at other windows yelling at the prisoners they were visiting. They couldn't touch him or be in the same room and that made it even harder to bear. They were allowed to visit only an hour and then made them leave. "Don't worry about me, Mom, please," Jeff called to her. She walked back and pressed her face against the glass. She would have to try to control herself for his sake. "I'm all right. Really, I am," she assured him.

The next day there was a hearing at the courthouse in Blountville to set bond. Shirley, Nelson and Donald attended, hoping against hope that bail would be set low enough for them to get a bondsman.

Six or seven deputies led Jeff and Chief into the crowded courtroom. Jeff's wrists and his hands were bound behind him. As he trudged in she saw iron chains around his ankles. Shirley covered her mouth to muffle her scream. He wasn't an animal to be chained up. As one of the guards shoved him into a seat she wanted to call out. But she kept her mouth shut fearing they would hurt him more.

The hearing lasted about an hour and a half. As she

looked at Chief a feeling of hatred such as she'd never before known swept over her.

Only one person testified at the hearing, a Kingsport detective named Stephen Page. He had discovered Mr. Keegan's body. "I found Mr. Keegan lying in a large pool of blood about fifteen feet inside the store. Mr. Keegan's throat had been slit from ear to ear and his head had been beaten."

Detective Page also read two statements given to the authorities by Jeff and Donald Strouth. Strouth's statement said that it was Jeff and a man named "Chase" who had committed the crime. He said that his knife wasn't used in any murder and that it was he who drove the car and waited outside.

Jeff's statement said that there was no man named "Chase," and an investigation by the police afterward agreed with that. He told how he had first met Chief. Then he described the day of the murder. Shirley sighed. It was exactly the same story as he had told it to her. She knew her son was telling the truth. Her jumbled thoughts turned this way and that. The one question that gnawed at her was, how were they going to prove his innocence?

She remembered Jeff had mentioned that the day the murder took place, a man in a dark pickup truck was parked across the street from him and had looked over at Jeff sitting in the car. If one person saw him, maybe there were others; maybe she could find them.

Suddenly her attention swung back to the courtroom. The judge announced bail would be set at $100,000. A new and troubling question struck her. That meant she had to come up with $10,000. Where would they get it?

Back home it was decided that Donald, Cindy and Shirley would go to Kingsport and try to find witnesses who might have seen Jeff that day. Nelson was going to work so he wasn't going. By this time Shirley and Donald had started falling in love, and although Nelson was jealous, he knew it was over between him and her. At least Shirley would have someone to lean on, and of course he would always be there for her—when he wasn't drunk, of course.

She had no answers but knew some had to be found, and quickly. Cindy, Donald and Shirley walked the street in Kingsport on which Mr. Keegan's Budget Shop was located. Cindy started on one side of the street, and Don and Shirley started on the other side. They had a picture of Jeff that they were going to show to proprietors of the shops, asking if they had seen Jeff sitting in the car the day of the murder.

The first shopkeeper barely let them get their question out. "I don't want nothing to do with that murder," he said and pointed to the door. A group of people had gathered and appeared to be watching them.

"It's Mrs. Keegan," Cindy said. "I don't know who the others are, but the lady in front is Mrs. Keegan."

In a few moments, a patrol car pulled up; two officers got out. A dark, heavyset man approached Shirley. "Just what do you think you're doing?" Shirley tried to explain.

"I don't care what you're doing, lady, I want you to get out of here and stop bothering these people," the heavyset officer said.

"But we're not bothering them," Shirley replied, close to tears. "I have to find someone who saw my son sitting out here in front of the store. He didn't go into the store the day Mr. Keegan was killed, and I need to find some witnesses."

"Like I said, lady, you and your family just leave town. You're not wanted here and I'm telling you to get out! We have the murderers now, and this town doesn't need your kind trying to stir up trouble. You're bothering Mrs. O'Shea by just being here."

"Shirley, we'd better go," Donald said.

She tried to protest but the look on the policeman's face convinced her. She left but vowed she'd come back. "There has to be someone who remembers that day and can help Jeff," she said getting into Donald's car.

They drove to a motel to figure out what they could do

next. Again Shirley came up with an idea. She called a local television station and explained what she was trying to do. Rob Peterson, the station manager, agreed to run a spot on the six o'clock news and then on the later edition at ten. Shirley was interviewed and nervously answered some questions about Jeff. She explained, "There were people on the street that day. Someone may remember seeing my son Jeff sitting in the car outside the store. There was a man in a pickup truck who saw Jeff. Please, if you have any information come forward."

The story ran on the six o'clock news. A picture of Jeff was flashed in the corner of the screen. At ten o'clock the story did not air at all.

A little after ten Shirley received a phone call from Rob Peterson at the station. "I'm very sorry," he said apologetically, "so many people called in and complained about the segment we had to drop it. They said they didn't want the mother of an accused murderer asking the public for help."

Shirley began to sob, "How can we prove he didn't do it if no one will help us. We have to find someone who saw him. And they don't want us to. They've already judged him guilty and don't want to know the truth."

Donald put his arms around Shirley. "Don't cry, Shirley, we'll find a way to prove his innocence. Somehow, we'll show them that Jeff didn't go inside the store."

Shirley sat there for a long time. She didn't say anything else. She seemed to retreat into some dark place in her own mind, silent, alone.

Suddenly she started. "Cindy," Shirley began, "Jeff said something about Chief making a call from the motel. Do you remember the name of the person he was calling?"

"I think he said it was someone named Chris. She paused, "Livingston, I think. Chief told him he had killed a man. He said his partner froze up on him and waited in the car. Listening to him Jeff and I were scared. He sounded so cold. I didn't know what we were going to do, but I did hear Chief tell Jeff that he killed a man." Cindy's voice cracked.

"Donald, won't the motel have a list of any phone numbers made from the room?" Shirley said. "Perhaps if we go to the motel and talk to the manager, he'll give me the number. Then, I'll call this Chris and see if he would testify about what Chief said to him."

"You could be right, Shirley," Donald nodded.

They decided to go back to the motel and try to attain the phone number of the person Strouth called. "It feels strange coming here," Cindy said as they got out.

"Eerie is more like it," Shirley added.

The hotel manager, a blond, freckled thirtiesh man nodded as Shirley explained why they had come. "The police have already been here and gotten the phone numbers," he said, "but the calls are still unpaid. If you'll pay for all of them, I'll give you a printout sheet of the numbers.

"I don't know how to thank you," Shirley said, blinking back tears. "Of course I'll pay. Anything."

She wasted no time in calling the number with the North Carolina prefix. An older woman with a gravelly voice answered.

"Does Chris Livingston live there?"

"He does," the woman said. "I'm his mother." Shirley gave a thumbs up sign to Cindy and Donald. Then she asked Chris' mother whether he knew Chief. The woman said that she knew Donald Strouth was a friend of her son's, but she added that she did not know where her son was that day.

Shirley explained, "I desperately need to talk to him." She told Chris' mother the story. "I'm praying he can testify at Jeff's trial and tell the court about Chief's confession to him." Chris' mother said she would give her son the message.

After she hung up she turned to Cindy and Donald. "We have to hope he'll help us, but we can't count on it. We have to keep searching, trying to find other evidence." Shirley shook her head. Another idea struck her. "Cindy, we should go back to Greenville, South Carolina, to talk to some people who might have seen Jeff wearing that army jacket during the month he lived there after the murder." Cindy nodded. "If only I hadn't given the police the only photograph of Jeff in it."

They went to Greenville anyway. Shirley talked to Roberta, the waitress at the restaurant Cindy had worked in.

"Yeah, I remember your son," Roberta said to Shirley. "He would come in the mornings and talk to Cindy."

"Do you remember the jacket he wore?"

Roberta wrinkled her nose. "Yeah, it was an army coat of some kind."

"Do you remember if you noticed any blood on the coat?" Shirley asked. She could see the couple in the next booth quickly leaning in her direction. She knew they were trying to listen to what they were talking about. She wished there was a private place to talk to the waitress, but since there wasn't, she would have to make do.

"No. I never seen any stains on that coat. I saw him all the time in here, and I never saw any blood on that coat."

"Would you be willing to give a statement to that effect?" Shirley waited for the answer.

"Sure. I'll give you a statement of what I saw. As long as I don't have to go in no courtroom. I don't like to be in the courtroom, but I'll give a statement and you can take that to the judge."

"Could we meet after your shift is over?" Shirley said, "We'll need a notarized statement, so it will stand up in court."

Their next stop was Manpower, the place Jeff had worked. The manager that Jeff had worked for, Mr. McGuire, also remembered the coat. "I never saw any stains whatsoever on it," he said definitively and gave them a statement to that effect. With the two statements in hand, they headed back to North Carolina, confident that they had at least some evidence to offer.

Despite this, they still needed to find money to defend

Jeff. Shirley never forgot that necessity, even for a minute. She knew the battle Jeff would have to fight would be a hard one. First, there was $10,000 to be raised for the bondsman just to get Jeff out of jail, then the lawyer's fee.

The sum seemed exorbitant and unobtainable by any means she could fathom. Still she couldn't, wouldn't give up.

Although Nelson was still there and would be until the fight was finished, they had started divorce proceedings. Shirley put the house up for sale. She knew they couldn't get too much out of it since they'd put very little down and most of the money they had paid in had gone for interest. But at least it would be something.

They continued to visit Jeff each Sunday, usually taking two cars because all of the kids wanted to go. Shirley, with Nelson and Donald, who had become her major allies, would drive over the mountain to Blountville.

Each time Shirley saw Jeff he looked worse. His weight was drastically dropping, and the dark circles under his eyes grew more and more prominent. When she asked the heavyset guard if she could bring in some food for Jeff, or pay for some to be brought in, he said, "If you are waiting trial for murder you are only fed two times a day. The sheriff says that these men don't deserve to eat anything and they are lucky to get any food at all."

"They have him convicted before going to trial," Shirley said sadly to Donald. "I feel so helpless. I hate the system and people who would do this to someone when they don't know for certain who is guilty and who is innocent."

"Shirley, nothing can be done right now," Nelson said shaking his head.

"Well, I don't know if I can stand much more of this," Shirley said. "Jeff tells me everything is fine. But I see him. I see the blackness under his eyes and the marks on his body." She began crying as she thought of her son sitting in his cell, alone, afraid, and under the constant tauntings of those who called him "murderer." She couldn't save her son from these people. "If we were one of the fortunate ones and had money, they would never do the things that they were doing to Jeff."

"Stop getting yourself worked up, Shirley," Nelson said. "I wish I could put your mind at ease, but I really feel that Jeff will only get a few years for being there."

"Nelson, I'm so tired of everyone saying he will only get a few years. I don't know what is going to happen but I have this feeling of fear."

The next day Shirley called Calvin Birch of the sheriff's department. Birch told her that they weren't looking for Jeff as a murderer.

"He's going to come out of this fine." Birch went on, "Detective Wilcox knows that Strouth did the murder. I saw the evidence they had on him myself. I told you before, they only want Jeff as an accessory." Shirley thanked him for trying to put her mind at ease. But it wasn't working. They had all lied to her and she was sorry she had let Jeff turn himself in. She should have been smarter, she thought. If she heard one more time that everything was going to be fine, she would scream. Shirley knew it wasn't going to be that easy; they were out for blood and didn't care whose it was.

More weeks went by. More hearings. Shirley hadn't been able to raise $20,000 for the attorney she had found, so they lost the $500 she'd paid him. The court finally appointed two attorneys for Jeff. One lawyer was James Beeler, a short stocky man in his mid-thirties with sandy brown hair. When he was first told to represent Jeff, Mr. Beeler had told the judge he didn't feel that he was qualified to handle the case because he had never handled a murder case before. But the judge told him he would have to represent Jeff. Teeny and Shirley went to his office to talk to him. He talked in a reassuring, soft voice and told them that he would do all he could do for Jeff as he believed in his innocence.

"It's going to be hard because Jeff gave that statement to the police like he did, but I assure you we'll do the very best we can. If Jeff had had an attorney when he went in to the police, he wouldn't have been allowed to tell the police he had been there the day of the crime. They never had any evidence on him. You never give any information without being represented." Mr. Beeler looked sad, and Shirley felt they'd have serious trouble proving Jeff innocent. He just didn't want to tell them that.

A few days later Shirley was contacted by Tom Edwards, a newspaper reporter in Kingsport. Mr. Edwards asked if she would agree to do an interview. "I'm interested in the case, and I believe Jeff is innocent. I want to write a story in the Kingsport paper to perhaps help in finding someone who would remember seeing Jeff in the car the day of the killing." Shirley agreed to it, and the article appeared the next day. He did an excellent job, but no one came forward with any information that could help them.

Nelson went back to New York to live, and Shirley began to see more of Donald, on whose counsel and companionship she had come to depend. She told him how worried she was that she had not yet been able to sell the house. Under normal circumstances she would have been more patient. The house had not been on the market that long and Nelson, who supported her efforts to help Jeff, was willing to go along with any decision she made on it. But time had become a critical factor. Jeff's life depended on a good lawyer. Shirley didn't know which way to turn. Donald offered to help, but he had little money saved. Her other children were doing everything they could; Tina had even gotten a job after school pumping gas. Every avenue Shirley explored ended in another disappointment. She prayed for a miracle but soon realized Jeff's life was going to depend on money. That wasn't fair, but that was the way it worked. Those with money got to live.

"I'll give you all the money I make!" Tina said crying.

She loved her brother and wanted to help him as much as Shirley did. "Won't that be enough?"

"No, Tina. A good lawyer wants $20,000 and more just to take the case. I have to find some way to get it, any way," Shirley said miserably, her voice breaking. If they didn't have it, Jeff would surely be convicted. What was she going to do?

"It's not a fair world when it's money that decides who will live and who will die, but that's what it boils down to. I don't know what I can do." Shirley started to cry, and Tina ran into her mother's arms. Together they cried until there were no tears left. "I don't know, Mom. I don't want to see Jeff die for what he didn't do. Do something, Mom, anything."

Shirley shook her head, "I would do anything. I just don't know what." As Shirley became more and more agonized, impractical schemes to make money ran through her mind day and night. Time after time she discarded them only to reconsider them again. Finally, abandoning hope of finding a legitimate way of obtaining the money, the memory of the bad checks Jeff had written flashed through her mind. Suddenly, she thought of a desperate plan. She would purchase merchandise with worthless checks, then sell what she had "bought" in a flea market. At this point she didn't care if she got caught and went to jail. What did her life matter? She had to save her son.

Asking Donald to watch the children, Shirley went to New York with Cindy and stayed in a hotel not far from where Nelson lived. She told them both what she was going to do. They tried to dissuade her, but Shirley was adamant. "I have to help Jeff." She went into the bank and opened a checking account, using false identification. Since she didn't have an address, she told the manager at the bank that she'd pick the checks up. Shirley said the kids around the street where she lived were always getting in her mailbox. It was the only excuse she could think of for not having the checks sent directly to her.

When the checks were ready, Nelson drove Shirley

and Cindy to the bank. Shirley's heart was beating so hard she was sure everyone in the bank knew what she was about to do, but everything went smoothly and soon she was outside heading for the nearest mall.

The first store Shirley, Cindy and Nelson walked into was a large department store. Shirley wore a blond wig to help disguise herself in case her appearance would be remembered. She had seen a woman do that once on a detective story on television. There were hundreds of people milling around. Shirley was afraid. It felt like everyone had their eyes on her and she almost gave up. Then she remembered Jeff. In her mind she saw the electric chair. She had to go on.

Hands shaking, Shirley picked out a few things and went up to the counter. Nelson stood a few feet away with Cindy as Shirley pulled out her checkbook. Smiling at the cashier, she chattered nervously about everything she could think of. The cashier asked for identification.

"What do you mean?" Shirley asked stupidly. "I only have a receipt for a driver's license that I had applied for in another state." Shirley watched as the clerk looked at the paper, then handed it back.

"You must have something else. A rent receipt, telephone bill or electric bill. I can't take a check without some sort of identification," the girl said reaching for the phone. Shirley panicked. Turning around she ran for the nearest exit. Once outside the store, Shirley ripped off the wig and continued running through the mall until she reached the car. It wasn't long until Nelson and Cindy caught up. She burst into tears and Nelson got behind the wheel to drive.

"I told you not to do it," said Nelson. "You're not a criminal; you can't get away with something like that. Just go home and see what happens at the trial." The three of them headed for the motel.

Tired and discouraged, Shirley and Cindy drove back to North Carolina the next morning.

"What are we going to do now?" Cindy asked. "We have to get the money for Jeff. We need a good attorney."

She paused, looked out the window then back at Shirley. "I'm getting hungry, are you?" Cindy seemed to be always hungry since her pregnancy so Shirley stopped to get her a hamburger. "Don't you want something?" Shirley shook her head numbly. She couldn't eat a thing, and felt nauseated.

As they sat there Shirley's thoughts darkened. She wondered why nothing she did seemed to help. It had never entered her mind that she couldn't just walk into a store and cash the checks. She should have known she would need proper identification.

Why was this happening to her? To them all? Jeff had done nothing wrong, yet he couldn't prove his innocence and it looked like neither could she. She sighed heavily. She would have to get the money. Next time, she would be smarter. Other people wrote bad checks, she thought, so could she. No matter that she had never even thought of doing such a thing and hated being dishonest. It was the only way to save her son's life.

SIX

The rest of the family were elated upon Shirley's return home. With Jeff in jail and her divorce final, the small family had come to depend on each other. When Shirley told her mother the reason she had been gone Teeny was horrified.

"You know people won't understand what you're doing if you get caught. It's going to go harder on Jeff and people are going to say you're crazy or worse," Teeny said. Shirley knew her mother was right; a lot of people would never understand.

"I can't help it, Mom. I have to do it to save Jeff. I would hope that any mother would understand why I have to go against the law. Am I supposed to let the State find him guilty and sentence him to die because I don't have the money to save his life? I'm damned if I do, and I'm damned if I don't," Shirley added. "There will always be people who want to think the worse of someone, and if they want to think I'm a terrible person, then I can't stop them. I know what I'm doing is wrong. I know I have other kids to watch over, and I'm trying to do my best by all of them. They all agree that the most important thing is to save Jeff." Shirley gulped back tears and watched as her mother poured a cup of coffee. Shirley knew all that had happened had taken a lot out of Teeny, but she was still the same old Ma and would stand by her daughter no matter what.

"Well, I don't know, Shirley. I just don't know what else you can do, but this is wrong. I can't see where you're going to come out ahead."

The conversation dwindled into silence. They both sat there for a long time. Then Shirley leaned forward, an intense look on her face. "By the way, Ma, I have something to tell you," Shirley said. "Donald and I are going to be married this week. I know this is sudden. But I know you'll understand, Ma, I need him. I feel so desperately alone."

Teeny smiled at her daughter. "Pop and I like Donald," she said. "We want you to be happy, Shirl. You're such a loving person. You deserve so much more than the unhappiness and pain you've had."

Donald and Shirley were quietly married. There was no talk of a honeymoon. There was no talk of anything but Jeff.

Not long afterward Teeny called. "Shirley, I've been racking my brain trying to think of something and I don't know if she will, but maybe Nana would help Jeff."

Shirley's grandmother lived in Lawrence, Massachusetts. She wasn't wealthy, but she lived quite comfortably and had no real bills to speak of. Shirley phoned her that night, asking her to loan them $10,000 for Jeff.

"Nana, I'll give you the title to my house, and Donald's trailer. He owns it free and clear along with an acre of land. It's worth much more than the money we need for the bondsman," Shirley pleaded.

"I'm sorry, Shirley. But I can't help you. I never loan out money, and Jeff got himself in this mess. It's up to him to get himself out. I don't believe in getting involved in the kids' lives."

"But, Nana," Shirley begged tearfully. "You're the only one that can help us. I can't raise that kind of money, and they want to kill Jeff. Doesn't that mean anything to you?" Tears streamed down Shirley's face.

"I'm sorry, Shirley. Ask your mother. I don't loan out

money, that's why I have it. Look, call me and let me know how it all comes out." She hung up the telephone. Shirley looked at Donald with a look of pure hopelessness. He held her close.

"She has money, and it's not like I owe a bill or something. This is my son's life and she could help save him. I almost hate her. She gave up my mother and her son when they were little. Her mother raised her kids and she never helped them either. Never gave her poor mother any money for their schooling or clothes. I should have known she wouldn't help us."

After Shirley's months of turmoil, it was difficult for her to understand her grandmother's seemingly callous attitude. All she could think of was that time was closing in on Jeff.

On each visit she made to see him, he looked worse and worse. His skin was waxy and pale; his weight continued to drop, his hands shook.

On her last visit with him, Jeff cried out to her, "Mom, please, please, help me. I haven't done anything. Why doesn't anyone believe me? Why are they keeping me here?" She had no words to answer his plea. She thought her heart would break.

After she left, Shirley knew she had to do something and right away. She decided to try the check writing one more time. But this time she would get more identification, so nothing would go wrong.

Sending for false identification out of a magazine, Shirley made up a new birth certificate by blanking out her name and replacing it with a different one. She typed the new name in and got the paper dirty so the white marks where it had been changed wouldn't show.

Shirley knew that this would not be enough; so she got another driver's license. She picked out a state that gave a license the same day you applied and went to the motor vehicle department there. She paid the man in back of her in line to use his car for the test. There were no problems.

Shirley wore a wig to the bank where she applied for a

checking account. The balding spectacled bank official looked at her for a long moment. Her heart skipped a beat. "The identification is sufficient," he said. "The account is approved." He walked her to the young fresh-faced teller.

"Kids always steal the mail from my mailbox," Shirley said. "I'll pick the checks up in person when they are ready." She felt extremely nervous. The weather was uncomfortably hot and humid. She began to perspire heavily, feeling faint. She kept going, though. Pictures of Jeff's sallow face and his eyes crying out to her for help kept going through her mind. The next day the holiday weekend began. She drove with Roger and Donald to a shopping mall. Picking up tools at the first store she went to, she headed for the checkout counter. She felt everyone's eyes upon her.

At any moment Shirley was sure, someone would tap her on the shoulder saying she was under arrest. Wincing in anticipation she wrote the first check. The clerk smiled, and said, "Have a nice day." Heaving a tremendous sigh, Shirley walked out and headed on to the other stores. By the time she had done this three or four times and nothing had happened to her, she began to breathe a little more easily, but inside feelings of shame and guilt still tormented her.

Outside Roger and Donald waited in the car. They didn't like what Shirley was doing, but neither had any idea where else to get any money and they both wanted to help Jeff.

Shirley went into Gears, a small department store, and bought three pairs of men's pants. Afterward she walked to the car and the three of them found a telephone. They looked up where another Gears store was located, got back in the car and headed for it. When they got to the new mall, they parked the car. This time Donald and Roger were to go inside and return the pants. After they came out, Shirley was to go in the store and buy more things to return to yet another store.

When Shirley saw them coming out of the store, she

went in and headed for the men's clothing department.
There she selected some black pants and walked up to one
of the clerks. She was filling out the check when she
glanced up and saw two men in blue uniforms walking
toward her. Sweat began pouring down her face. Something was wrong, she thought trembling all over. She tried
to calm herself. There was no possible way they could
know what was happening. But still they came toward her.

"Excuse me, ma'am, but what are you doing?" the
small dark-haired one with the moustache asked quietly.

She tried to act nonchalant. "They can't know," she
told herself. She had just bought those pants a few minutes
ago in the other store. Neither Donald, Roger nor she herself had been seen inside the stores together, yet she knew
they had figured it out somehow.

"I'm just buying some clothes for my husband. Is
there something wrong with that?" Shirley could feel herself becoming faint.

"Yes, ma'am. I think you're writing bad checks," he
said fingering his moustache. "Your husband or boyfriend
just returned a couple of pairs of pants just a few minutes
ago."

She tried not to break down. How did they figure it
out? She couldn't believe she was going to be caught now.
She just couldn't be sent to jail—not until she had enough
money to help Jeff. "I don't know what you're talking
about. I'm only doing some shopping for my husband and
kids."

The detective looked at her with pity in his eyes. Then
he turned to look toward the entrance of the store. "I see
your boyfriend has come back in the store and is peering at
us from behind that clothes rack over there," he said.

Shirley knew she'd have to bluff her way through. She
looked in the direction the man indicated, and, sure
enough, there was Don peeking at them from behind the
racks of clothes. "Everything is okay," she said. "I have
money in the bank. It's just that it's a holiday weekend and
we forgot to keep any money out. We deposited all our

money, and we wanted to take our kids who are back at home out for dinner and a movie later."

He didn't seem satisfied. "If you aren't doing anything wrong, why is the ringleader across the room trying to look so inconspicuous?" He looked toward the wall and Shirley almost fell over when she glanced in the direction he pointed.

If she hadn't been so scared, she would have laughed outright. There was Roger leaning up against the wall. He had on a ridiculous hat and reflecting sunglasses, looking more like a character on the Muppet show than anything else. What did he think he was doing anyway? He sure didn't look 'cool' if that was the image he wanted to portray.

The other store detective went over to Don and started to question him. He called the officer over, and they talked for a few minutes before coming back to where Shirley was standing. People were beginning to look at them, aware that something was going on.

Shirley's legs felt like rubber, and she wondered how crooks could do these things all the time.

"I'm going to let you go," the detective said with a slight smile. "But only because your boyfriend said pretty much the same as you did. It still doesn't make much sense to me. Come Monday morning, I'm going to the bank and see if you have the money there. And if you don't, I'll be back for you."

"Thank you," Shirley said. "The money will be in there." He copied the false address from her driver's license and said they could go.

The other older detective followed them to the entrance of the store. "Let's get out of here," Shirley whispered. "Let's go back to the motel, pack our clothes and leave right now before he changes his mind." She wasn't going to be able to do this, she decided, not even for Jeff. It was too scary and dangerous.

Shirley trembled all the way back to the motel room.

She felt like they were being followed, but didn't see anything in the rear mirror.

"I'll never get the money we need for Jeff," she began
crying.

"Don't cry, Mom," said Trevor, who had been waiting
in the room for his mother. "We'll get the money somehow."

"I hope you kids realize that what I'm doing is wrong,
and someday I'll have to pay it all back—and probably
spend some time in jail for doing it. Don't ever do anything
like this, ever. The only reason I am is to save Jeff. I can't
think of any other way."

"We know that, Mom. Don't worry, we won't do anything bad." Shirley tried to smile at Trevor, wishing she
didn't have to involve them. But right now the only thing
on her mind was Jeff.

"Why did you come back in the store?" she asked
Donald. "You were already outside. Even if I were caught,
it's better than all three of us."

"You know I wouldn't leave you in there alone," said
Donald. "We're in this together, and we'll get out of it together. If there were some way I could stop you without
turning you in, I'd do it. But since you're going to do it, I
feel safer about you if I'm nearby." He reached over and
kissed her. She was trembling all over. Would this nightmare never end?

The next morning they all went home. On the drive
Shirley continued to feel sick. She felt pain in her stomach.
She didn't think too much of it at the time, but a few weeks
later she knew the cause. She was pregnant.

This made her even more desperate; she began to
think again of her grandmother's credit card. One day she
decided she had to get it. Donald had to stay in North Carolina to work, so her brother Roger went with her. Nana
was glad to see them. They talked about all that was going
on in Jeff's case. Nana kept saying she hoped he came out
well in it, but she still refused to help out monetarily. While
they watched television Roger went to find her credit card.

In a short while, he signaled to Shirley he had gotten it and they prepared to leave. She felt guilty, but thoughts of Jeff in that hell he was living in drove her on.

She dropped Roger off at David's house and visited with him for awhile. Shirley loved her brother and wished he lived closer to the rest of the family. David was only a little taller than Shirley, with soft brown eyes and dark brown hair. It was longer than most people wore these days, but he was sweet and kind, and he worried about his big sister. His tears mixed with Shirley's as they kissed goodbye. The love they all shared was strong and knit them together.

On the way home, she stopped at Nana's house to spend the night. Suddenly Shirley felt terribly ill. Going into the bathroom she noticed that she had started to bleed.

Nana called Nelson in New York since he was only five hours away. "I'll be there as soon as I can and drive her the rest of the way back home," Nelson said. When Donald called a short time later, Shirley said Nelson was on his way.

"No, he's not," he said. "I'm flying up there, and I'll bring you home myself. Why didn't you call me when you found out about it?" It was the first time she had seen Donald angry. She put her grandmother on the phone. Nana told him she hadn't wanted him to come all the way up there when Nelson was so close.

"I'll meet them in New York as soon as I can book a flight out," he said and hung up.

Nelson arrived in record time. He hooked his car behind Shirley's and they headed for New York. "Thanks for coming to get me," Shirley said. The pain was getting stronger now.

"I'd come anywhere to get you if you needed me." Nelson placed his hand over hers and squeezed. She could see the love in his eyes and knew he was hurting. "Just because we're not married anymore doesn't mean I can't help you."

The ride was hard on her. Every bump in the road

seemed to bring more pain and nausea. Shirley started to bleed more heavily. She had a feeling she wasn't going to make it and was relieved when they finally reached the airport in New York. Don's plane had already landed, and he was waiting for them. He came running over and pulled Shirley close. She could see the worried look in his eyes.

"How are you feeling?" he asked. "Why didn't you go into the hospital?"

"Well, I wanted to be home when it happened. I know I've lost our baby, but I just didn't want to be in the hospital so far away from home."

"I tried to get her to stay there in Lawrence, but you know how stubborn she is. I figured I'd better be with her, and not let her drive by herself."

"Yeah, thanks for driving her here," Donald said as they walked to the car. "I know how she is. One day her stubbornness will get her in trouble."

"Don't talk as if I'm not here," Shirley said to them both. They each had one of her hands and guided her to the car.

Her knees buckled. Nelson and Donald both grabbed her. Half carrying her to the car, they sped to the nearest hospital. Donald and Nelson carried her into the emergency room. The nurse there needed information, and she began to ask the usual questions. Both Donald and Nelson were answering at the same time, one on either side of Shirley holding each hand.

Finally the nurse glared at both of them exasperated. "Which one," she demanded, "has more of a right to be here?"

"I was married to her for seventeen years," Nelson half shouted at the nurse.

"But I'm married to her now," Donald said in return.

"Look, both of you go out in the waiting room," Shirley said as she tried to smile through the pain. "I love you both. Now go out, I'll be fine." They both reluctantly left.

"I've never seen anything like that," the nurse laughed

as she started questioning Shirley again. Shirley lost the baby that night.

Nelson came to see her the next morning. "I'm sorry, Shirley. I love you so much and hate to see you in pain." Sitting on the bed, he held her close and let her cry.

"I'll always be there for you if you ever change your mind. I'll never find anyone to love like I do you. And please, stop worrying about Jeff. He's going to come out of this just fine." He held her hand, and she could see tears falling down his cheeks.

"I guess I can leave today," Shirley said changing the subject. She didn't want to think about the child she had lost.

"Maybe God is telling me that I will keep Jeff," she said to Nelson. "Maybe this is His way of telling me He won't take the child away that I already have." Still, despite her optimistic words, she felt an emptiness, like a part of her was lost. But she knew she couldn't spend time feeling sorry for herself.

"I don't know about things like that," Nelson said, "but I still think you're crazy to do what you're doing. Those court appointed attorneys will be okay. You're just going to end up in jail along with Jeff. What good are you going to be then to him? Or to the other kids?"

He wasn't telling her anything new. She knew she would have to pay for what she was doing someday. But it didn't seem to matter, not if she could save Jeff. "I don't care what happens to me," she said. "And I'd do the same for any of the other kids, too. As for the lawyer, the one they appointed doesn't know anything about a murder case; how can he help Jeff? I have to see if I can get Jeff a good lawyer, someone who will know what to do. I have to," she began crying.

At that moment Donald walked through the door and bent down to kiss Shirley. "How are you feeling, honey?" he said wiping away a tear. He looked at Nelson, "Thanks for being here with her."

"Take good care of her," Nelson said to Donald, shaking his hand. "I'll always love her." He turned and left.

Shirley forced herself to get ready to leave. She was still weak and dizzy. She fought the dizziness and tried to put one foot in front of the other. She felt she had to go on no matter how awful she was feeling.

"Please, Shirley, let's just get you home," Donald said. "I'm afraid you're not strong enough for this. After all, you just lost a baby last night. The doctor doesn't want to let you go home today, but since you insist he can't keep you here."

"I'm sorry, Donald. But I have to do this. Time is running out for us. Donald Strouth's trial is coming up soon, and Jeff will be tried right after it. We only have a few weeks to raise the money for a lawyer. Every minute counts. I need to use the credit card all the way back to North Carolina, and we still have to sell the stuff we buy. You have to let me go on." She knew she wasn't being fair to him. He was worried about her, but still she felt compelled to go on.

Going to store after store buying tools, appliances, and other things she thought might sell at a flea market, she kept pushing herself. Donald tried to get her to stop, but she was driven by a force even she didn't fully understand. Soon the car was full. Now she would have to stop and rest. Sweat was running down Shirley's face, and she was almost happy to be forced to rest. Still she knew her grandmother would be reporting her credit card stolen before too long and then she would be forced to stop for good. The thought that she still might not have enough money to help Jeff terrorized her.

Once back in Asheville, they went to see Jeff. They had to look through a small peephole in the steel door and yell through it. "Have you found an attorney yet?" Jeff yelled back through the hole, straining to be heard against the loud voices of other people who were visiting their own relatives that day.

"We haven't found one yet, but we'll be up here this

week to see what we can do," Shirley yelled back through the door.

She struggled to see Jeff through the peep hole. What she saw made her more unhappy. His physical condition was not improving. His eyes had sunken in, and the black underneath made him look like a prisoner of war. His bones stuck out of his white tee shirt. His jeans hung on his lean frame and were tied together with a rope to keep them up. Shirley cried when they left. The tears were of hopelessness and rage.

On the weekend Shirley and Donald went to the flea market selling what they had gotten during their trips to the stores during the week. They usually sold the things for half price. Sometimes they made good money; sometimes not.

Donald had given Shirley the small amount of money he had in his checking account. Every night they counted what they had and tried to figure out what they needed. He offered to open more accounts. "We don't have much time left," he said sadly. "I can't go on watching you kill yourself trying to raise the money, and I just don't have anymore."

"But I don't want you to be wanted by the law, too," Shirley cried. "It's enough that I'll have to leave when they find out; I don't want to ruin your life too." Shirley couldn't change his mind. He was determined to help her raise the money to save Jeff's life. She marvelled at this man who loved her enough to ruin his life to save her son, someone he hardly knew.

More checking accounts were opened in Donald's name in different cities in North Carolina. It was a little faster than just using the credit card, as Shirley usually tried to limit her credit card purchases to under $50 so the card would not be called in for verification.

Then Nana telephoned Shirley. "Shirley, did you take my Visa card? I haven't been able to find it since you were here."

"Yes," Shirley replied. "I'm ashamed that I had to

stoop that low. I know it was wrong, Nana, but I had to do
it. I had to get money for Jeff's attorney. It means his life,
can you understand that?" Shirley was crying and hoping
her grandmother would forgive her.

"I can't understand why you would do such a thing
even to help your son. I love you, Shirley and I wouldn't
tell on you, but I have reported the card stolen to the bank.
The police were here and asked me a lot of questions, but I
never mentioned you. Please be careful." She couldn't understand the love Shirley had for her children that would
drive her to go against the law to save Jeff. Perhaps a lot of
other people would never understand either. But Jeff was
innocent. Shirley couldn't stand the thought that the State
could put her child in a chair and run electricity through
his body until he was dead. She had to fight in every way
she knew how to save him. Right or wrong, she had to.

Shirley never lost her nervousness or guilt. At each
checkout counter she wrote the checks or used the credit
card. Then she would take the merchandise to their motel
room at night. People were doing their early Christmas
shopping, and no one seemed to notice the amount of merchandise they unloaded from their car in the evening. The
sounds of Christmas carols brought tears to Shirley's eyes.
She remembered the Christmases past and felt miserable
thinking of this one.

Always she continued to fear being caught. Sometimes
she wore glasses; sometimes not. She had two wigs that she
wore in the stores. One was blond; the other was black. She
thought if people tried to describe her, it would be hard to
do because one would remember her as having blond hair,
and another would remember her as brunette.

One night Shirley went into a small shop. Donald had
gone to another one. She placed some items on the counter
and waited for them to be rung up.

"I'll need more identification," the coffee-skinned
young clerk said. "This card is not enough." She looked at
Shirley, waiting for her to give her some other identification before ringing up the sale.

Shirley tried to remain calm. This was the first time she had encountered anyone wanting more identification. "Well, I don't have my license on me. I just don't carry all that stuff when I go shopping. I'll come back later and get these things when I get my license," Shirley said as she reached for the card the clerk was holding in her hand. But the clerk started walking to the phone.

"I'll just call it in and verify it," she said. "Then you won't have to come all the way back." She smiled as if she were doing Shirley a favor. Shirley felt a chill all over her. What was she going to do now?

"Oh, that's all right. I don't mind coming back in," Shirley said nervously. She looked around to see if she could spot Donald in the mall anywhere. "Just give me the card and I'll be back later." The clerk made no response. She had the card in her hand and began to dial the phone. Shirley began walking away. Seeing Donald inside the front entrance, she gave a sign that meant she was in trouble. He quickly went over to Shirley and she explained what had happened. They half ran to the outside exit. Frantically she pulled off the wig and put it in the paper bag she was carrying. Two security policemen walked past them. They were in such a hurry they didn't even see Donald and Shirley cowering in the corner. The detectives headed for the store Shirley had just come out of.

As soon as the men were out of sight Donald and Shirley ran to the car. Shirley felt like passing out. "That was a close call. I'm so scared," she said, her teeth chattering. Her teeth always chattered when she was scared and they wouldn't stop until she calmed down, which this time she didn't. Donald drove to the motel room and they hurried inside. Shirley fell on the bed. "Why is everything going against us," she whimpered, her teeth still chattering. "How will we save Jeff if nothing goes right?" she cried.

Donald tried to console her. "It will be alright. We'll find a way." He paused and looked at his wife, "I love you so much," he said tenderly and kissed her reddened eyes. "Now take a hot bath and watch some television. I'll go back to the mall and get more merchandise." Shirley nodded gratefully. After he left she ran the tub and exhaustedly got in. The soothing water made her feel somewhat better. Getting out, she slipped into her nightgown and lay down on the bed. Every channel on the television had something to do with Christmas. She turned the TV off. Her mind returned to Jeff. He wouldn't be with them this year to open presents under the tree, to eat the turkey she fixed every year, to share in the whole family gathering together. This year would not be a happy one for any of them. And next year, she shuddered, there was the possibility that Jeff might not even be alive to see it.

Once back in North Carolina, Shirley called famed attorney F. Lee Bailey's office in New York hoping she could appeal to him to take the case. She would beg him if she had to, explaining that Jeff was innocent and without a really good attorney he was probably going to be convicted and put to death. Shirley only got as far as the secretary, whose melodious voice patiently explained that Mr. Bailey was currently on a case, but quoted some round figures regarding fees. His starting fee was $50,000, and that wasn't for murder cases. They sometimes ran into the millions. Shirley swallowed hard. They could never raise that kind of money no matter what they did, and at this point she would have done anything. They would have to search for an attorney whose fee was more reasonable and pray he or she was good enough.

Cindy's baby came on August eleventh. Shirley stayed with her during labor. "I'm here for your daddy, little one," she said when the nurse first handed the infant to her, "because he can't be." When Shirley first looked into the baby girl's blue eyes she felt immense love. The baby looked just like Jeff. Jeff had wanted to name the baby after his mother, so they named her Shirley Anna Maria Dicks. Everyone called her Maria from the start.

Shirley called the jail and pleaded with the sheriff to let Jeff see his baby as soon as Cindy could bring her. The sheriff agreed.

At the prison, they were locked in a small airless room. A guard stood outside the door. His name was Henry Kogan, a burly Irishman, who always had a kind word for them. He was one of the nicest guards at Blountville. He even congratulated Jeff and posed for a picture with the baby.

Shirley watched with pride as Jeff held his first child tenderly in his arms. But she felt helpless at seeing her child hurting and not being able to do a thing about it. She couldn't take his pain away; she couldn't stop her own pain.

"We've got some money saved," she said to Jeff as he checked Maria's tiny fingers and toes carefully. "I think we can get an attorney before too much longer. Don't lose hope; we'll fight this thing together." Jeff gave a weak smile and told her not to worry about him.

When Henry Kogan came in to say their time was up, Shirley's tears started again. She wondered how one person could have so many. She wondered if she would ever run out of tears and pain. When she looked at Jeff she saw tears welling up in his eyes also as he gave Maria a last hug and kiss and handed her to his mother. Then he embraced his wife. Afterward he turned to Shirley, and she felt his ribs sticking out as he put his arms around her. She was shocked by how thin he'd become.

"I love you, Mom, please be careful and take care of my little girl for me." He looked away, and Shirley knew he didn't want her to see the tears falling down his face.

At home Cindy didn't take very good care of the baby, but Shirley told herself that Cindy was young and would come around in time. Jeff's sisters, Tina and Laurie, took over most of Maria's care whenever Shirley couldn't be there.

Tina was tall with long brown hair and hazel eyes. Laurie was tiny, blond and blue eyed. They were both beautiful, each in her own way, and Shirley loved them dearly. She was proud of them for caring for the baby, but she worried that their own youths were being disrupted.

Several times she tried to talk to Cindy about taking better care of the baby. Cindy said she was just too depressed. So Shirley tried to keep peace in the family for Jeff's sake. She told her daughters not to mention anything to Jeff. "It will only upset him, and we all know he doesn't need anything else on his mind."

Despite her feeling that Cindy should put her child first, Shirley felt sorry for the young girl. She obviously couldn't handle both the responsibility of a new baby and her husband's imprisonment.

A few days later Wilcox telephoned Cindy to testify at Chief's trial in Blountville. After Cindy hung up she turned to Shirley. "Mr. Wilcox says they're going to put me up at the Mayville Hotel. He'll take me there first to get settled."

"That's a pretty creepy place," Shirley said, "in a bad part of town."

"Will you come with me, please," Cindy pleaded.

"Of course I will. I wouldn't leave you alone with that man," Shirley said vehemently. "I wish we'd all never met him. Him with his lying promises about only questioning Jeff 'cause he knew Chief had done it."

SEVEN

After the murder of James Keegan, Donald "Chief" Strouth had fled to High Point, North Carolina. There he met with a friend, Chris Livingston at a convenience store. He told Livingston he had killed a man in a robbery. When Livingston asked if anyone had been with him, Strouth said no; his partner had "froze up" on him. After the meeting with Livingston, Strouth called his girlfriend, Sharon Carlson, who was in Elizabethton, Tennessee, and begged her to drive over the mountain to pick him up. The car he had bought with money from the robbery had broken down. Somehow he convinced Sharon, who had earlier told him to leave her alone, to drive over to High Point and pick him up. On the way back to Johnson City, they stopped alongside the road near a rest area.

There Strouth told her his pants had blood on them and, "I have to change them." After he got out and put on another pair, Sharon told him to rip them up and throw them away. Walking into the woods a little way, he dug a hole, put the jeans in, and shoveled dirt over them. Afterward Chief and Sharon continued on to Johnson City, where they rented a mobile home.

Unbeknownst to him, Chief had been spotted by several people around downtown Kingsport the day of the murder. They gave his description to the police, who made a composite drawing. It was circulated about two weeks before he was finally found. On March 8, Strouth was arrested at the trailer. Now, after more than five months in custody, his trial was about to begin.

Detective Wilcox and another detective drove over to North Carolina to pick up Cindy and Shirley. Wilcox told them they were to be put up at a hotel near the courthouse. "I know," Shirley said. "Cindy already told me your plans." She drew out the last two words and gave Wilcox a dirty look. As they drove over the winding, twisting road to Johnson City, and then over to Blountville, Shirley watched Detective Wilcox intently.

"You know, it's not going to be the same at Jeff's trial," he said. "We know that he didn't take an actual part in the killing. All he's going for is accessory."

"I don't believe a word you're saying," Shirley replied. "You told us when he came in, the warrant would read, 'accessory' and yet it was 'murder one.' " Wilcox flushed. Obviously he didn't like to be talked back to, but they needed Cindy's testimony, so he sat back. He frowned and stared at Shirley hard for a few minutes. "I'll drop you at the hotel first," he said. Then he gave a smile that wasn't really a smile at all and looked out the window. Thinking about staying in that seedy hotel made Shirley nervous.

She felt in her purse for her small twenty-two. She often carried it when she drove at night with just the kids or while alone. She never had any bullets in it; didn't even own any. She didn't think she could ever really use it. But she felt safer just carrying it, and she figured if she should run into trouble, it would scare someone away. She knew the hotel they were going to was in a bad part of town, and since Cindy and she would be virtually on their own, she felt the need of some protection. She planned on dropping the gun off at her room before going to the courthouse. But Detective Wilcox didn't drive to the hotel as he had said he would.

Instead he pulled up to the huge, antiquated gray stone building that was the Sullivan County Courthouse. "I thought we were going to the hotel first, so we could put our suitcases in the room," Shirley said to Wilcox. He got out of the car and told them to get out. His voice was very curt now, his eyes glaring at her.

"We don't have time. We're late as it is." Wilcox barked as he stood outside waiting for them. "You can leave your suitcases upstairs in the chambers. We'll take you to the hotel later." He was already ahead of them, climbing the courthouse steps.

Once in the chambers, they put the suitcases down. Shirley turned to Cindy, "I'd better put the gun in my suitcase. Don't want to take it in the courtroom."

"I guess that's a good idea," Cindy replied as she looked around the office. As Shirley took the gun out of her purse, Wilcox yelled out, "What the hell are you doing?"

"I'm putting my gun in my suitcase since we're going into the courtroom. I thought we were going to the hotel first, so I had it in my purse." Shirley started to close the suitcase, but Wilcox screamed at her again.

"You can't have that here in the state of Tennessee." He held out his hand for her to deposit the gun in. "Give it to me right now!"

Shirley's voice shook, "I have a permit for it. Since we're not staying at a decent hotel, I figured I might need it." She handed the gun to him. "It isn't loaded; I don't even have any bullets for it." He glared at her and grabbed the gun from her hand.

"Well, you can't have it here. I'll give it back when you get to North Carolina."

"I never intended to bring it here in the first place. You're the one who didn't take us to the hotel first. It wasn't our idea." Shirley stood her ground. She didn't like the idea of staying at the rundown hotel, nor that Wilcox had again broken his word.

"I said you can't have it until you leave, and that's all there is to it," he snapped. "Now both of you go down to the courtroom, and you," he pointed at Cindy, "sit outside until you're called."

Shirley and Cindy walked down the steps from the chambers. The halls were crowded with seedy looking prisoners and even seedier lawyers.

Cindy sat down on a scarred wood bench unable to go inside since she would be testifying. As Shirley walked into the courtroom people whispered loudly and turned to stare at her. She knew they were talking about her being the mother of the other boy involved in the murder. Her face flushed with embarrassment as she took a seat.

Shirley looked around; she could see the Keegan family on the other side of the room. The looks they gave her seemed filled with hatred. Shirley felt a shiver go up her spine. She knew they felt her son was somehow involved in the killing, and she couldn't blame them for the bad feelings they relayed toward her. She just wished she could tell them that Jeff didn't do it and how sorry she was. But she knew she wasn't supposed to speak to them. So she turned her attention to the prisoner.

Chief sat sprawled out at the table in front of her wearing the jeans and plaid shirt his attorney had supplied him with. Stony faced, he turned to glare at the spectators. Only once did he turn toward her, and Shirley stared into his eyes. She shuddered; they were steel blue, expressionless as if he were drugged or stunned. Next to him sat his court appointed attorneys Larry Dillow and Patrick O'Rourke. District Attorney Carl Kirkpatrick and Attorney Greely Wells at the opposite table represented the prosecution. The bailiff told them to rise as the judge, Edgar Calhoun, a small man with light brown hair, entered the courtroom.

"Be seated." His tone was icily formal.

After nine hours of questioning, six jurors were chosen. They were to be sequestered for the night at a motel. Cindy and Shirley were taken to their hotel until morning, when a car would be sent to take them back to the courthouse.

Shirley had been right about the place. As they walked into the lobby a stench filled their nostrils. The room looked as though it had not been cleaned in weeks. A stained sink and toilet stood in the corner. The beds creaked and cockroaches flitted about. If Shirley's car had been there, they surely would have gone someplace else even if she had to pay for it herself.

"Well, Cindy," Shirley said despondently, "I guess we don't have much choice in the matter. Try to make yourself as comfortable as you can."

The girl nodded.

They both tried to sleep hoping they were tired enough that their surroundings wouldn't matter. But both were glad when morning came. At dawn both women rose in silence and began to get ready.

The second day was almost a carbon copy of the first. Shirley felt relieved when shortly before five P.M. the twelfth juror was selected.

After Carl Kirkpatrick's opening statement the next morning, Donald Strouth stood up in the courtroom. Murmurs began in the courtroom. The judge banged his gavel decisively. There was silence again. "Good morning. My name is Donald Strouth, and I'm on trial here for my life." His voice was colorless, subdued. "These men are my lawyers and I hope you give them your attention. Thank you." Still expressionless, Strouth sat back down at the table and began doodling with a pencil on a pad of paper that lay in front of him.

The spectators shifted in their seats: first one way and then the other. Shirley sensed a general unrest fill the room. Shirley looked over and saw Jeff's attorney, James

Beeler. He had come to the trial to observe and try to get
some idea of how Jeff's might go. She knew he didn't have
to be there but wanted to do all he could to help Jeff. Jeff—
Shirley's thoughts turned to him. What would his trial be
like? Would the same animosity she couldn't help feeling
from the spectators be there when her son was tried? She
looked forward and tried to focus on what was happening.
Perhaps, like Mr. Beeler, she could learn from Strouth's
trial.

The first witness called to the stand was Steven Page,
one of the police officers who had discovered the body. The
pictures that had been taken at the murder scene and other
various articles of evidence were shown to him to identify.
When Mrs. Keegan, a small, brown haired woman, her face
pale and strained, was called to the stand to testify, she
walked slowly to the front of the courtroom. She paused to
glance around her at the spectators, then looked at Shirley
for what seemed to be a long time before she sat down.
After answering a few preliminary questions, she told the
jury about her husband and how he carried some money in
his front pocket. Then tearfully she explained how she had
found her husband's body when he didn't come home for
dinner.

A fake fur jacket alleged to be taken in the robbery was
entered as State's Exhibit Number 1.

A little after twelve, the Court recessed for lunch. Shirley was only too glad for the break. Tired and uncomfortable sitting in the courtroom by herself, she could feel the
animosity from the other spectators and realized sadly that
many people blamed her son along with Chief for the killing.

Cindy and Shirley walked across the main street to
Curtains, a tiny storefront restaurant. Peering in she saw
the attorneys and some of the witnesses inside. "I wish we
could go somewhere else," Cindy said.

"It's the only restaurant in town," Shirley frowned.
People began to whisper and Shirley felt every eye on them
as they entered.

"Let's take a seat at a table in the back," she said. "I don't want to be sitting close to Wilcox or the others." Shirley frowned.

"There are newspapers over there," Cindy pointed to a wire rack. "Should I get one?" Shirley nodded. Cindy took one, brought it back, handed the newspaper to Shirley and sat down. As she read the news account, Shirley gasped.

"I don't believe this," she said to Cindy. "Listen to what it says. 'Keegan Murder Trial Security Tightened.' Shirley began to slowly read the words, " 'Security was drawn even tighter around the murder and armed robbery trial of Donald Wayne Strouth. The extra security was clamped down yesterday after the noon recess when Judge Edgar Calhoun dryly announced that certain facts surrounding the trial had led him to authorize sheriff's department deputies to frisk all spectators before they would be allowed in the courtroom. Deputies were then stationed at each door after all occupants of the court were taken out and searched. From then on all persons with the exceptions of the attorneys, police and press personnel were frisked each time they entered the court.

"We are concerned about the threat on our client's life," said defense attorney Patrick O'Rourke. A high ranking official directly related to the case said that a gun had been confiscated from Shirley Dicks, mother of co-defendant Jeffrey Dicks, earlier in the day.' "

"But that's not what happened," Cindy said, her eyes widening.

Shirley was furious. "What a lie. They tried to make it sound as if I had the gun on purpose to kill Chief. What was I going to do with the gun, throw it at his head and kill him? There were no bullets in it, or anywhere else in my belongings. 'Confiscated?' Brother, they're sure doing a good job of making us look bad." Shirley folded the paper back up and pushed it aside. Again she had done the wrong thing, and it was all stacking up against Jeff. Everything she tried to do ended up in making Jeff look like a criminal.

Would she never learn? She thought, "I can't believe they tried to say I threatened Chief's life. He's the only one who can tell the truth about Jeff: He's the only one who can free Jeff." Shirley passed a hand across her aching head.

Cindy shook her head and finished her lunch. "I think it's time we went back over. Everyone else has already gone. Guess they had a pretty good idea of what you were reading. If I was them, I wouldn't have stuck around, either." She sighed, got up, put on her coat and they left.

Back in the courtroom all was quiet. The witness called next was Colleen Ebsen, who lived in the same apartment building as Jeff and Cindy.

One of the prosecutors, Carl Kirkpatrick, strode forward.

"What is your name?"

"Colleen Ebsen," the attractive brunette answered softly.

"Back in February of this year were you living at 718 Maple Street, next door to Jeff Baker and Cindy Baker?"

"Yes, sir," she said in a hesitant voice.

"Now, the man by the name of Jeff Baker, did he have any employment that you knew of or where did he work?"

"Well," she said slowly, "he sold Fuller Brush is what he sold. I mean that's the only thing that I knew of."

"Did they have guests periodically?"

She shook her head affirmatively.

"Yes, sir. That one they call Chief and Sharon Carlson and, of course, Jeff's parents," she paused, "and that's all."

"Now how did Chief get to the apartment?"

"He would drive his girlfriend's car."

Kirkpatrick leaned toward her.

"On the day that Jimmy Keegan was murdered, did Jeff leave the apartment?"

"Yes," she murmured.

Kirkpatrick's voice had hardened.

"And did Strouth arrive there?"

"Yes."

"Did they leave the apartment together?"

"Yes," she nodded.

He cast a lingering look at her.

"How long were they gone?"

Again she hesitated.

"About half an hour," she stopped, looked around, then continued, "or something."

"When they returned did you see them?"

"Yes."

"Then what happened?"

"They went into their room. After about five minutes they all left."

He wanted to be sure the jury understood his point.

"Chief, Jeff and Cindy?"

"Yes."

"Did they ever return?"

"Not that I know of."

He nodded and switched to another topic.

"What is the next activity that took place in the room that they were living in?"

Colleen seemed to be confused and hesitated, "Well, his mother and his stepfather came on Sunday and they got the stuff out of the room that belonged to Cindy and Jeff."

"After that, did you see any more of the Bakers or of Sharon Carlson or Mr. Strouth?"

"No, sir."

Kirkpatrick looked toward the defense table.

Dillow waved his hand.

"No questions, Your Honor."

"You may step down and go back to the witness room, and don't discuss with any of the other witnesses your testimony," Judge Calhoun admonished the witness.

Chief's red haired, pretty girlfriend, Sharon Carlson, was called next and duly sworn. As she turned to face the jury, Shirley could see Sharon's lower lip quiver with nervousness. She said she had known Chief about five months at the time of the murder. She spoke so softly, the Court asked her to speak up. She told how Strouth had come to see her the day of the murder in a car she had never seen before.

"Did he tell you where he had gotten the car?" Kirkpatrick asked quietly.

"He said he bought the car."

Kirkpatrick's voice hardened.

"Of course you knew he didn't have money to buy the car with. Did you ask him where he got the money?"

Sharon visibly trembled.

"I asked him what he'd done and he said he was doing what he . . . he done what he knew how to do. I asked him did you rob somebody or something and . . . he said yes. I was mad at him for doing something I knew would cause him trouble. I said you can't come back to my house," she sighed. "He said he was going to leave and said he was going to go to Chris' house."

Kirkpatrick stepped back.

"Now, at that point, did you all part company?"

"They left," she said softly. "Jeff and Cindy left with Chief."

"Now, when was the next time you heard from the defendant, Mr. Strouth?"

"He called me on Friday night, and . . ."

Kirkpatrick cut her off.

"By this time you had learned from listening to the news that Jimmy Keegan had been robbed and murdered?"

"Yes."

"What did Chief ask you."

"He asked if anybody had been around asking about him. I told him no. I asked if he was coming back. He said, 'Do you want me to come back?' I said, 'I'd like you to come back.' I told him I'd drive to High Point and meet him."

"And did you meet him there?"

"Yes. We went riding around," she sighed heavily. "I asked him what Jeff's part in this was and he said something about 'Jeff froze on me,' or something about Jeff freezing on him."

Kirkpatrick quickly moved the testimony to another topic.

"That's the same place Chris Livingston lives?"

"Yes."

"He told you on many occasions that he and Jeff went in and killed Mr. Keegan, hasn't he?"

Again he tried to get Sharon to implicate Jeff.

"No," she said quickly, steadfast in her testimony that Strouth acted alone. "One time he said he hit that man and the man went down and he . . . before he knew it . . . he said he hit him with a rock."

Kirkpatrick continued.

"Did he have a knife?"

"I bought him a hawkbill knife."

Kirkpatrick nodded.

"Now when Chief came back from North Carolina, what was he wearing that day."

"Blue jeans."

"And you observed and discussed with him the fact those blue jeans had blood all over them, didn't you?"

"There were blue jeans that had dark spots on the legs of them."

"Did he tell you he needed to change his pants?"

Sharon's face was troubled.

"He said . . . these pants have blood on them and I have to change them. I stopped the car. He got out and took off his pants and he had some . . . he had some more clothes in my car, and he put on another pair of pants. He started to lay them down on the side of the road and I . . . I said to throw them away. To rip them up. So he ripped them up and threw them."

Kirkpatrick turned toward the jury and again his voice was forceful.

"These blue jeans you speak of, you later went to that same area with Mr. Bower from the police department and recovered them, did you not?"

She hung her head.

"Yeah."

The jeans were marked as Exhibit Number 11 and filed.

Kirkpatrick had only one more question.

"And did you give Mr. Bower a bill of sale for a 1964 Comet automobile?"

"Yes," Sharon said softly.

Kirkpatrick gave a slight smile. "Thank you, Miss Carlson. I have no further questions at this time."

The next witness was Tony Becker, the used car salesman at the lot where Chief bought the Comet. He told how Chief had come in and paid for the car in cash. He pointed out Chief in the courtroom as the one who bought the car in the name of Jeff Baker.

Next, Chris Livingston, the friend Chief had called on the day of the murder, testified. Livingston, a dark and slight young man, looked uncomfortable as he walked to the stand.

Shirley leaned forward to see him better. It was Livingston whom she had tried desperately to reach, since he might be able to clear Jeff.

After Livingston had been sworn in and asked a few preliminary questions Kirkpatrick got to the point.

"Mr. Livingston, on February the 16th of 1978, did you see Donald Strouth?"

"Yes, sir," Livingston said clearly.

"What did he say?" Kirkpatrick inquired.

"He said that he'd hit some man in the head with a rock and killed him in Wilmington and that he was running from the law."

Kirkpatrick, still hoping to implicate Jeff but not taking any chances that he'd get an answer he didn't want this time, asked, "What else, if anything, did he say?"

Shirley's heart skipped a beat; she prayed Livingston would say something to prove Jeff had not been there.

"We just talked in general after he said that."

Shirley sighed disheartened.

"Did you notice what kind of clothes he had on?"

"He had a pair of jeans on, and I don't know what kind of shirt."

"Did you notice anything particular about the blue jeans?"

"They were dirty and stained down the front of his pants."

"Did you ask him about the stains?

"No."

Kirkpatrick hurried on.

"Did you see him with a car on that day?"

"Yeah. It was an old beat up Mercury Comet."

After dismissing Livingston, Kirkpatrick indicated he would call Cindy to the stand.

"This is the girlfriend of Jeffrey Dicks, who is privy to most of the knowledge from beginning to end," Carl Kirkpatrick told the Court. "I would suggest that there be a short recess to allow the jury to sit without discomfort throughout the entire examination."

Shirley was glad to have a chance to stretch her legs. Sitting in the courtroom hour after hour on the hard bench was depressing and tiring. And watching Strouth sitting like a peacock directly in front of her was almost more than she could bear. Since his mother was sitting behind her, once in a while Strouth would turn around and glance at his mother, sometimes giving Shirley a glare. She had heard he hadn't lived at home in many years and his attorneys had to pay his mother's way over to the trial.

Cindy was waiting for Shirley, and they walked down to the lobby to get a cold drink. "I hope I do okay," Cindy said taking a drink of coke. Her long brown hair shone, and she didn't wear any makeup. She looked to be about fifteen instead of nineteen. "I get so confused when they talk to me, they make me forget what I'm saying," she said, turning to her mother-in-law for reassurance.

"Just tell the truth," Shirley told her. "And it won't be all that bad." She hoped it wouldn't, but she worried Cindy was in for a long and hard time of it. Soon it was time to return to the courtroom. Shirley watched Cindy walk unsteadily to the stand. Her voice shook as she told the Court that she and Jeff hadn't been married when the crime took place. They made it sound like the only reason they did marry was so Cindy wouldn't have to testify against Jeff.

"Who were your closest friends in Kingsport?" Kirkpatrick asked, turning toward the jury.

"Sharon Carlson and Donald Strouth."

"And after you and Jeff moved to Kingsport, did you continue your close relationship?"

"Yes, even though my mother-in-law advised against it."

"On February 15th did the defendant come to your apartment?"

"Yes. He was talking to my husband. They said they were going to go down to the welfare office. They left, came back, and left again. Then they came back and said we had to leave. I noticed blood on Chief's hand and on his clothes and I said . . . what happened to your hand? He said, 'I cut myself.' So we left for Bristol."

At the end she took a deep breath.

"What kind of pants was he wearing?"

"I believe he had on blue jeans."

"What kind of coat did he have on?"

"They both had army coats. Jeff's was long and Chief's was short.

"When you went out and got in the car, where was the car parked? And had the car been moved since the last time you'd seen it?"

"I believe it had because when I seen it, it was not parked in the same place."

"When was the last time you'd seen it?"

"That morning. I had walked outside and it was parked farther down."

"Now during this time, did you have occasion to see the fur coat? The coat Strouth gave his girlfriend Sharon Carlson."

"Yes. On the way back, I looked in the back seat and there was the brown coat, and I asked Strouth where he got it. He said, 'I bought it from the man at the Budget Shop.' I asked how much he'd paid for it and I forget what he told me. Then he said, 'I robbed the old man and I hurt him.' He said, 'I cut his throat. I had to slit the man's throat.'"

"Did he say why he had to slit the man's throat?"

"No," for the first time Cindy's voice was strong and clear. "I turned to my husband and asked him if he knew anything about it, and he said he did not. We drove to Johnson City and went to a gas station, and Strouth went in to buy a car."

"After he purchased the car, where did you go?"

"We went to pick Sharon up. Sharon and Chief were talking, and then Sharon got out of the car and got into her car and she left. Then Strouth and me and Jeff went to the Broadway Motel."

"Tell us what happened then."

"We were sitting in the room and it came on the news that the man had been killed. Jeff said he was going to call his mother. He called her, and Strouth made a phone call to a boy in High Point and talked to him. Then he said to Jeff to go to Florida. Jeff said, 'No,' he said, 'my mother is coming.' So Strouth left, and he left a number for us to get in touch with him the following Sunday; but we never called him."

"Where did you and your husband go then?"

"We went to Greenville, South Carolina. Then we went to Erie, Pennsylvania."

He looked at the girl intently and then asked, "Did you know the police were looking for you?"

She nodded, "Yes."

Kirkpatrick let the jury have a few minutes to consider the remark. Then he returned to the subject of the relationship between Cindy, Jeff, Strouth and his girlfriend.

"When you first moved to Kingsport, did you and your husband continue with your friendship with Strouth?"

"Yes, even though my mother-in-law advised against it."

"How were you able to support yourselves since Mr. Dicks was no longer working at the Giant store?"

"Jeff's mother brought us our money and food to us."

"Now, during the week that you were in South Carolina, did you all work?"

"We both did."

"How did you get to Pennsylvania?"

"Jeff's mother."

"She came and picked you up?"

"Yes."

"Now on March the 19th of 1978, did your husband surrender in your company at the Asheville Police Department?"

"Yes, sir." Her voice was all but inaudible.

Kirkpatrick turned to the defense counsel. "You may ask."

Cindy was cross-examined by Mr. Lauderback. He tried to discredit her testimony by asking her if she was aware of any agreement "by which your testimony here today against Donald Strouth will benefit your husband?"

She looked him directly in the eyes and said, "No. I'm just going to tell the truth."

Kirkpatrick, obviously surprised, quickly asked another question.

"When you lived in Knoxville, where did you stay?"

"I lived at Barrett Hall and then moved to Motel Monday."

"What is Barrett Hall?"

"It's a place for girls who don't have a home," Cindy said softly.

"When did you meet your husband?"

"In Knoxville."

"I believe after you left Greenville, South Carolina, his mother went back and burned all the clothes, didn't she?"

"My father-in-law burned everything that was in the apartment."

"And one of the things was the long green coat, wasn't it?"

"That's correct."

"You got married on March the 4th, I believe you said."

"Yes, sir."

"Do you have any children?"

"I have a daughter almost three weeks old."

"And is Jeff Dicks the father?"

"Of course," Cindy said flushing.

"And of course, at the time you got married you realized that if you got married, you wouldn't have to testify against your husband, didn't you?" Kirkpatrick said with a look of distaste.

Cindy shook her head.

"No, sir, that is not it," Cindy's voice quivered; she was visibly upset by Kirkpatrick's innuendos.

"When you left Erie, Pennsylvania, I think you said you were up there about two weeks, where did you move back to?"

"We came back to North Carolina and my husband surrendered to the police there."

"Now was that his mother's idea to come back from Erie?" Kirkpatrick snapped.

Cindy had pulled herself together and said calmly, "My mother-in-law left that decision up to my husband. She called him and told him that he was wanted for questioning in the murder and she told him, 'You don't have to come back.' A look of pride came on her face, "And Jeff said, 'Well, I want to because I didn't do anything.'"

But Kirkpatrick wasn't giving up that easily.

"Did she go up there and get him?"

Cindy looked him straight in the eye.

"She came up and got us."

Once again, the jury was dismissed for the night. After dinner, Cindy brought Chris Livingston, who had testified earlier that day, to the motel room with her.

"Mom, this is Chris. He told me more about Chief, and he says he'll come back and testify for Jeff."

"Hello, Mrs. Dicks," Chris said to Shirley as he sat down on the old wreck of a bed. "Cindy told me they're going to try to railroad your son on this murder."

"Yes," she replied dispiritedly. "It kind of looks that way, even though they told us earlier that they only wanted him to testify against Chief," she sighed. "I guess they were lying about everything right from the start. They didn't even call Jeff to testify. They didn't need him with all the others." She shook her head wearily.

Chris nodded sympathetically. "Well, I'll be glad to come back when Jeff has his trial. That Chief is a weird one. He told me that his partner froze up on him and didn't come in. He didn't call him by name, but that's what he said."

Shirley's eyes filled up with tears. "You're sure," she said. "It means so much." He nodded.

"That would help, I'm positive," she told him gratefully. "I know the State pays its witnesses when they come to testify, so I guess we'll have to do the same. We can only pay you a week's wages and your plane fare down here. We can't scrape up more than a thousand dollars. I hope that will cover your expenses. We just don't have any more."

"It'll be all right with me," Chris said. He shook his head. "I can't see no one doing a friend that way. Chief is really my brother's friend, but I've known him for years. I never really trusted him, and sometimes he acts real crazy, but when he called me, I said I'd meet him." After talking a bit longer, Chris left after Shirley thanked him and promised to let him know when her son's court date was.

The next morning at the courthouse, a guard announced they all would have to be searched before going in. Annoyed and embarrassed, Shirley looked around and was startled that Mrs. Keegan was waiting in line next to her. She knew she shouldn't talk to Mrs. Keegan, but felt she had to.

"I'm real sorry about your husband," Shirley gently said to her. "My son was there, but he didn't go into the store. He never knew what Chief was doing that day. I know that Jeff would never have let Chief hurt your husband." Shirley waited, hoping the woman wouldn't start yelling, or crying. Mrs. Keegan spoke softly, and without hostility.

"Thank you," she replied. Mrs. Keegan looked very tired, as if she were ill. "I believe that your son didn't harm Jimmy, and I really hope he gets a fair trial. The police tried to make me say that I had seen both of them running past my window that morning, but I'm not going to lie. I didn't see anyone that morning, or hear anything either. Seems like I've been hassled ever since this whole thing started." She pushed a few strands of her hair from her face, and Shirley noticed how pale she looked.

She had read Mrs. Keegan had heart trouble.

"Maybe you should go home and rest," Shirley said worriedly. "You really don't look that well." Shirley offered to help her sit down somewhere, but she declined.

"I asked the police earlier if I could go home and rest, but they said they may need to recall me, so I can't go. I said I had a telephone and could be here in fifteen minutes, but they have no heart. They just want a conviction. I want the guilty ones to pay for killing Jimmy, but I don't want anyone to pay who was not involved. I'm really not physically able to be here, but the police are mad because I wouldn't say I saw both boys that morning." Mrs. Keegan brushed a few strands of brown hair flecked with gray away from her face again. Beads of perspiration ran down her face.

Shirley wanted to talk longer, but she was next in line to be searched. The guard asked to see her purse. After that they were ushered into another room, where hands were run up and down their bodies to make sure no one was carrying a weapon.

Court was reconvened. The State called Dr. James Wilford to the stand. He was a pathologist and had examined the body of Jimmy Keegan. Shirley thought how painful his testimony would be to Mrs. Keegan and wished she would have been spared at least this.

"Dr. Wilford, did you have occasion to examine the body?"

"Yes, sir, I did."

"Describe the condition of his body and injuries you found on his body." Kirkpatrick looked at the jury soberly.

The doctor's voice was grave. "Mr. Keegan's body had multiple traumatic injuries. He had a neck wound which extended the entire width of the neck from the base of the skull, the mastoid process on one side to the mastoid process on the other. It cut in half the jugular vein on the left side."

Kirkpatrick pressed on.

"Would you be able to determine whether or not the blow to the head would have killed him?"

The doctor nodded.

"The wound did produce damage to the brain."

"Would this have caused unconsciousness?"

"Yes, sir," he said politely.

"Would it be sufficient to kill him immediately?"

Wilford rubbed his chin.

"It would not be a sufficient injury to cause immediate death, no."

"Would the fact that the cut was a smooth cut, not being jagged and not having hesitation or stopping points along the way, would that indicate to you that the person who was being cut was either conscious or unconscious at the time they were having their throat cut?"

"It would indicate that there was not any great deal of struggle during the time the wound was being inflicted."

"So the wound would have had to be inflicted on an unconscious victim?" Kirkpatrick inquired.

"Yes, sir."

Kirkpatrick gestured widely. "Now, Your Honor, we submit at this point that the photographs of the scene of the crime are significant to show that the victim's throat was cut while he was in a state of unconsciousness, that he did not struggle after the point in time that his throat was cut. He lay still and that he died in a pool of blood. We would also submit," he turned back to his witness bending over as if a person had been lying at his feet, pretending he had a weapon in his hands, "let me ask you this, Doctor: During the course of cutting of a man's throat, if the person was standing behind the victim and the victim lying in this manner with his head in front of my . . . or right here at my feet, and the cutting had been done in a manner across his throat in this way, would there have been a spurting of blood from the arteries in the throat?"

"Yes, sir."

"Would the spurting of blood been consistent with the blood stains which are located on State's Exhibit Number 11? You have seen these trousers, have you not?"

"Yes, sir. The blood stains on that article of clothing would be consistent with the bleeding that would come from such a wound."

Kirkpatrick could make his point now.

"And would they be consistent with the cutting being done while the victim was in an unconscious position lying on his side or lying on his back?"

"Yes, sir."

"Would this picture be an aid to you explaining the spurting of blood which it's the State's contention was spurted onto the trousers which you have seen just a few moments ago?"

"I feel like it would demonstrate the origin of the blood," the doctor said definitively.

J udge Calhoun, his face somber, injected his conclusions: "Now, there have been witnesses that have placed the defendant in the area of the crime. There is also a pair of jeans that has also allegedly been connected with the defendant. The throat wound being the cause of death, the position of the body showing a blood pool and the absence of blood on the hands, which the doctor explained, make a photograph relevant. However, the only photograph that shows the entire body and hands, I hold they are relevant to the doctor's testimony on the issue of when and where the throat wound occurred and also as to . . . on the issue of the blood on the trousers which have been connected to the defendant. If the inflammatory nature of the photograph is outweighed even though it may be relevant, then it is not admissible. I feel that the one photograph that passes the test is Exhibit Number 14, and I hold that one is admissible, and no other photograph is admissible into evidence of the victim's body."

Kirkpatrick began again, "Now, when an artery is cut on a living human being specifically in this area, what happens with reference to whether or not the blood oozes or what happens with reference to the blood?"

Wilford patiently explained, "When an artery is cut there is a jet of blood because of the pressure in the artery which will project out from that artery."

Kirkpatrick nodded. "Now, Doctor, I show you State's Exhibit 14, which you have previously examined. Would you come down here in front of the jury. Can you give us an opinion to a reasonable medical certainty as to whether or not the victim in this case, if his throat was cut while he lay unconscious on the floor in his shop?"

Wilford unhesitatingly answered, "My opinion is that his throat was cut and that he died from loss of blood without ever having moved from that spot."

"Doctor, the pants which have been entered into evidence as Exhibit Number 11 and which have spots on them which have been testified to are human blood which are shown on these trousers, would they be consistent with the spurts that would come from the neck of a person whose throat was being cut if the person cutting the throat was standing over them in this manner, the red pen being the head and the stroke coming in this manner as I am demonstrating from my left to my right?"

"Yes, sir, it would be consistent with that."

"Dr. Wilford, after this man's throat was cut and based upon your opinion that he was unconscious at the time that his throat was cut, for what length of time would he have lived, in your best judgment?"

"He could have lived for fifteen minutes roughly."

"Doctor, if in fact, a man were conscious when he received an injury such as you have described to his neck, would such a person struggle and thrash about in an attempt to save their own life?"

"Yes, it is my opinion that he would have made some effort to stop the blood and move around some way."

Shirley felt sick to her stomach and weary of mind by the time they recessed for lunch. Cindy was waiting for her in the hall. "Please hurry up," Cindy called, "I'm hungry."

"You're always hungry," Shirley said, catching up to her. Shirley didn't tell her daughter-in-law that food was the last thing she wanted. The day was hard enough. Even a little respite seemed a relief. They could see the attorneys heading toward the restaurant across the street. "I wish there was another restaurant in town," Shirley observed again. "I hate to eat with the D.A. and all the others," Shirley murmured as they walked slowly down the courthouse steps.

"Just give them hateful looks. That oughta scare them off," Cindy said laughing.

"It feels good to share a small laugh for a change," Shirley replied as they went inside. Cindy ordered the blue plate special. Not wanting to make her feel odd, Shirley ordered a sandwich and coffee, but when it finally came she couldn't bring herself to eat. Minutes later it was time to go. Shirley and Cindy, along with attorneys from both sides, hurried back to the courtroom.

Shirley took a front row seat on the wooden bench in back of Strouth and in front of his family. She wanted to see how they reacted to each other. Most of the time, she observed, they sat like statues. Guards stood all through the courtroom, as they had throughout the trial, as if they thought Chief could somehow escape; or maybe they thought that Shirley really would gun him down as the papers had insinuated. She tried to get comfortable on the hard bench but couldn't. She found herself wishing the State would have invested some of its tax dollars into cushions. A slight smile played about her lips as she realized that even in the midst of such misery the mind could conjure up such silly things.

Then her attention turned back to Strouth's lawyer, who was speaking. No witnesses were to be put on the stand in Strouth's defense.

Carl Kirkpatrick stepped forward and the prosecution began its closing argument. "Ladies and gentlemen, at this point in time you have heard all of the evidence, all of the testimony, all of the proof that you're going to hear regarding the guilt or innocence of Donald Strouth, who has been brought here before you and tried this week to answer the charges of armed robbery and murder in the first degree. We have charged him with committing a murder during the perpetration of a robbery of James Keegan on February the 15th, 1978. Mrs. Keegan was the one who found her husband's body lying in a pool of blood in his place of business at approximately noon on that day and she ran out to call for help. Officer Page was the man who came there. He found the corpse of Jimmy Keegan lying in a pool of blood with his throat cut from ear to ear.

"Why was Jimmy Keegan killed?" His voice conveyed rising anger, "Jimmy Keegan was killed to prevent him from identifying Donald Strouth and Jeffrey Dicks as being the individuals who robbed him." Shirley ground her teeth together hearing her son's name. Wilcox had lied again, she thought angrily. "Well, folks, that's just what we've done, I submit to you. We have overwhelmingly proved that Donald Strouth is guilty of felony murder, a murder committed during the course of the robbery of Jimmy Keegan. We've done that through the testimony of people who told you that he did it, and we've done it through showing it to you, giving it to you; it is real and it exists, the fruits of the crime, the stolen coat. The coat that came from the Budget Shop that was given away by this man's girlfriend because she knew that it came out of the Budget Shop and that it was the fruits of crime and as she put it, that it was 'hot.' 'I knocked the old man down.' Yes, folks, they knocked him down."

Shirley put her hand over her mouth to stifle her cry when she heard the word "they." She knew then that the prosecution would also go for the death sentence on Jeff. The police had lied when they said it would be different at his trial. Shirley had known that deep in her heart.

Kirkpatrick was still talking, mimicking Strouth. " 'I had to slit his throat.' Yes, folks, this man slit his throat. This man stood over Jimmy Keegan's body and slashed from left to right and slit his throat, and that poor old man's blood oozed out onto the floor until there was no longer any life in his body. And there's the man who cut Jimmy Keegan's throat causing him to die. I submit to you that there are no alternatives, there are no lesser included offenses. It's first degree murder."

Kirkpatrick walked up and down in front of the jury box. His voice had a steel edge now. "Chris got on the witness stand. 'Did you see Mr. Strouth over in North Carolina?' 'Yes, I did.' 'Did you notice anything about his clothes?' 'Yes, sir. They had dark stains on them.' 'What did he say to you?' 'He said he had killed a man with a rock and the law was after him.' And then he is brought back to Elizabethton by his girlfriend, Sharon Carlson. 'What did he say to you, Miss Carlson?' 'He said Jeff froze on me. He said, 'I hit the old man and he went down.' And he said, 'I've got blood on my pants and I've got to get rid of them,' and they did, in that dump where this police officer was later taken to approximately a month later by Sharon Carlson, and where those blue jeans were found that you have seen, that you've touched, and that the FBI says had human blood on them splattered from the cuffs up to the knees, which blood spatters the doctor says are consistent with the type of slashing of a throat by which James Keegan was killed.

Kirkpatrick's voice rose almost to a crescendo.

"James Keegan, the only eye witness to the robbery perpetrated by this man and his friend. There is the man who I submit to you cut James Keegan's throat causing him to die, causing him to bleed to death there on the cold hard floor. And I submit to you that there's only one answer you can come to, that this man is guilty of first degree murder."

Kirkpatrick sat down.

Slowly Larry Dillow walked to the front of the room and looked at the jury. His face was somber.

"Ladies and gentlemen of the jury, at this stage you decide the guilt and the innocence. I want you to think about the proof of burden and what the State hasn't proved as I go through my argument. Now, Sharon Carlson, ladies and gentlemen, testified as I recall that at no time until after Mr. Strouth came back from North Carolina was anything wrong with his trousers. She said she didn't see anything until Mr. Strouth, as I recall, said something himself about blood on his trousers. That's when the pants were disposed of. Now, also there are no connections between those pants and Mr. Strouth. Then there was Cindy Dicks, and I'll ask you this: Who had more to gain out of saying Strouth did the murder? She's the only one, ladies and gentlemen, that's got anything to gain out of this. I want to thank each and every one of you, and I want you to remember your oath. Go over the testimony. Go over what these witnesses said. The State gets two chances at arguments. I've done everything humanly possible. On behalf of Mr. Strouth, I want to thank you."

Judge Calhoun asked, "Are we ready for the State to close the arguments?"

Carl Kirkpatrick strode forward for the last time. His voice was filled with confidence and fervor.

"Ladies and gentlemen of the jury, I'm going to make this short. The State has proved its case beyond any doubt. They raised the issue saying Cindy Dicks had a lot of reason to come in here and pack it all on Strouth. I want you to listen closely. Jeffrey Dicks was an accomplice of Strouth, and the act of one, no matter which one cut Jimmy Keegan's throat, is the act of all. Helping her husband out, my foot. She's confessed him guilty to first degree murder. So if her motivation was to come here and lie to you, she lied herself into a mess because she has protected her husband by confessing him guilty of murder in the first degree.

"As I say, Mr. Dillow, Mr. Lauderback and Mr. O'Rourke have done all they could do and are very capable and competent lawyers. It's a violent, vicious crime that was committed on an unconscious man that was lying on the floor that had gone to work that day just trying to make a living, and he was murdered in as cold blood as you can because Mr. Donald Wayne Strouth didn't want to take a chance of going to the penitentiary for a few years if he got caught for armed robbery; so he was willing to kill to prevent that. We ask that you find the defendant guilty of that."

The jury came back in only an hour and twenty minutes. They had come up with a verdict, but when Judge Calhoun questioned the foreman he found out they hadn't understood that they were to decide on the armed robbery charge as well as the murder charge. They were taken back to deliberate. After another half an hour, the jury came out again.

Strouth was brought back in. The buzz of whispers

rippled through the room. He walked slowly to the table and sat down. He showed no emotion as the foreman read the verdict: "We the jury find the defendant guilty of murder in the first degree." Shirley watched Strouth's face. It remained imperturbable. He was given forty years in the state penitentiary for the robbery. He was found guilty of murder. Still, he sat stone-faced. She shook her head. If only Jeff had listened to her and stayed far away from this cruel man.

The second phase of the trial began. The jury would decide if Strouth would get a life sentence or if he would receive the penalty of death.

At that point, the full story of the disturbed young man Donald Strouth was unfolded. He had three juvenile court petitions brought up against him while he was growing up in Maryland. One was for possession of marijuana; one as a habitual runaway; and a third for burglary. The first time he ran away from home, he was ten years old. Once grown, Strouth spun fabricated stories about his past. He claimed he was an Apache Indian chief of a tribe in New Mexico. (His parents were found out to be from Virginia and Tennessee.) He even gave his age wrong. One officer testified that when Strouth had been arrested for the theft of a minibike in Elizabethton he had a knife and a pair of brass knuckles on him. He told the arresting officer at the time that he had "connections in New York" and would get a machine gun and blow the policeman's brains out.

Wilcox testified. He told of two statements taken from Strouth after Mr. Keegan's murder. One said he wasn't at the scene of the crime at all. The second one said that he remained in the car all the time. Then the prosecution outlined reasons why the State was asking for the death penalty. Strouth's previous convictions would act as mitigating circumstances, they said. In an angry voice District Attor-

ney Kirkpatrick asked, "Is there any moral justification for
killing an unconscious man?" He shook his head definitively. "Chief would kill again," he went on, "and in fact
testimony at the trial told of an oil-soaked towel that was
placed over an electric heater in an attempt to burn the
Budget Shop down." He stared at the jury and asked in a
hushed tone, "What would have happened to people who
entered the shop if a fire were in progress?"

"If Dicks did it all," he continued, "what's the blood
doing all over this man's pants? Did the blood spurt all the
way out to the car, where he says he was sitting? Mrs. Keegan has lost her husband. She will be paying for this crime
the rest of her life. Where must we retreat to, until finally,
we say, 'No more.' "

"If this is not the proper case for the imposition of the
death penalty," Attorney General Wells added, "then I submit to you that you will never see one."

Patrick O'Rourke presented the closing arguments for
the defense. He touched little on the facts of the case, but
spoke of the ramifications of the death penalty.

The jury had sat through the entire trial, where the
main issue was the death of James Keegan. The bloody details depicted during the trial were nauseating. A life was
taken by Donald Strouth—Jimmy Keegan's life. The taking
of someone's life is horrendous. Both sides agreed. So, now
the jury was asked to do the right thing and put Donald
Strouth to death.

As much as Shirley despised Strouth, she found herself agreeing with the defense attorney. It didn't make
sense. As he said, "Does killing a man because he killed
make it right?" It was the first time she had ever seriously
thought about it. Everyone waited, holding their breaths
for the verdict. They did not wait long.

The bailiff asked Strouth to stand as the verdict was
read. Judge Calhoun's voice was grim.

"Ladies and gentlemen of the jury, have you reached a
verdict?"

"Yes, sir, we have, Your Honor."

Judge Calhoun looked the foreman straight in the eye and he looked back. For a moment it was as if they were the only two people in the courtroom.

"And what is that verdict?" the judge asked coldly.

Strouth would die in the electric chair.

EIGHT

Wilcox's words at Strouth's trial linking Jeff to the murder kept reverberating in Shirley's mind. She was convinced that the same thing would happen to Jeff as Strouth, innocent or not. They all seemed in a hurry to close the books on the crime, and men like Wilcox were obsessed with winning no matter how it was done.

Shirley knew she had to get money quickly if she was going to save her son, and although she hated it, the only way to do it, she thought bitterly, seemed to be by writing checks and buying merchandise which she could return. Before long Shirley had accumulated $6,000. Four thousand more and they could get Jeff out on bond. The trial date was coming up fast, though, and she had a strong feeling that they wouldn't be able to raise the whole ten thousand in time.

"I don't think we can do it," Shirley told Donald one morning over breakfast. "Jeff's hearing is coming up, and I just don't see us having the whole amount by then."

"Maybe, maybe not," he said. "But I don't see any other options to choose from." He looked over at her lovingly, but Shirley knew Donald was worried too.

"There might be one," she said. Donald gave her a suspicious look. He wasn't going to like what Shirley had to say, but she had thought about it for some time and felt it was her last hope. "I've been thinking it over for a long time. I should have acted on it earlier, but I didn't really believe it would come down to this." Shirley hesitated, got up and, going to the refrigerator, took out a Pepsi. Donald was waiting for her reply; he didn't know what to expect from her anymore.

"What?" Donald asked, giving her his full attention. He knew Shirley was serious, and he was half afraid to hear what it was. Shirley had been under so much pressure, he was afraid she was cracking up.

"I'm going to break Jeff out of jail." There, she had said it. It was out in the open. "I know it's a crazy idea, but I just heard where someone had taken a helicopter and broken an inmate out of a prison." She looked at Donald pleadingly. Her anguish had shattered the last shreds of her control and reason. Donald was horrified at what his wife was suggesting. He watched as tears rolled down her cheeks and felt love, along with anger, at this woman.

"You're what?" Donald stared at her, his eyes widening. "You're nuts. I hope you're just letting off steam and talking, because it wouldn't work. You can't just walk up to the jail and tell them you want Jeff." He shook his head in disgust and took a drink of coffee. He hoped she was only joking, but Shirley was dead serious.

"It would work. I've thought it all out. The jail is a small place, and on visiting day there's only one guard in there. Then, in the other part of the jail, is another one." She knew Donald would never understand the desperation that had brought her to this point. Maybe, she thought, she was going crazy, but her only thought was to save her son. She couldn't stand by and watch them murder Jeff in cold blood.

"You'd better start thinking what the other kids would do without a mother. What you're talking about is something that'll end up getting you in a lot of trouble that no-body will be able to get you out of. You may be killed in the process. Did you ever think about that when you were getting this stupid idea?" Sometimes he could just ring her neck. She was such an exasperating woman, and as much as he loved her, he would not take part in anything that crazy.

"I really think I can do it," she said, tears spilling down her blouse. Why didn't anyone understand what she was feeling. Surely other mothers would do the same. If they knew the fear, the pain and the helplessness that she felt. If it were their child in danger of being put to death for a crime he didn't commit.

"You and who else?" Donald asked, shaking his head in the familiar way that he always did when she said something stupid.

"I figure all I need is about three men to help me, and we could do it on visiting day. Two of them could go down to the sheriff's office. There's only a couple men in there. They could tie them up while I went to the other side. Then, the other one could help me while I'm visiting with Jeff. I could pull the gun there—"

"Oh, come on—" he started with a laugh, rolling his eyes upwards.

"It wouldn't be loaded. But they don't have to know it. Just one guard is in there when we visit. All I have to do is find someone to help me. Maybe I could ask around. I just know—"

"No! It's too dangerous!" Donald yelled.

Shirley was surprised. "You never yell at me," she said.

"Well, this time you could get yourself killed. It's better to yell than sit calmly while you try to pull off this crazy scheme. I won't let you do this crazy thing. I know how worried you are over Jeff. But this is just something you cannot do. Anything could go wrong. The whole thing with Jeff is making you crazy. Give it a chance and see if we can raise the money before court comes."

They were still arguing about it as they headed out to the car to go to her mother's. "You can say what you want," Shirley said, "but I've got it all thought out. And I have thought of something happening to me. I already made out my will, and I gave Ma power of attorney over all my things here."

"I suppose you gave her the other kids too?" Donald said starting the car up. "I can't believe you would just say to hell with Trevor, Laurie and Tina. Don't you care about them anymore?" Shirley didn't answer. No one was going to understand how her thoughts were all on Jeff at this moment. She would do the same for any one of the kids, it's just that Jeff needed her more now.

They were silent the rest of the trip. Shirley's parents lived about six miles out of the city, in Fairview, North Carolina. Shirley and Donald had planned a special day there. Cindy and the baby, Maria, had gone ahead.

Pulling up in front of the freshly painted house with red, pink and white flowers everywhere, Shirley saw Teeny outside. Up close Shirley could see how the stress of Jeff's problems had taken a toll on her. There were bags beneath her soft brown eyes. As tired as she looked, Shirley thought she kept on taking good care of herself, never letting her hair go gray. Her hair was as red as it had been when Shirley was a child. Shirley smiled.

In contrast, Pop looked much older. His hair, what he had now, was white, and his potbelly hung over his belt. Despite this physical evidence, he adamantly denied any weight gain. He was always chewing on something which he tried to hide.

"It's just my tongue!" he would yell if accused. "Stop watching everything I do." Ernest hated it when people fussed over him, but the kids all worried about the extra weight gain, especially since his heart attack. The doctor had warned him to lose weight, but he never could seem to.

Now he stood beside his wife holding his first great-grandchild in his arms talking to Maria as if she understood every word her great-grandfather was saying.

It was good to be together again. As they enjoyed the hours of late afternoon, the Jeff problem almost took a back seat in their minds, but then, as always, the subject came up.

"You need to talk to your daughter," Donald told Ma. Shirley gave him a warning look so he would shut up, but he kept on. "She's got this crazy idea to break Jeff out of jail. She thinks it's all going to be so easy. I think it's plain stupid, and I'm letting it be known here and now that I don't want any part in it."

"Shirley," Teeny said as she drank her coffee, "isn't there anything we can do to change your mind?" Shirley knew it was hard on her mother. Not only did she worry about Jeff, but now she was worried about her. She hated to cause her mother more pain but felt that she didn't have any choice.

Shaking her head, Shirley tried to change the subject. "Are you two going to see Jeff this weekend? Donald and I are going to Florida to set up at the flea market. We'll be down there the whole week. Trevor will go with us, and the others will stay at the house. There's a hearing next week in Blountville, so we'll be back for that. Please go. I want Jeff to have someone visit him while we're gone."

"We will," Ma said sighing. "You be careful going down to Florida. I wish you didn't have to do this. You know that you'll have to run, too, once they find out what you've done." Shirley knew her mother was only trying to help, but she felt anger that she couldn't understand her either. "Well, I don't think they gave us a choice in the matter," she said, getting up from the table. "We can't get an attorney without money, and we'd never make that kind of money in ten years legally. What else can I do? Just sit back while I watch them railroad Jeff into the electric chair?"

No one had an answer. The formerly happy afternoon finished in silence. A few days later Shirley, Donald and

Trevor left. Florida was hot and sticky when they got there. Donald and Trevor went over to the flea market at six every morning, and she followed later. They were doing well, and the money was coming in.

Despite this, Shirley felt miserable. "I wish as much as my mother does that we didn't have to do this," Shirley said sadly to Donald as they stood at their booth. "I can't believe what has happened to my family. I can't understand why. That's the question that keeps gnawing at me. I've always worked hard, been honest and tried to teach my children right from wrong. Now look at us. My son's being tried for a dastardly crime he didn't do and we've become petty crooks to try to get enough money to prove him innocent," she began crying.

"I don't know why, Shirley," Donald said. Gathering Shirley into his arms, Donald held her tightly, wishing he could take away the pain.

She watched as Trevor sold something to a customer. He was short for eleven years old, with light brown hair and blue eyes. He had two dimples that showed every time he smiled, which was all the time. He gave an excellent sales talk and sold the items. Shirley knew he shouldn't have been a part of all this, but she didn't know what else to do. Shirley knew many people would say that there were other choices she could have made. She hoped they would not judge too harshly until they had walked in her shoes. Sadly, she watched Trevor writing up a sales receipt. The whole family felt they had to save Jeff at any cost. Trevor walked over to show his mother the money he had gotten from the customer. "I know I'm helping my big brother," he said quietly.

She turned away, so he would not see the tears in her eyes. When she composed herself, Shirley took Trevor's hand and they walked down the countless isles of booths listening to the vendors pitch their products. For a few minutes Shirley could almost forget the reason they were there—almost. The flea market had a carnival-like atmosphere. Everything anyone could think of was for sale there, from an old Avon bottle to the latest best-selling paperback. The woodsy aroma of hamburgers and the pungent scent of french fries wafted through the air. Music poured from all directions. Any other time Shirley might have enjoyed it, but now her mind was back in Tennessee with Jeff.

At the end of the week, they loaded up the U-Haul and headed back to North Carolina, about a thousand dollars richer. All Shirley could think was that it wasn't enough.

They arrived home the day before the hearing. How inviting the small brick house looked when they finally drove in the driveway. Holding Maria, Cindy came out to greet them. "Well, how did you all do?" she asked. "It's been lonely without you. Tina and I had a fight, but we're friends now." As usual, everything came pouring out of her mouth at once. Shirley noticed how childlike Cindy acted and wished again she was more mature.

"Let me see the baby," Shirley said, reaching out for Maria. I missed her so much while we were gone." She rubbed her face against Maria's face, thinking her the softest, most beautiful child she'd ever seen.

Inside, Shirley's older daughter, Tina, waited. After giving her mother a hug and kiss, she whispered, "Did you know that Cindy never changed the baby hardly at all? Even when she cried, Cindy just left her in the bed and wouldn't pay any attention to her. Laurie and I had to take care of her. Cindy kept running off, and she was gone for a long time, never saying where she was going or anything." Tina gave Cindy a hateful look, and Shirley wondered what was wrong with Cindy that she didn't want to care for her beautiful baby.

Shirley felt bad hearing of Cindy's treatment of Maria, but she was so tired and knew that no amount of arguing could change things. She suggested to Tina that they save their strength for the next day; it would probably be needed more.

As they climbed up the stairs at the courthouse the next day, Shirley felt a sense of lightheadedness and fatigue. She wondered when this would all be over with and how it would ever end. She didn't understand half of what was said in the courtroom, and only her love for her son gave her the strength to carry on.

As they brought Jeff in to sit at the table in front of the judge, he smiled at his mother and she smiled back. She winced. He looked just as bad as he had the last time she'd seen him.

The hearing lasted three hours. Shirley told them everything she knew—how she had been threatened with a jail sentence if she didn't cooperate; how the detectives said they would hunt Jeff down and shoot him and Cindy; and their promise that Jeff would be charged only with aiding a robbery, not with murder.

Wilcox and the other officers who had questioned Shirley at the Holiday Inn earlier denied everything.

"I told Mrs. Dicks that it'd be to his benefit to surrender than for us to be hunting him down," Wilcox said as he smiled at Shirley. She knew he was baiting her, and for once she kept her mouth shut. She felt like jumping up and screaming at this man for standing there in front of the judge and lying. She would ask to take a lie detector test to prove what she said was the truth.

Jeff gave his first public statement at the hearing. He knew Chief said he was going to the store that day for a robbery; Chief was always making stories up, and Jeff hadn't believed him.

"Nothing at all was ever said about hurting or killing the old man." When Strouth had come out of the Budget Shop, Jeff said he didn't know what really had happened.

Judge Calhoun overruled all the motions presented at the hearing. He did schedule another hearing to be held on November 10 on a possible change of venue move to give the State attorneys time to examine affidavits from county citizens concerning the chances for a fair trial for Jeff within the county.

"Well, I guess we expected him to overrule most of the things," Shirley said to James Beeler, Jeff's attorney. "They have the power, and that judge doesn't know if the detective lied or not. Why can't I take a lie test and prove we didn't lie?" Shaking his head sadly, the attorney quickly looked away from her, and she knew he didn't want to tell her how bad it was looking.

Beeler said, "We'll just have to wait and see if we can get a change of venue. Maybe to Knoxville; people there would be more apt to give a sentence of so many years. Here in this small town, they might be more prone to go for the death penalty." He paused. "Of course, I'd be really surprised if Jeff would ever get that. Shirley, why don't you and Cindy go home and I'll keep you posted on what is going on."

"Can we speak with Jeff for a few minutes?" she asked.

"No. They won't allow that. They already don't like you, so we'd better not ask for favors." Shirley felt like fighting to see her son but decided not to start anything. They watched as Jeff was taken out of the room under heavy guard. The desperate look in his eyes haunted Shirley for days after.

They went to Asheville and got ready to head back to Florida again. It was apparent that they weren't going to get enough money in time to get Jeff out on bond; Shirley was convinced the only way was her plan of breaking him out.

Unable to sleep at all now, her eyes began to have a frantic fevered expression. She couldn't get the jailbreak out of her mind night or day. "I'm going to go downtown and see if I can find some men who will help in a jailbreak," Shirley said a few days later to Cindy. "Do you want to go with me?"

"Sure. I'll go with you," Cindy said. "I don't know what else to do, and we might find someone who wants to earn some money. Remember the time we tried to find someone to say they were Jeff so we could get married and we did? That plan of yours worked; maybe this one will to." Cindy began to brush her long brown hair methodically, stopped and looked at her mother-in-law. "If we do, I'll help with the jailbreak too."

Shirley shook her head. "No. I don't want you to be involved in that part of it. It might be dangerous. I have to find a couple of men to help us. You and the others can wait down the road in the campers. Then when we get Jeff out, we'll all take off." Shirley didn't want any of the family to be involved in the jailbreak itself. She would take all the responsibility herself—and the punishment too. If anything should go wrong, she would never forgive herself if one of her family got hurt or arrested.

As Shirley and Cindy pulled up to the squalid bar, they could hear loud music playing and the raucous voices and laughter of the men inside. The night was inky black; not even one star lit the sky. They walked slowly to the door. Shirley felt fear churning in her stomach. She wasn't used to being in a place like this, and she pictured all kinds of things happening. She worked at the Holiday Inn lounge, but that was a respectable place; this bar was seedy looking and the men inside looked tough. Still she knew that was what she needed; there was no turning back.

In a few moments, two dark, greasy looking men came over to their table and sprawled in the empty chairs leaning toward them. "What are you doing?" Shirley yelled to them above the music. The men laughed as though she had said something funny, and she felt scared. She didn't want them to know she was afraid so she half smiled and gave Cindy a look. "Do either of you speak English?" she asked them.

"Little bit," one of them replied smiling through tobacco stained teeth at Shirley. As he opened his mouth the smell of whiskey made her gag, and Shirley wished it were over with so they could leave. "You want to party?" the man asked.

"No," Shirley said, pushing further away from him. "But would you and your friend like to earn some money?"

"Sure. Doing what?" He laughed as he gulped down another swig of beer, most of it missing his mouth and running down his chin. The other one just kept grinning from ear to ear, obviously understanding very little of what she was saying.

"We need three men to help in a jailbreak." She had barely gotten the words out when one grabbed the other's arm muttering to themselves what could probably be translated into something like "crazy broads."

She could hear the two men talking in loud voices, telling others what she had told him. In her mind she could see herself and Cindy lying on a dark street, dead. There was raucous laughter and dirty gestures made in their direction.

"Let's just get up and slowly walk out," Shirley whispered to Cindy.

"Okay. But what if they won't let us leave?"

"Just follow me, and for once don't say a word to anyone."

They eased out of their chairs and headed for the door. A tall, bald, fat man stood in front of the doorway staring into Shirley's eyes. She panicked. She didn't know if the man was serious or having fun at her expense. She was sure he had seen her look of fear and knew the women weren't the kind to be in that type of place.

"Laugh," Shirley said to Cindy. "Pretend that we're having fun." Cindy looked at her as if she had gone crazy but did as she was told. As Cindy laughed stupidly, they quickly walked around the man and ran to the car. Loud laughter followed them. As Shirley drove away, they finally dared to breathe more easily.

"That was some strange laugh," Shirley said to Cindy as they drove off. "I've never heard anything like that before. Sounded like a hyena."

"I was nervous," Cindy laughed. This time the laugh

was for real, and soon they both were laughing so hard Shirley could hardly drive.

When they got home Tina ran to the car as soon as it stopped. She was crying.

"What are you doing?" Tina demanded. "I'm afraid you'll get hurt. There must be another way, please." Tina was crying hard, and Shirley knew the pain she was causing her. What was she to do? No matter which way she turned, someone was going to be hurt. Yet she couldn't just sit back and not try to save Jeff. Turning to Tina, she tried to smile, and getting out of the car, Shirley put her arm around her daughter and hugged her tight.

"Tina, please trust me," she said. "I have to try to help your brother. I would do the same for you or any of my children."

Tina seemed a little soothed at her mother's words. "Promise me you'll be alright."

"Yes, Tina."

Together they walked inside the house and settled around the kitchen table. Laurie had made a fresh pot of coffee and poured a steaming cup for everyone. Though she managed to make small talk, inside all Shirley could think of was Jeff and how she had to find some people to help get him out. Meanwhile Tina was crying again and trying to talk her mother out of the crazy idea of a jailbreak.

"I don't want you to do it," she said. "You might get hurt. I'd die without you, Mom." Shirley wished she could spare Tina, but her only thought now was of Jeff, who, without her help, might be put to death.

"Let's not think about it anymore tonight," Shirley said and tried to comfort her without lying. She had a long drive ahead the next day, back to Florida to do more selling.

"Are they going to kill Jeff," Laurie asked suddenly. Shirley could see her younger daughter was close to tears and wished she could tell her it was all a bad dream. But it wasn't a dream; it was all too real.

"No. I'll never let them kill Jeff. Now don't you go

worrying about that," Shirley answered fervently. "I think we all should go to bed. It's been a long day, and I imagine you're all as tired as I am."

She went to her room, undressed and had just decided to turn off the light when the phone rang. It was her mother calling to tell her about a man who had come in the store where she worked. He had bragged he had a lot of "boys" who did things against the law. She said the man was willing to talk to Shirley, if she was still going to go through with the jailbreak plan. Teeny didn't approve of what her daughter was doing, but she didn't want her to go back to the bars and maybe get into more trouble.

"Ma, let me have his number," Shirley said. "I'll call when I come back from Florida."

That night she dreamt of sand in an hourglass running out. She knew the dream was about Jeff. His trial was less than two months away. Jeff was looking worse every week, and it broke Shirley's heart to see him suffering so much. He had lost so much weight. He looked like a stick with two hollowed out eyes. Shirley wasn't exactly sure what had happened to him in jail, but she knew it wasn't good.

The trip to Florida went pretty much as she'd expected. They made some money but not enough. As soon as she returned, Shirley called the man that her mother told her of. His voice on the phone was cold and gruff, "I'll go to Tennessee with two of my men and look around. You make a map of the area and one of the jail."

"I'll do that right away," she promised. "Do you have a plan?"

"It'll be easy. We'll tie up the only man that is at the other end of the jail. You get the one at the visiting point." He rushed on. "Our charge for the job is $5,000. I'll call and let you know how to get it to us and where to meet me next week."

Shirley waited but he never called. Shirley decided she would have to take matters into her own hands. She wasn't quite sure how though. That Sunday, as they drove to the jail to visit with Jeff, Shirley could see police cars

from the Tennessee line all the way to the jail. She wondered what was going on. They pulled in the lot near the
jail and parked as usual. It was almost eerily quiet. There
weren't even any trustees walking around outside.

When they got in to see Jeff, it seemed like all eyes
were on them. Instead of just one guard, there were three
—one of them a huge, bear-like woman. All were armed.
When they asked Jeff what was going on, he shook his
head, "I don't know, no one will tell me." On the ride back
to North Carolina police cars were everywhere. Shirley
was curious but dismissed it, until a few days later when
the newspaper from Kingsport came.

"Listen to this," Donald said to Shirley as he began
reading the paper. "It explains what we saw Sunday. The
headline reads, 'Jailbreak Plans Foiled. Roads leading out
of Blountville were heavily guarded for an "expected jailbreak." The sheriff there had received a tip a few days before. They had ten extra deputies stationed all around the
jail. Officers on the roads kept watch over the jail with bin-
oculars. They remained in position for hours, changing off
shifts with other uniformed men after so long. The sheriff
said that his tip came from a reliable source and that it was
expected to take place during a regular Sunday visitation.
He said that the jailbreak could never have succeeded. He
said later that the officials confirmed that Jeff Dicks was
the center of the intended jailbreak.'"

"That's why the man never called me back," Shirley
said. "He must have gone to the police and told them I was
going to break Jeff out. I hate him. Nobody can be trusted.
Nobody cares."

Donald shook his head angrily. "I guess you're right.
He must have gone to the police. I only hope they don't
take out a warrant for your arrest. They can, you know. I
tried to warn you not to try something so stupid, but no,
you wouldn't listen. You never listen." Donald's face was
agonized. "You're going to get into trouble and I can't stop
you. Nobody can. You gave that man a diagram in your

own handwriting of what the jail looked like." He glared at Shirley, who broke into tears.

"Everything is working against me." She curled up in the chair, defeated.

She was ready to give up. "Everything I try only makes Jeff look bad," she mumbled.

"Well, what are we going to do now?" Cindy asked. "How are we going to get Jeff out of there? You said that your plan would work. I guess it didn't work after all," she said dejectedly.

"I don't know," Shirley answered slowly but vehemently. "But I'm certainly not giving up. I'll never give up. I'm going to Jeff's hearing tomorrow. Then I'll figure something out." In fact she had no idea of what she could do now. She only knew she had to do something.

As Shirley, Donald and Cindy sat in the courtroom the next day, Jeff was brought in. There were chains around Jeff's neck and legs as well as cuffs on his hands. Shirley wanted to shout that he wasn't an animal; they didn't need to chain him up. Looking at him that way was more than she could bear. He had always been such a good boy, helping whomever he met. How had he gotten into this mess? More than anything she wanted to take him far away, away from the pain these people were inflicting on him and the hatred they felt for him. She sat there mesmerized, staring at her son.

Although he was skin and bones, his eyes haunted, he looked neat and clean in the new dark blue suit. His short curly hair was combed nicely, and Shirley thought how much she loved him. As he sat down at the table next to the attorney, he looked over and gave her the gentle smile she always loved, and tears came to her eyes. The courtroom was heavily guarded. It looked as though they expected a large mob of people to rush in.

Suddenly she saw Judge Calhoun come in, bang his gavel and begin the proceedings. He said, his eyes impaling the prisoner, that Jeff Dicks would be turned over to the State Department of Corrections for his own protection.

"From there," his voice grew colder, "he will be taken from the Sullivan County Courthouse in Blountville to an undisclosed prison."

As Judge Calhoun got up and began walking out of the room Shirley yelled out to him, "How is my son going to get a fair trial; you're already prejudiced?"

The judge, seeming not to have heard, kept walking.

"Let's get out of here," Shirley said to Don and Cindy. Her face was pale and waxy, her eyes as haunted as Jeff's. "They aren't going to let us even visit with Jeff before taking him away."

As they started out of the courtroom, Jeff's attorney came running over. "You'd better get out of here fast," he said. "Judge Calhoun just realized what you shouted to him, and he told the sheriff to arrest you. Get on back to North Carolina, and call me later on tonight."

Shirley could see the irritated look in his face and knew she'd done it again. But how could she stop? They were railroading Jeff. And she had to speak up to stop them, or else somehow spirit him away.

But now Shirley would have to stop dreaming of his escape. All that was left to do was to continue raising the money for a good lawyer. And hope.

NINE

Not long before Jeff's trial Shirley's brother, Roger, told her of an attorney he'd heard of. Barry Bixby had earned a local reputation for defending people on drug charges. Drug charges were a long way off from a case such as Jeff's, but considering the short time they had left until Jeff went to trial, Shirley decided to see Mr. Bixby at his office.

Barry Bixby's offices were located in the Northwestern Bank Building on Pack Square. The plush offices in his section were all new. Shirley's shoes sunk partially into the dense carpeting.

Shirley was accompanied by both Nelson and Donald. Nelson had driven down from New York. It was no doubt difficult for both men to be thrown together, but they were both making the best of it because of their mutual concern for Jeff. They had not waited long when Barry Bixby walked in.

Shirley was a bit surprised to see how young he was. Barry's smooth cheeked face looked like a college student's. He stood about five-feet-eight, and his longish black wavy hair kept falling over in his eyes. "I've already talked over the preliminary aspects of Jeff's case with Roger." He turned to Shirley. She filled him in on the rest of the story.

After they had discussed Jeff's case, he offered his services. "I'm sure I can get him off on probation," he said, giving a handsome white toothed smile. "Since the police know Chief murdered Mr. Keegan, and Jeff didn't go inside the store, they'll be easy on him."

"I don't think it's going to be very easy," Shirley shook her head wearily. "Mr. Wilcox is going for the death penalty on Jeff too. I don't know the law, but from sitting in on Strouth's trial, I just don't know . . ."

"Not to worry," Barry smiled at Shirley. He had an air of confidence about him, and Nelson was convinced.

"See. I told you Jeff would be fine," Nelson said. He patted Shirley on the back. "She's been so worried about Jeff, thinking they were going to give him the death penalty. I told her over and over that couldn't happen. After all, this is the US of A and we have the best justice in the world."

Of course it sounded marvelous, but Shirley felt Barry didn't have to sell them quite so hard. As she had learned over the last few months, sometimes words are spoken quite loosely.

"I only have $6,000 now, but I'll give you some every week," Shirley said to Barry. "I've been writing checks and using my grandmother's credit card to buy merchandise. Then we sell it at the flea market. I guess Roger told you about that."

Barry frowned. "Yes, we spoke about that. A bit of warning though. Keep the checks under a hundred dollars. You don't want felony charges against you too." Barry stood up and held his hand out. He didn't seem to mind about how the money was gotten, as long as he was on the receiving end of it. "You can give my secretary the money; she'll give you a receipt. And leave the address of where you'll be staying in Florida. Just in case warrants against you for the checks start to come in, I'll give you a call and warn you."

"All right. It was nice meeting you. Now perhaps Shirley can stop that worrying and doing stupid things to get money," Donald said getting up from the easy chair.

"Take care," Barry said. "My secretary will give you a receipt for the six thousand. I'll go up to see Jeff this weekend and talk with him about the case."

"What do you think?" Shirley asked Nelson once they were out of Smith's office. "Does he sound like he knows what he's talking about?" She felt she couldn't trust her own judgment anymore, she had been wrong so many times before.

"I think he sounds real smart," Nelson said. "I told you that Jeff wouldn't get very much time out of this, but you wouldn't listen to me."

"I don't know," Donald said. "I don't think anyone can predict the outcome of the trial. He seems sincere, and I guess he knows his law. Guess we'll just have to wait and see what happens. At least now we can take it easy for awhile." Shirley was lost in thought as they drove home. She wanted to believe they had nothing to worry about, but she still felt a nagging apprehension.

It stayed with her during her trip to Florida. She tried to shake off the feeling and to keep her mind on making as much money as she could for Jeff's defense. While she was away she thought about him day and night. Two weeks later when they returned, it seemed to her as if it had been months since she'd seen Jeff.

The first thing Shirley did was make plans to visit him. Now that Jeff was in prison in Knoxville, they would drive the long way through Blountville and pick up Cindy and Maria, who were still living in a trailer near where Jeff had been imprisoned. Now he had been moved to Brushy Mountain.

When Donald and Shirley finally arrived in Blountville four hours later, there was no answer when they knocked on the trailer door. Shirley was puzzled. "That's funny," Shirley said to Donald. "Cindy knew we were coming. It's so cold out, I can't imagine her out walking with the baby."

"Well, the door isn't locked, so let's go in and wait for her," Donald said as he opened the door, walking inside.

Shirley shivered. "This trailer is as cold inside as it is outside. I wonder why the heat isn't on?"

"I don't know," Donald said, looking around. "Hey, Shirl, there are bags of trash all over the place. I wonder if she moved out and didn't tell us."

Shirley walked over to the sink, which was piled high with dishes. "I can't believe anyone would be living like this," Shirley said as she walked out of the kitchen and through the living room. "We can't wait too long or we won't get to see Jeff either."

"It sure does stink in here. I can't believe she left such a mess. Two people shouldn't have that much trash in the two weeks she's been living here." Suddenly they heard a sound coming from the back bedroom.

"What's that?" Shirley said, getting ready to head out the door. She wasn't about to go back there. Donald walked back.

"Shirley, better get in here," he yelled. Shirley ran back. Maria lay on the bed covered by a blanket. Little Maria was blue with cold, and all alone.

"You poor thing," Shirley cooed to her, bending down to pick the baby up. She immediately began to clean her. "Donald, see if you can find some clothes to put on this poor child. It's so cold inside, and being wet, she's freezing."

"I can't find anything clean anywhere. Clothes are all over the floors in the bathroom and living room. I found a sleeper that's not as dirty as the rest of them. Put that on her while I go to the neighbors to find out if they've seen Cindy." Then Shirley began to think something might have happened to Cindy. She shook with fear as she dressed Maria.

Donald didn't come back for over an hour. "What's happened to her Donald?"

"I couldn't find her. I asked everyone around here if they'd seen her. One lady said she left a couple hours ago with some people in a car. The lady figured the baby was with her, otherwise she would have come over here."

"I can't believe this," Shirley said. She was so angry she could hardly contain herself. "What's the matter with that girl, leaving a baby all alone like this." Shirley fumed. Just as they were getting ready to leave with Maria, Cindy came through the door.

"I didn't think you'd be here so early," she said quietly.

"That's obvious. What do you mean leaving Maria here all alone?" Shirley shouted. "She's just a baby, Cindy. You don't leave a little child like that. Something terrible could have happened. She could have suffocated or—"

"Well, I wasn't gone that long," Cindy yelled back. "I have no husband anymore and I'm tired of taking care of a baby all the time." She slammed a book down on the table and got a glass of milk, with a dirty glass. Shirley started to say something but her words were gone. For once in her life, she was speechless. She couldn't believe what Cindy had said, and her lack of concern for her child. Shirley had always loved her children beyond anything, even her life.

"Let's not argue," Donald interjected. "Jeff has enough on his mind without seeing you two fighting."

"You and Maria are coming back to North Carolina with us," Shirley said to Cindy. "You can stay at the house with Nelson and the girls, and we'll take the baby to Florida with us when we go back down. I won't be able to rest back home, picturing that baby as I saw her today." She didn't leave room for argument, and Cindy seemed to know it was time to shut up.

"All right," she said. She threw some clothes together in bags. She seemed happy to hear that someone else would be caring for Maria.

They drove to Knoxville in silence. Shirley knew Jeff had it hard enough already, and she was determined not to let him see her cry anymore. She wouldn't let him know about the things she had seen today, or the fact that Maria had been alone while Cindy was off running around. It would serve no purpose other than hurting Jeff. There was nothing he could do about it, and Shirley would see to it Maria was taken care of from then on.

Jeff shuffled into the visitors' area. He looked bad, just as Shirley had expected. "Jeff," she cried out.

"I'm just fine, Mom," he said hugging her. "You worry too much." He looked searchingly at Shirley. "You know, Mom, you have to be careful," he said half-whispering. "I don't want to see you sitting in a jail somewhere just to help me out. I don't like the idea of your writing checks like Nelson tells me you're doing. You don't know how bad it can get inside a jail cell. I love you so much, and I never want anything to happen to you."

Shirley felt angry that Nelson had told Jeff when he was already suffering so much, but she knew this wasn't the time to voice her angry feelings.

Jeff tried to keep the conversation rolling. "I talked to Barry Bixby. He seems okay. I still like Mr. Beeler, though. But if you think Barry's better, then it's all right with me."

Suddenly Shirley's resolve not to let Jeff see her cry broke and she started sobbing. Patting her hand he tried to comfort her. "I can't help it," she cried. "I can see how you're suffering, and it hurts so much that I can't do anything about it. Everything I do turns out wrong. That stupid jailbreak idea just got you locked up in a worse place."

"Don't do this to yourself," Jeff said trying to console his mother. But it just made her cry harder. "Now you stop worrying. I'll be fine. Really."

To Shirley, Jeff was still her little boy; now she watched as he held Cindy close. She could see the love he felt for his wife and decided to say nothing about her treatment of Maria. As they said goodbyes, Shirley wondered if there would be anything left of the old Jeff by the time he got out of there—if he got out. She shuddered.

When they got home, Cindy asked if she could have a talk with Shirley and Donald. "Is there some place where we can talk without Tina and Laurie around?" She rightfully sensed the feelings between her and Shirley weren't exactly congenial anymore, and she approached her hesitantly. "It's about Maria," she said twisting a handkerchief in her hands. Shirley noticed how nervous she was acting and immediately thought something awful must be wrong with Maria. Donald had been quiet, and he said they could go out and sit in the car. The three of them walked out to the car; Cindy got in the back seat. She sat there for a few minutes without speaking. Shirley was getting more and more anxious by the time Cindy started.

"I tried to tell you before that I can't handle it. I can't handle her." Cindy searched Shirley's eyes, looking for some sign of understanding. Then she looked over at Donald since Shirley didn't seem to have much sympathy for her. "I can't stand it when she cries. That's why I leave her alone. I've been having to do it lately. I leave her so I won't hurt her." Shirley watched as tears rolled down Cindy's cheeks and felt anger such as she'd never known.

"What do you mean?" she yelled louder than she meant to. Donald put his arm around Shirley and told Cindy to go on.

"I got to where I was starting to do things to her when she cried. Like, one time I hit her so hard I had to take her to the emergency room at the hospital. I told them the little boy next door threw his metal truck at her, and that's how she got hurt. Another time I pulled her arm out of the socket and told them at the hospital she had fallen on the floor. And another day she was crying so bad, I took a pillow and put it over her head." Cindy looked away from Shirley and flushed deep red. "I almost killed her," she said so low Shirley thought she'd heard wrong. She tried to block out the picture hurtling through her mind of Maria laying in her crib neglected and, as she now learned, abused.

Cindy continued. "I went to the orphanage in Knoxville the other day and told them they could have her before I really hurt her. I hope you aren't mad at me. But I just can't take care of her. I can't do it anymore. I'm sorry. I really am." She sat there with her hands folded in her lap.

Shirley tried to feel some pity for her. But she couldn't feel anything but anger. Anger and hatred.

Reddening, Shirley tried to get control of herself. Donald looked at his wife, saw her struggling and turned to Cindy. "Thanks for telling us about all this, Cindy. I know it must have been hard on you. At least now you're doing the right thing." He reached his hand around to the back seat and took Cindy's hand, holding it for a few minutes. Shirley, on the other hand, was raging. She couldn't understand child abuse, and Maria was her own blood.

"Almost," Shirley said, trying to hold the anger in. She could see the look Donald was giving her, and she heard Cindy sobbing. But she didn't care what Cindy was feeling at this moment. "Maria is Jeff's baby. I can't let you just give her away. If you don't want her—if you really don't want her—I'll take her and raise her as my own." Cindy nodded. She looked relieved that Shirley wasn't going to yell at her. Shirley still felt anger that a grown woman could harm an innocent child, but she didn't say more.

"That's okay with me," Cindy said. "I didn't even think about you wanting her with the kids you have now and all the trouble you're having trying to free Jeff."

"It wouldn't matter how many children I had. I love that child, and I'll see to it that she's never hurt again," Shirley said passionately. "I could never let you give her to strangers. Jeff loves his baby."

"I know that," Cindy replied, "and maybe if he'd been here things would have been different. But I don't know how to take care of a child." Any other time Shirley would have felt sorry about the way Cindy had grown up, but this was not the time for that.

"It seems to me if someone grew up in an orphanage, knowing her parents had given her up, she would love her own child. And not want that child to grow up unwanted like she had been. It don't make sense to me." Shirley sighed, and threw her hands up. This was too much for her to cope with.

"I didn't think you'd understand. Only Jeff understands me. Are you going to tell him what I did?"

"No, of course not. I wouldn't do that to him. I don't care to protect you because I don't know how you could have hurt a small child. I had Jeff when I was seventeen, and I did all right. You're nineteen years old. . . . Oh just forget it. There is one thing, though. I want you to go to our attorney and fill out papers giving the baby up and telling all you did to Maria. That way you can never come back and say you want her. If I adopt her, you will never get her back. I won't ever let that child be abused again."

Cindy hung her head. "I'll do it," she said quietly. "Thanks for not telling Jeff about it."

"Thank you, Cindy," Donald interjected. Shirley wondered how Donald could be so wise and understanding to Cindy. She stared at him. She hated the feelings of rage she felt, but she cringed when she thought of Maria with a pillow over her head.

The next day Cindy and Shirley went to see Barry Bixby, and he drew up the papers for Shirley's legal adoption of Maria. Cindy made out a statement confessing the things she had done to Maria. In the agreement Cindy was allowed to see Maria whenever she wanted to—when Shirley was around. Cindy would still live with the family; Shirley had promised Jeff she would take care of his wife, and she would keep that promise.

At Christmastime the family took a motel room in Knoxville. They had to be at the prison at 8 A.M. if they were to see Jeff, and it was a lot easier to be near the prison to avoid the long drive in the early morning on Christmas Day.

They decorated a little tree in the motel room and put the children's presents beneath it. Not that Shirley felt like celebrating, but she didn't want the children to go without a real Christmas—at least as close as they could get to a real one.

But the colored lights and the brightly wrapped packages only made Shirley think of past Christmases. It had always been a wonderful time for all of them. Always, the entire family gathered for the opening of the gifts and the holiday turkey. Quick flashbacks came to Shirley's mind. In them, her happy, laughing children ran all over the house with their new toys. They had a special glow on their faces that was not present at any other time of the year.

Then she thought of the holiday Jeff would have this year. There would be no Christmas feast. No presents. Nothing. Shirley had tried to send a small tree in for him. But the warden wouldn't let him have it. She had also sent in a CB radio.

She thought he could set it up and she could park outside the prison so they could talk. But the warden said he couldn't have it. Shirley didn't know about prisons and what prisoners could have or couldn't have. She had sent in a lot of other things in brightly wrapped packages. The guards had to unwrap them all. She hadn't known you couldn't send in wrapped packages. The thought that Jeff would only know what he had known for months—the steel bars clanging open and closed, and the sound of the keys clipped to the guards' clothes jingling as they went down the walk, pierced her heart.

Despite the sadness they all felt when they arrived Christmas morning, Nelson, Donald, Cindy, the kids and Shirley pretended they were having a merry Christmas. Jeff did the same. It was hard to keep from crying, but Shirley was determined not to ruin the visit. To watch everyone pretending for the others to be happy, when inside each one there was only fear and unhappiness, was agonizing. They talked about everything except what really was on all their minds—the trial.

The visit was over much too soon. As they were leaving, a look of glazed despair began to spread over Jeff's face. His expression was one of mute wretchedness as he held Cindy tight and kissed her. "I love you, Cindy. I worry so much about you."

He asked Shirley to stay a few minutes. Unable to speak, she nodded.

"Mom, I haven't said anything about your adopting Maria. I'm relieved. I know how frightened Cindy has felt about raising a child. She wanted an abortion, and it was only because I made her carry the baby that Maria was born. Mom, Cindy tried to be a mother, but some people are not cut out to be parents."

"I'll try to take care of Maria just as I promised you," Shirley sobbed.

"I wish I could help, I wish I could care for her myself like I planned." He looked around in despair. "Now I may never be able to. I keep asking myself why. I haven't done anything to be punished for," his voice broke. Shirley's misery was so acute that she felt physical pain. She hugged her oldest son and couldn't stop the tears. She could feel his misery, saw the haunted look on his face, and knew her child was in hell.

Soon they were heading homeward; there was no singing or happiness this Christmas Day. At home, one of them was missing—might always be missing.

The day after Christmas, Donald called Jeff's lawyer, Barry Bixby. Barry told Donald everything was looking good. He was all ready for the trial to begin. He said he had everything under control and would take care of it all. Shirley had asked him many times if he had subpoenaed all the witnesses she had told him about, like the Fuller Brush manager, Mr. Carlton, to show Jeff was working, and character witnesses who could tell them what Jeff was really like. She especially wanted him to call Chris Livingston. Each time she would talk to Barry, he would brush aside her suggestions and tell her he would take care of it. He was the attorney, and she need not worry.

Nelson went back to New York and took Laurie with him, telling Shirley that way she would be able to focus all her attention on Jeff, who really needed it. Shirley didn't argue. She could only fight one battle at a time.

Meanwhile, Barry Bixby was pressing them for more money. Shirley decided to take Trevor and Maria down to Florida to sell again at the flea market. It was the only way to ensure Jeff would be represented by a competent lawyer. The trial was only a few weeks away. Even with it, Shirley felt Jeff's life was hanging in the balance. Without good legal help she was surer and surer he would have no chance at all.

The wind was gale-like as they drove the pickup truck along the freeway on the way south. The U-Haul behind it swayed back and forth. Suddenly, the truck went out of control.

"We're going to crash!" Shirley yelled to Trevor. "Hold onto Maria and get down on the floor." She gripped the wheel tighter and tried to go with the tires, but the U-Haul swung from side to side. She felt the pickup truck go out of control. In front of her the driver of the eighteen wheeler stepped on the gas and gave her more road. She could see Trevor's eyes. Stark fear shone out. He was clutching Maria on the floor. He was speechless. She prayed to God to see them through this and tried to maneuver the truck to the right side of the road.

Suddenly, she heard a loud crack. Through the rearview mirror, a flash of silver and orange streaked into the air as the U-Haul flipped on its side, breaking away from the pickup truck. Her heart constricted. Sweat poured down her face. Then she somehow managed to bring the truck to a stop. In a shaky voice Shirley thanked God for saving them and opened the door so they could get out.

"Are you all right, Mom?" Trevor asked in a small voice. He was still clutching Maria to him. She began to cry.

"Yes. I'm fine. We're lucky that hitch didn't hold. We would have crashed right along with the U-Haul." Shirley trembled all over. "But you were wonderful, son. You took good care of Maria." She beamed at her son and took Maria out of his hands.

"You were brave," she said to Trevor. "And you did just what I told you to do. I'm proud of you." Pride came into his face replacing the fear as Shirley hugged him. Peo-

ple came running over to see if they were all right, and she
assured them they were.

"I called the police and they're on the way," a white
haired man said, shaking his head as he looked at the
truck. "You're one lucky family." In a few minutes a
cruiser pulled up behind them and parked.

"Are you okay?" the young red haired freckle faced
officer asked.

"Yes, we're all fine. We didn't get hurt. Just kind of
scared us." Shirley watched as the officer, who didn't look
much older than Jeff, walked over and picked up some
merchandise off the side of the road. He didn't seem to
notice anything was wrong. She still couldn't stop shaking.

"Do you want to go to the hospital?" he said walking
back to her.

She tried to smile. "No. I always shake and my teeth
chatter when I'm scared. I guess it's some sort of reaction.
But I'm okay now. I was so scared the kids would get hurt.
I guess I was going too fast for the hill, but I hadn't realized
the wind was so strong." Shirley knew she was rattling on,
but she felt dazed and suddenly very tired. She wished she
could lie down but realized it was a stupid thing to think
about.

Trevor was busy retrieving the merchandise from the
U-Haul and putting it back in the truck. When the officer
finished making out his report, he helped Trevor pick up
the rest of the things.

"You have enough stuff here," he said. "Where'd you
get it all?" He smiled. Shirley's heart skipped a beat. She
didn't know if he suspected anything or not and tried to
think of something plausible to say.

"My brother has a store in New York," she stammered. "He's going out of business, and we're trying to sell
some of it for him." As she spoke she noticed price tags
blatantly in view with the names of several major department stores printed on them. Her heart began to pound.
She expected him to ask why some tags said Gears and
others said L-Mart or Nickel's and tried to formulate some

kind of answer. He looked at her quizzically for a few seconds but said nothing.

A wrecker came and hauled the trailer off. "I'll write down the address where you can get the merchandise after you get another trailer to load it all onto," he said. Shirley started to object. "Don't worry, I'll see to it that it will be safe." Shirley took a deep breath wondering what to do next. "You can leave now," he said gently. He hadn't called in her driver's license. She was waiting for that. If he had called it in, he would have found that she was wanted for writing bad checks. Barry had told her there were some warrants out already. She couldn't believe none of her fears had materialized. Quickly, she gathered up the kids and settled them in the car.

They drove to a nearby motel, and Shirley called Donald.

"I had a little accident," she began, her voice quivering.

"Are you alright," he cried into the phone. "Are the kids alright? I knew I shouldn't have let you go alone. Where are you?"

She interrupted, "Donald, it's okay, really. We're all fine; the truck is fine. It's the U-Haul that is gone, and we have to pick up the merchandise that was in it. They have it at a storage place. I have the address here," her voice trailed off.

"Thank goodness. Now don't worry. I'll rent another U-Haul and be there by morning. As long as you're sure you and the kids are really all right."

"We are," Shirley paused, "but come as soon as you can."

Donald left home immediately and got a new trailer. Several hours later he arrived at the motel. Under the cover of darkness, he and Trevor picked up the merchandise and loaded it in the new U-Haul.

The next morning Shirley rose at dawn. "We have to get started," she said. "I know we've all been shaken up a bit, but we have to go. We've lost too much time. We can't rest here even for a day." She sighed heavily. "The trial will be starting next week. We have to get together as much money as we can if we're going to save Jeff."

Trevor looked at his Mom's anguished face. "Don't worry, Mom. We're all okay. We know how much Jeff needs us, and more than anything we want to help him." He smiled reassuringly at his mother.

And Shirley's heart broke once more.

TEN

Greenville, the place where Jeff's trial would take place, was a small, white-washed southern town that looked, on first glance, to contain simple, down to earth people. It was cold and blustery the day Shirley and Donald arrived there from Florida. They could see their breath in puffs of smoke every time they breathed out. They went straight to the hotel and saw Teeny's car already parked there. Donald checked in while Shirley went to her parents' room. Family members had come from near and far to support Jeff. Shirley's sister, Brenda, and her two brothers, Mike and Roger, were there along with Shirley's two daughters, Tina and Laurie, Nelson, and Cindy. Maria was at home being watched over by Nelson's sisters. They were drinking coffee and talking among themselves about insignificant things. They tried to cover their fears, but the tension was palpable.

When they went out to eat lunch that afternoon people stared and exchanged furtive looks and whispered conversation. Obviously word had gotten around that a murder trial was about to begin. It was big news in the small town, and everyone tried to get a look at all of the people involved and their family members. No one smiled. The gawking and whispers made Shirley feel terribly uncomfortable.

She sensed an unfriendliness in the town, as if Jeff had already been tried and sentenced by the public.

That night Shirley met with Barry Bixby, Jeff's lawyer, who was staying in the same hotel. His blond heavily madeup secretary looked on, making Shirley even more uncomfortable. "I want you to be on your best behavior, Shirley," he told her. "No outbursts in the courtroom, no matter what's happening." He spoke as if she were a child.

She knew he was right. "But I can't seem to keep quiet when people are hurting my children," she said.

"I know it's hard, but it'll look bad for Jeff, and you don't want that."

"I'll really try," Shirley said earnestly. She meant to keep her word. She sat down in the chair and waited for Barry to tell them how he was going to represent Jeff. He had been very evasive in the past, and Shirley never could get him to tell whom he had called to testify but he continued to harp on Shirley.

"Another thing I want to tell you and Donald. The FBI was looking for you in Asheville about the check charges. They might come here to talk to you both." Fearfully Shirley looked at Donald. She turned back to face Barry.

Her voice trembled, "We'll have to leave."

"I'll tell them that you can't say anything until the trial's over. Then you can leave town." Barry smiled at Shirley and sat down next to his secretary.

Shirley looked around the room. For the first time she noticed the bed was unmade. A lacy nightgown lay on the chair beside the bed, and when his secretary saw Shirley looking at it, she blushed. Shirley was startled. She knew Barry was married. Shirley stared at the lawyer for a moment and wondered if she had made a mistake.

"I have a lot to go over," he said rising.

Beeler, the other lawyer walked into the room. Shirley nodded to him. "But I need to know who you are going to call. What are you going to do?" Shirley pleaded.

He shook her questions off. "Like I've told you in the past, Shirley, there is no way Jeff is going to get the death penalty. You hired me to represent him, now let me do my job. You all just go back to your room. I'll see you in the morning, and try not to worry."

Shirley didn't know whether to believe him. So much depended on him. She sighed. Jeff's life depended on him. "Have you gotten the Fuller Brush manager over here? Mr. Carlton is his name. Remember, I gave you his phone number and address so you could get in touch with him." Shirley pressed him. Beeler walked to her side, now holding some papers in his hand but not saying a word. Shirley knew the prosecution was going to say that Jeff wasn't working and that he needed the money from the robbery. It didn't matter to them that Chief had spent it all on a car in Johnson City, she thought.

"Don't you worry about who I've called and who I haven't," he said, opening the door. "I've got it all covered. Just let me do my work, and you just watch what you say."

She stood there not willing to go. "Did you ever get a hold of Chris Livingston?" she asked.

"I said I'd take care of it," Barry said, irritation plain in his voice. Shirley saw Mr. Beeler look down at the papers in his hand and noticed the quizzical look on his face. It seemed to Shirley that he didn't agree with the way Barry was running the case, and it showed. A twinge of fear began in the middle of her stomach.

The next morning, the first day of Jeff's trial, was dark and bleak. Shirley felt like it was a bad omen. After dressing and eating a light breakfast they hurried to the courthouse. They wanted to be there early so Jeff would see them when he was brought in and know they were supporting him.

Since Shirley had been told she would testify, she along with Nelson and Cindy were not allowed in the courtroom. The rest of the family took their place in the front of the room, on the left. The victim's family were seated on the right side.

Jeff was brought in. He had on the new beige suit Shirley had bought him, but he was gaunt, his eyes haunted as he glanced around, gave his family a faint smile and sat down at a table in front of them with his attorney.

During the day that followed, over fifty people were interviewed as prospective jurors. The hours dragged by. The next day was the same.

The first day of the jury's selection was mostly handled by John Rogers, a Greenville attorney whom Barry Bixby had specially retained for the jury selection process. Rogers took on a folksy manner with the prospective jurors. Using his local knowledge, he would say cute phrases such as, "Now you don't have a dog in this race, do you?" a seeming attempt to pull the hearts of the men and women to his side.

The jurors were put in a room off the courtroom as the alternates were selected. Their laughter and general vivacity could be heard from behind their closed door. It unnerved Shirley. She wondered, at first, if they realized how serious this all was. She knew the answer, it was her son— not theirs.

After two long days, a jury of eight women and four men were finally chosen. Wilcox walked past Shirley every chance he could and gave her Cheshire cat smiles. Each time he did it she wanted to dash out, to call him a damned liar, but she bit her lip to keep the words back. He knew the effect he had and seemed to enjoy the torment.

The newspapers they rushed to buy each night compared Jeff to Donald Strouth at his own trial. Strouth had rarely if ever looked at the jurors and spent most of his time doodling on a scratch pad. Jeff, the reporters pointed out, not only looked more attractive than Strouth had, but he rose with respect as each and every juror was introduced.

Shirley and Donald tried to talk to Bixby many times during those two days. Most of the time he turned them away, saying he was "too busy." The woman Shirley had met in his motel room, the one he called his secretary, was with him all the time. "We don't have the time," he kept saying, "to be bothered answering questions."

Toward the afternoon of the second day he did tell

them that the district attorney wanted to make a deal. If
Jeff would plead guilty, he could take a life sentence now.
The death penalty would not be considered. Barry said he
had told Jeff, but Jeff had refused because he said he wasn't
guilty.

During those first days Shirley learned that under Tennessee law, anyone taking part in a crime during which a
murder occurs is also guilty of the slaying, even if they did
not actually take part in the murder itself. Even though Jeff
had not taken part in the crime and didn't know it was
occurring, he had been in the car. That frightened her. She
told her mounting anxieties to the attorneys. Barry Bixby
continued to tell her that her fears were senseless. "Nothing will happen to Jeff," he kept saying. "I fully expect he'll
get probation, and he'll walk out of this courtroom with
you." Shirley looked searchingly at James Beeler, who
stood beside him. She felt this man would not lie. He said
nothing, but his face was grave; he looked very concerned.

Finally it was time for opening statements.

Striding to the front of the courtroom Greely Wells
began the prosecution's case. "Good morning, ladies and
gentlemen. I would like to make a brief statement to you.
I'm not going to say the names of all witnesses, I just want
to give you an outline of what we feel the proof from the
State is going to be. Jimmy Keegan was an elderly businessman living in a run down section of Kingsport, Tennessee, Sullivan County. He was about seventy years old and
operated a small used clothing store on East Sullivan
Street in Kingsport, called the Budget Shop. Directly behind this store was a white house, running on an alleyway
behind the store where he and his wife lived.

"Jeffrey Dicks moved into an apartment in Kingsport
about four blocks from the store. He was living with his
girlfriend, Cindy Haines, who is now his wife. After moving
to Kingsport, they were visited by Donald Strouth and his
girlfriend, Sharon Carlson. I think the proof will show that
Mr. Dicks was unemployed and that he and his girlfriend
were living on his mother, Shirley Dicks, who was supply-

ing them with money to pay their rent on the apartment and money to buy food. The proof will also show that Donald Wayne Strouth was unemployed and was being provided funds by his girlfriend, Sharon Donaldson."

He droned on. "On February 15, 1978, Mr. Strouth came from Elizabethton to Kingsport; he went to the apartment where Mr. Dicks was living. That Mr. Strouth and Mr. Dicks went to the Budget Shop with the intentions of robbing Mr. Keegan. I think the proof will show that there were two sets of footprints leaving the back door of the Budget Shop after the murder had taken place. The defendant and Donald Strouth entered the Budget Shop, and struck Mr. Keegan on the head with a rock, and slit his throat." He paused and looked from one juror to the next until he had locked eyes with each one. His tone deepened as he began to talk again. "His wallet was gone, and the front door of the shop was locked."

Now his voice gathered force. "Evidence will show that two sets of footprints led through the backyard, toward the alleyway. Mrs. Keegan went down and found her husband dead, lying in a pool of blood. Mr. Strouth and Mr. Dicks ran back to his apartment, got in a car belonging to Sharon Carlson, and drove to Bristol and then to Johnson City where the proceeds of the robbery were used by Mr. Strouth to buy a car. They got in with Sharon Carlson, and Donald Strouth gave her a fur coat that they had taken from the Budget Shop. I think the proof will show the defendant with part of the proceeds he got from the robbery rented a motel room in Johnson City, and he and Strouth split up never to rejoin. Strouth went to North Carolina in the car that he purchased with the proceeds from the robbery, and Mr. Dicks called his mother, Shirley Dicks, and asked her to come and get him and his girlfriend.

"On March 9th, Mr. Strouth was arrested at the residence of his girlfriend, Sharon Carlson. After that his bloody jeans, the ones Mr. Strouth was wearing during the robbery and murder, were recovered from a trash dump where she had thrown them."

He walked back and forth in front of the jury box.

"The testimony will show Mrs. Dicks did come to Johnson City to pick up her son and his girlfriend. She took them to Greenville, South Carolina, and obtained an apartment for them. She later moved them to Erie, Pennsylvania.

"Testimony will show Agent Wilcox and other law enforcement officers, after the arrest of Strouth, went to Asheville, North Carolina, and had a conversation with Shirley Dicks. She was informed they were looking for her son, Jeff Dicks. And following that she was followed by Wilcox and others." His voice hardened. "While outside her residence, they observed a ball of flame, hurtling out the back door of the residence where she was living. Subsequent to that, the charred remains of a long, green army coat, was recovered from Mr. Dicks.

"Following that conversation Mr. Dicks came to Asheville and turned himself in to North Carolina officials. What I've said is not to be taken as evidence because it isn't evidence. It is what I expect our witnesses are going to testify to. Thank you very much." He sat down.

Judge Calhoun asked, "Does the defense have an opening statement?"

Barry Bixby answered, "Yes, Your Honor." Slowly he walked toward the jury box, paused and took a deep breath. "Ladies and gentlemen of the jury, while you're listening to this evidence, I would ask you to realize that you think very closely among yourselves, not with your rational minds, but with all of your common experiences that you use everyday in your life, and consider Jeffrey Stuart Dicks a living, moving man, a human being with a heart and mind and soul. That while he's not been able to stand here and tell you anything yet, and his relationship with you is minimal at the most, that he is entitled, regardless of what he looks like, regardless of what the State says, regardless of what you think at the outset of this trial, to the most precious King's Robe around him, the presumption of innocence.

"He has pleaded not guilty in this courtroom and has maintained that he is not guilty throughout this trial. Keep in your mind that not only is he human, but that his mother, Shirley Dicks, is human, that he's married to Cindy Dicks, that he has a daughter who he named after his mother (Her name is Shirley Ann Maria Dicks. She was born in 1978), and that he is entitled to all of the benefits of the law.

"Now, there is something to be said among people that the first thing they hear is the most likely to be believed, and I ask you, ladies and gentlemen, to keep your minds open. The State puts on its evidence first, then the defense puts on its evidence. Of course, the State has the privilege of making the first opening statement, and after the evidence is all in, the State makes the first summation and then the defense makes its summation, and then the State has the privilege to make another summation.

"Remember, ladies and gentlemen, do not allow the State to make you sit here and smell blood when it may not be on the hands of Jeffrey Dicks; and we will prove to you that it's not." He looked into the faces of the jurors for a sign of sympathy or support. There was none. He forced himself to go on.

"The State tried the case first against Donald Strouth, also known as Chief. He called himself an Indian, that he is the leader, that he did do the heinous things that the State says that he did, that he was guilty of a terrible brutal act.

"We don't deny that; you'll hear that evidence, and we don't deny it. But you'll hear Jeffrey Dicks testify, and you'll hear other testimony to the effect that in his mind and in his heart, he had no contemplation that this man who called himself Chief, and remember the implication of that name or that designation, was a leader whose ambitions had become distorted, perverted; and you will hear testimony from Jeffrey Dicks that while he befriended Chief, he had no idea in his mind that this man named Chief was capable of the kind of terrible acts that he perpetrated on James Keegan.

"You'll hear testimony from his mother, that while she did help her son, while she did involve herself in these things, she was doing it as his mother, and that she was doing it as a person who thought that her son was involved in something that he'd never contemplated being involved in.

"I just ask you to do this: I ask you to consider in the first phase of this trial that you are a juror who will hold the State to its proof beyond a reasonable doubt and to a moral certainty as if you or one of yours was on trial."

Detective Wilcox was the first witness to be called. He strode arrogantly to the front of the courtroom and settled himself in the witness chair. He told how Jeff had turned himself in after he and the other detectives had questioned Shirley. He said he and the other detectives had followed her home that night and had parked outside the house.

"What did you observe as you sat in the car outside Shirley's residence?" Kirkpatrick asked smoothly.

Wilcox looked toward the jury, a tight grim smile on his face. "We were sitting where we could observe the rear and front of the house. Something which was a ball of fire came out of the back of the house, a round type ball of fire which I would describe as probably the size of a small, well, a half bushel. It looked like it was something rolled up. We made some comment to each other about someone was burning up the house, or burning something up." He shook his head in mock dismay.

"And later, did you recover a green overcoat which had been burned?"

"Yes, sir."

"Later, did you have occasion to go to the state of North Carolina, to see the defendant in this case, Mr. Jeffrey Dicks?"

"Yes. We took him into custody," he said tersely.

"Did you advise him of any legal constitutional rights that he had as a person who is charged with a crime?"

"Yes. I advised him at that time that he was charged with first degree murder and also armed robbery."

"Did he indicate he wanted to talk to you?"

Impassively, Wilcox said, "Yes. He did wish to talk to us. He gave us a statement."

As Bixby began the cross-examination, Wilcox gave him a cocky, self-assured look.

"Now in searching for Mr. Dicks, did you contact his mother?"

"That's correct."

"Did you contact her yourself?"

Wilcox nodded his head affirmatively. "We went to North Carolina. Myself, Officer Paterson and two Buncombe County investigators appeared at her place of employment, and when she showed up we asked her if she would talk to us, and we took her to an office and interviewed her."

"Did you all take her to a room to talk to her, all of you?"

"Yes."

The muscles around Wilcox's mouth tightened; it was the only emotion he betrayed. "I told her that her son was charged in Tennessee with first degree murder and armed robbery."

"Are you sure you told her first degree murder?"

Wilcox snorted in disgust. "I told her that her son was charged with first degree murder and armed robbery. I told her I thought it would be in her son's interest to surrender himself, that, if he did not, we would eventually arrest him." Wilcox's eyes were hard.

"You deny then, I assume, that you told her he was only wanted for armed robbery, and that it would be better for that reason to come back and tell the truth. Do you deny that you mentioned that to her only?"

"There was no mention made of that only," Wilcox said matter-of-factly.

"What time was this interview."

"It began about 7:00 P.M. until 12:00 A.M."

"You and other officers were there with this lady; nobody else was present from 7:00 until 12:00?"

"The manager of the motel came in on several occasions to get something out of the desk drawer."

"So, some five of you were all there interrogating her?"

"We were not per se interrogating her; we were interviewing her."

Barry Bixby wanted to bring out the intensity and duration of the questioning to which Shirley had been subjected.

"You talked for five hours about this homicide."

Wilcox hesitated and then went on, "Well, partly the five hours was used to try to solicit the information that we knew she possessed pertaining to information that her son had told her in reference to this killing and robbery."

Bixby appeared nervous, his hands visibly trembling. Wilcox was cool and matter-of-fact.

"Did she contact you later about her son coming back?" Bixby went on.

"She contacted Mr. Calvin Birch on a Saturday following the interview and advised that he would surrender on Sunday at 4:00 P.M."

"And he did that, didn't he?"

"Yes."

Bixby got to the real bone of contention, the green overcoat. "You made some statements about seeing a ball of fire come out the back door?"

"Yes," Wilcox nodded.

"Now, you're not leading the jury to believe that you went there on that occasion and got that fireball and it turned out to be a green coat?"

"No, sir."

"You've gone to many schools and received training on interrogating alleged defendants?"

"I attended the FBI National Academy. I have interrogated many witnesses."

"The sole purpose of the interrogation of Mr. Dicks was to gain his statement and evidence to be used against him in court, is that true?"

Wilcox skillfully made the point his. "The sole purpose was to obtain the truth."

"The purpose of this interrogation of Mr. Dicks, the sole purpose or a purpose was to gain a statement to be used against him?"

"One of the purposes was to gain a statement, yes, sir; not the sole purpose, no, sir, not to be used, just primarily, against him."

"When you began taking this statement, you knew what Mr. Kirkpatrick and Mr. Wells would have to prove in court to convict this man, didn't you?"

"No, sir. I had a general idea what facts were needed, but I didn't know precisely, no, sir."

"Did Mr. Dicks appear to be a passive individual when you took his statement?"

Kirkpatrick rose to his feet, "Your Honor, we object to that."

The judge nodded, "Sustained. That would call for a conclusion."

Bixby shook his head but continued. "He wasn't in any way violent, was he?"

He shrugged, "No, sir, he was not violent."

"He never cursed you or . . ."

"No, sir, did not."

"That's all. I'd like to reserve the right to call him back for cross-examination at a later date, later time."

Judge Calhoun said to the witness, "You may step down."

A short recess was called.

Barry Bixby came out and talked to Shirley about Wilcox's testimony. She was enraged at hearing of the lie about the "burning ball of flame" coming from her house. "How could he say something like that?" she exclaimed. "The houses are only five feet apart, and anyone could have seen something burning like that at night. I'm not that stupid. Nelson burned the coat the same day I brought Jeff's things home from the apartment. He had been drinking. He insisted it all was a bunch of junk, and I was too tired to protest. I'll take a lie test to prove it, or have them give me truth serum. Nelson and I will both take one. Then make Detective Wilcox take a test to show that he is lying. How can a cop sit there and lie to put an innocent boy to death? I just don't understand it."

"Don't worry about a little thing like that," Barry said brushing away her concerns. "Won't make any difference. I'll have you testify about the coat when you get on the stand." He turned to talk to Beeler for a moment. Beeler looked worried, Shirley noticed, and her own heart beat faster.

Shirley continued. "If the coat was all stained and I wanted to hide it I could easily have just bought another coat that looked like that one. They wouldn't have known the difference. Why didn't I do that?" she wondered aloud. "And besides, if they saw something burning and they really thought it was 'evidence,' they would have run over and grabbed it. It's illegal to burn that time of night; so they'd have had every right to do that. I'll tell you why. They didn't know the coat was burned until Nelson went in and told them. That's why they asked Jeff where the coat was, because they didn't know. They're lying!" Shirley cried out, "Can't you make them tell the truth?"

Hearing her cries, Nelson, who had been standing a few yards away, hurried to her side. "Calm down, Shirley," Nelson said. "There's no use in getting upset right now. Everything is going to come out in the long run. Don't forget, God is watching over us and He wouldn't let Jeff be killed for something he didn't do." He led her over to the bench, where they sat down.

Just then, Teeny, who had been in the courtroom, came running over. "Mr. Beeler was right," Shirley said to her mother. "Things don't look good. The other day I asked Bixby where Jeff's witnesses were. I haven't seen any of them standing around the court, and he just said to let him do his job. Perhaps we made a mistake in hiring him. Him and Beeler aren't getting along either. I heard them talking in loud voices last night. I think they were arguing about something."

"I don't know anymore," Teeny said to her daughter. Her face was pale and worried.

Investigator Robert Paterson was the next to testify. His testimony proved to be the most crucial and the most controversial. He said that they found two sets of footprints in the back lot leading away from the Budget Shop.

"I can't be hearing what I think I am," Teeny said agitatedly.

"What's wrong?" Shirley asked.

Teeny's voice shook as she spoke, "Well, first Paterson said they found two sets of footprints." Shirley gasped. "He tried to make it sound like one was Chief's, the other Jeff's," Teeny went on. "But then, when Bixby asked him if he had pictures of them, which would have been normal since he'd taken pictures of everything else, he said the camera had malfunctioned during those shots."

Shirley was the one who was incredulous now.

"Don't you think it's funny," Teeny asked, her face flushed, "that all of the bloody, colored pictures of the body came out perfectly, yet those of the footprints were completely ruined? And," Teeny added angrily, "they never took plaster footprints as they usually do in a murder case."

It was getting worse and worse, Shirley thought. Her hopes that Jeff would get a fair trial and that the truth would come out were fast fading.

"I'm sure Detective Paterson was lying." Teeny went on, "There was no way all those pictures didn't come out."

Shirley nodded. "The back lot is where the drunks and

winos came to drink and, of course, there would be many footprints. What they were trying to make the jury believe was Jeff hadn't taken the car that day, and that he had gone inside with Chief." Shirley wrung her hands together. "I'm getting more and more frightened. Mom, you'd better go back in and hear what else is happening." Teeny nodded and hurried back to the courtroom.

A short while later Mrs. Keegan took the stand, but she broke down and had to be excused until she could regain her composure. Shirley knew Mrs. Keegan felt terrible, and felt pity for her, but she also knew this was sealing Jeff's chances. The jurors felt compassion for her, as they should, but then they turned hate-filled eyes toward Jeff.

After her testimony, Barry Bixby talked to the jury and cautioned them not to make a decision until all the facts were heard. He also reminded them that Donald Strouth had been found guilty beyond a doubt of James Keegan's murder.

The next person to take the stand was the used car salesman from the lot where Chief had bought the car he later used. This time Becker testified that he couldn't remember who actually bought the car, though under cross examination by the defense, he admitted that in the trial of Donald Strouth he had testified he had sold the car to Strouth.

When Shirley heard that, she got madder and madder. "What are they all doing?" she raged to Nelson. "Each and every one of them is changing their testimony from Chief's trial to Jeff's!"

Shirley's anger turned to terror when she heard from Teeny about what Sergeant Dan Bower, who had gone with Strouth's girlfriend to retrieve Strouth's bloodied blue jeans from the side of a road, said. Nowhere in his testimony did he express the fact that the jeans were Strouth's. Moreover, it was not mentioned by the prosecution that it had been proven by two witnesses that Strouth was the owner of the jeans. When the defense questioned Bower directly about the jeans being Strouth's, the prosecution agreed to stipulate that they were Strouth's. But the damage had been done. The jury had heard so much about the jeans, they didn't care at this point who had worn them.

When Bixby questioned more about the footprints other inconsistencies surfaced.

"You consider yourself to be a professional officer. You have taken plaster casts of footprints, taken photographs of evidence, haven't you?"

"Yes. I have general knowledge of a camera. I'm not a professional photographer."

"You relied on your ability and Sergeant Page's ability to make photographs of the evidence there at the scene, did you not?"

"To be honest with you, I didn't take any pictures that day."

"Do you realize Sergeant Page testified that you had made photographs too?"

"Well, I did later, but not right then."

"Do you know if there were footprints?"

"I knew there were footprints."

"But you have absolutely no picture of any footprints, or not even any evidence of a plaster cast of any footprints, do you?"

"I don't have, no, sir."

"And Sergeant Bower, you say that you walked up that little space between the two buildings."

"Yes, I did."

"And this is the time you saw footprints?"

"Yes."

"You don't know whether those were Sergeant Page's footprints or Donald Strouth's footprints or Jeff Dicks' footprints, or whether there were any footprints there or not, do you?"

Again, as with the jeans, so much had been made of the prosecution's supposed proof that the fact that there was no real evidence to support the contentions was paid little attention.

"I don't know whose footprints they were, I can tell you there were footprints in there."

"You've been in Kingsport long enough to know that that area is an area where there's lots of people such as drunks, people that get back in that alley and deposit their alcoholic beverage bottles in that area, don't they?"

"Well, I know that's an area for drunks, but I've never worked in uniform. I don't fool with them, and I don't know where they hang out."

"And there's no way to tell if a footprint is fresh or stale, is there not?"

"I'm not an expert on that either."

"A lot of the pictures were made a long time after the crime. How many films didn't develop?"

"Two, I believe."

Bixby shook his head in disgust.

"That's all," he said, his feelings creeping into his voice.

The final nail was driven in Jeff's coffin when Chief's girlfriend, Sharon Carlson, was called by the State to testify. She was instructed by the court not to say anything Chief had said to her, as it was regarded as "hearsay" and was not admissible. Barry Bixby, knowing how imperative her testimony was to saving Jeff, tried to reach a compromise with the Court.

"Well, Your Honor," Bixby began, "if Donald Strouth is a co-defendant and he made an exculpatory statement with respect to Jeff Dicks, then we have a right to ask him about it. And if he's not available for testimony, if he cannot be made available for testimony, and his attorneys object to his testimony based on the Fifth Amendment, then it becomes necessary for us to ask this lady right here what he said."

It made no difference. The Court ruled anything Strouth told Sharon Carlson—his confession to her that he was the only one who killed Mr. Keegan and Jeff did not have a part in the crime—was ruled as inadmissible. The jurors were not going to be able to hear anything Chief had said. They had been taken out while the attorneys argued over the point.

Shirley's heart sank when she was told. How could they ever prove Jeff was innocent if they weren't allowed to bring in testimony which proved that Strouth had admitted he alone had killed Keegan?

Wells knew he had won a significant point. "Your Honor, the State would make a motion that the Court directs no questions be asked of this witness designed to elicit hearsay statements made to her by the co-defendant, Donald Strouth."

Calhoun said, "You may cross-examine her about any statements she may make, but any statements made by Donald Strouth are not admissible in this case against the defendant."

Bixby made one last try. "We'd like to subpoena Donald Strouth."

Calhoun shook his head. "It's kind of a late date to be subpoenaing Donald Strouth."

Bixby said, "Well, if Donald Strouth made an exculpatory statement with respect to Jeffrey Dicks, then we have a right to ask him about it. If he cannot be made available for testimony, if his attorneys object to his testimony based on the Fifth Amendment, then it becomes necessary for us to ask this lady right here what he said. I believe that would be the law very definitely."

Wells nodded, his face sober, but he could not suppress the hint of a smile at the edges of his mouth. "It would still be hearsay."

The rest of Calhoun's ruling increased his good spirits. Calhoun was adamant. "My ruling is this witness cannot testify as to hearsay statements made to her by a co-defendant. You've had months to prepare for this case. Bring the jury back in."

"Your Honor, could you instruct the witness as to the effect of the ruling," Wells said.

Calhoun gave Sharon Carlson a withering look, "You understand you are not to make any statement as to what

Mr. Strouth said to you. That's hearsay in this trial as to this defendant. Do you understand that?"

She nodded. Shirley knew Sharon had wanted to tell the whole truth, but now she would not be able to.

Bixby tried a new tack. "I want to make another motion: that her testimony in the former trial be made a part of the record for this trial outside the presence of the jury."

Calhoun wasn't about to allow it. "Mr. Bixby, you know how to get such testimony in the record. You have a law license. Now let's proceed."

Wells inclined his head in the witness's direction. "Your name is Sharon Carlson?"

"Yes, sir," she said. Her voice had a purring, almost rhythmic quality.

"Was Mr. Strouth employed?"

"No, sir."

"Was Mr. Dicks employed?"

"He was selling Fuller Brush."

"When you saw Strouth the day of the murder, was anyone with him?"

"Jeff was with him in one car, Cindy was in my car."

"What did you do at this point?"

"I walked over to Cindy and she . . ."

Judge Calhoun stopped her, "Don't."

Wells picked up his cue. "Don't testify as to what anyone said," he said curtly.

Bixby began again.

"Did anyone give you anything?"

"Chief gave me a fur jacket."

"Miss Carlson, let me show you what has been marked Exhibit Number 4, and ask if this appears to be the fur coat Donald Strouth gave you."

She nodded.

"Yes, sir."

"What did you do with the fur coat?"

"I gave it to Peggy Miller."

"Were you given anything else?"

"Chief said there was a calculator . . ."

The judge stopped her; he made no effort to camouflage his irritation.

"Madam, the question is were you given anything else. You may answer yes or no."

"I can't say . . ." Sharon pushed a strand of red hair that had fallen in her eye back into place.

"Well," Calhoun took a deep breath and let it out. "You can't say what anyone said other than Mr. Dicks."

Again Wells took direction.

"Let me show you, Miss Carlson, State Exhibit Number 15, which appears to be a pair of blue jeans, and ask you if you have ever seen those blue jeans before?"

"These were Chief's pants. These are the ones he was wearing the day he came back from High Point, North Carolina."

"What did you do with these pants after he came back?"

"He took them off and laid them on the side of the road. I told him . . ."

"You can't say any conversation now."

Wells said, "That's all the questions I have."

Barry Bixby moved forward. He looked tired, no longer as sure of himself as he had been earlier.

"Your Honor, I would like her to read her part of this transcript in this former trial and identify it as her testimony in the Strouth trial outside the presence of the jury."

Kirkpatrick rose. "For what purpose?" he said. It was more a statement than a question. However, Calhoun answered.

"If she can read it and identify it as such, it might be a way of getting it introduced. All right, at this time we'll take a recess and let her read it."

Again it was Bixby's turn.

"You have known Jeff Dicks for several months, haven't you?"

She hesitated and finally said, "Yes."

"And during that time, Jeff was selling Fuller Brush products?"

"Yes."

"In the morning that Chief left with your car, was he drinking or had any pot?"

"No."

"That evening, he was drinking beer?"

"Yes."

"Was Jeff drinking?"

"No. He was sick . . ." Sharon, who had come there to tell the truth, all she knew, had been unnerved by being stopped so many times . . . "I don't know. He was nervous."

"When you went to see Chief at High Point, he discarded the hawkbill knife?"

Wells said, "Objection, Your Honor."

"Overruled."

"Did I see him do it?"

"Well, you knew he discarded it, did you not?"

Calhoun intervened again, "If your answer depends on something someone told you other than Jeffrey Dicks, you can only state what you saw."

"I didn't see him discard the knife."

"You said something about what happened in Kingsport that day?"

Wells wasn't about to sit still.

"Objection, Your Honor."

Looking extremely uncomfortable Bixby said, "I'm sorry."

Then he went on.

"You were sitting in the car talking, and was the conversation related to . . ."

Again Wells jumped up.

"Objection, Your Honor."

Again Calhoun ruled with him.

"Sustain."

Bixby was clearly out of his depth now; he struggled to get on with the questioning.

"Would you describe the hawkbill knife you bought for Chief."

"It had a wooden handle, and a hawk . . . you know what a hawkbill knife looks like."

"Do you know if he carried it around with him after you gave it to him?"

"I assume he did."

"You didn't appear voluntarily to the grand jury, did you?"

"No, I was scared. Officer Wilcox told me if I signed the papers, he would not charge me with committing a crime."

"You signed the statement?"

"Uh-huh. I was scared not to. He told me to quit playing games. He told me I could get the same sentence Chief got for helping him."

"And in your earlier testimony, in the case against Chief, you were offered a joint or a beer?"

"I believe so."

Calhoun looked sober as he said, "This witness may be excused."

Teeny was incredulous as she told Shirley what had happened in court. "I can't believe that we're living in the United States of America, the land of so many rights. Where was Jeff's right to a fair trial?" she asked plaintively. "Why couldn't the jurors hear all of the evidence before passing judgment on him?" Shirley felt her stomach churning; perspiration ran down her face. She wanted to shout, to run, to do something, anything to relieve the agony she felt. She couldn't believe this was our justice system working.

They went to lunch. As with Chief's trial, the town was small and most of the people from the prosecution ate at the same place they did. There wasn't much of a choice.

At the restaurant Shirley saw Barry Bixby. She walked over to him. "I don't understand," she said, "why Sharon

Carlson wasn't allowed to tell the whole story. How will they know Chief was proven to be the only one that killed James Keegan?'' she asked.

Again he put her off. "Why don't you let me worry about that." Shirley was too worried to be side-tracked so easily. She asked Bixby where the witnesses for Jeff were. So far only her mother, Nelson and she were in the hall waiting to be called. He didn't answer and walked away. By this time she was frantic. After all, they were the ones paying this man to represent Jeff, and he wouldn't even tell how things were going.

Her mind in turmoil, she hurried back to the table and told her parents that she didn't trust Bixby anymore. "Well, there's nothing we can do but just wait it out," Teeny said wearily. She was sipping at her coffee, the only thing she'd ordered. Nobody had much of an appetite. They were surviving on coffee alone. Shirley's dad looked the worst of all. Ernest's condition worried Shirley. "You ought to go back to the hotel to rest," she said, but he wouldn't hear of it.

"I want to be there all the way through the trial for Jeff," he said firmly.

Silently they paid the bill and walked back across the street to the courthouse. While they were in the room downstairs waiting to be called to take the stand in the courtroom, a short, slight man neatly attired in a blue suit approached Shirley. "I want to ask you a few questions about some checks you've written," he said, identifying himself as an FBI agent.

Shirley took a deep breath, "I can't answer any questions at this time." Barry Bixby, who agreed to represent her in this matter, heard the conversation and walked over.

"She'll talk to you once the trial is over. She isn't in any condition to talk at this time." The man gave Shirley a sympathetic look.

"I'm sorry to have to bother you at a time like this," he said. "I'll come back."

Dr. James Wilford, a small, compact man wearing glasses was the next witness called. He had already testified about the condition of the body and the wounds of Mr. Keegan at Strouth's trial and was called to do so again at Jeff's.

At this time the State brought in colored photographs of James Keegan, just as they had when Chief was tried, showing the victim's neck wounds and all the surrounding blood. The jurors were also told about the bloody jeans. This time, however, the prosecution seemed to imply that the jeans were Jeff's. It was a ridiculous theory. Shirley was incredulous when she heard it. The jeans belonged to a small person. Jeff was six foot three. Anyone could see they couldn't be his but, she thought despairing, no one did.

Having been sworn, Wilford supplied his credentials as a physician. Then Kirkpatrick began to ask question after question about the body itself. It seemed as if the State wanted to impress the jury with the bloody details of the crime. As if these acts, by their horror, called out for further retribution, for someone else to blame despite the fact that Strouth alone had committed them.

"Would you describe the injuries that you found on the body of James Keegan?"

"There were multiple traumatic injuries on the body, including a depressed skull fracture in the right temple area of the skull. There were contusions over the right side of the face and in the right ear. There were lacerations of the right ear extending through the cartilage of the ear, separating from these lacerations. The cut on the neck was very smooth, done by a very sharp instrument. The edges were very smooth, and the muscle was also cut smoothly underneath. It could not have been done with a dull instrument."

"Could you determine was this done with a single stroke or was it done with many hacking movements?"

"It was done with a single stroke," the doctor answered definitively.

"If a person was conscious, what would be the reaction of a human being that was having their neck cut? A person would attempt to get away from such injury, struggle?" Kirkpatrick inquired, looking at the jury somberly.

The doctor nodded, "It is reasonable to assume that someone would grasp his neck and try to deflect the instrument."

"After the arteries were cut, and the knife continued on its path, would that artery or the area of flesh have a tendency to close over the artery to stop the spurting from coming out further?"

"The flesh doesn't close over the arteries, but the arteries contract and the flow would diminish eventually from this type of vessel."

"At what distance, do you think that blood would spurt from a human being's neck who was being cut in this manner?"

"It would easily squirt twelve inches, a foot to two feet, with no problem."

The questions went on and on as Kirkpatrick tried to implicate Jeff in the killing of Keegan.

"Can you determine whether or not this man was unconscious or conscious when his throat was cut?"

"I feel like it is reasonably medically certain that he was unconscious."

"What is the significance of the cleanliness of the cut or the smoothness of the cut instead of a jagged cut?"

"If a person were to struggle against a weapon like that, the cut would not be smooth and sharp from one side to the other."

Kirkpatrick's voice was now rising to a crescendo, "Except under what circumstances? What would prevent a person from not struggling, Doctor. Are there two things that would prevent him from struggling?"

Wilford answered quietly, "That he were restrained or that he was unconscious."

Either way, Kirkpatrick was ready to clinch his point, "Now, you said it would take him about fifteen minutes to bleed to death. Had he received medical treatment promptly, would his life had been spared?"

"Prompt medical attention would most likely have resulted in the victim living."

Kirkpatrick gave Wilford's answer a few minutes to sink in. Then he went on, "Doctor, based on the reference to the blood on the pants, if there had been another person there, would it have spurted on his pants too?"

"Yes, sir."

"And whether he was lying down or standing up, are you in a position to make that determination with reasonable medical certainty?"

"I can't make that determination from what I saw on the body, no, sir."

"All you're saying is he was either unconscious or restrained?"

"Yes, sir."

Kirkpatrick turned away.

"You may ask," he said to Bixby, a faint smile on his face.

Bixby nodded. He wasn't smiling back.

"Doctor, you didn't go to the scene where this man was found did you?"

"No, sir."

"Now the attorney general has asked you a question that is very interesting, and that is, did you know whether or not this victim was standing when his throat was cut? Now, if he had been standing, Doctor, wouldn't he have been conscious?"

"He could have been supported, but there are problems with certain positions with producing a wound like that."

"Well, the wound that you're talking about is consistent with the way the victim was lying according to this picture, is it not?"

"That's right."

"And if the victim had been restrained, then he still

could have put up a struggle, so that the wound would have
been jagged? In other words, in your opinion, is that
right?"

"Yes, sir. It is always possible to restrain with enough
force, you know, to totally immobilize somebody."

"But, Doctor, in this particular situation, with this
man lying there and being unconscious, is this perfectly
consistent with the wound on his neck, the smooth
wound?"

"Yes, sir."

"And whenever a person is being attacked, his adrenal
glands, whatever, begin to pump, his muscles become
much more powerful, do they not? In other words, he
would have much more reserve of energy and muscular
control or just, say, power than he would in a normal situation, wouldn't he?"

"This will to live gives some added strength," Wilford
said quietly.

"Based on your reasonable medical certainty, Doctor,
and based on all of the observations, particularly this picture, your examination of the victim, he was lying on the
floor when his throat was cut? What I'm saying is that it is
more reasonable than any other assumption, isn't it, Doctor?"

"Yes, sir."

Bixby's line of reasoning seemed to have gone nowhere. He sighed, "That's all. You may step down."

It was time for the defense's case. Barry Bixby, already
battle weary from the many court rulings which had gone
against them, felt ragged and tired. Moreover, he had decided, much against the family's and Beeler's advice, to
call few witnesses. He struggled now to present some sem-
blance of defense and called Nelson Dicks to the stand.

Nelson, in his only suit, walked forward looking uncomfortable and ill at ease and settled his lanky frame in the witness chair.

"Mr. Dicks, do you remember when Jeff had been suspected of being involved in the killing of James Keegan, and when did you first learn of that?"

"About a week or so after it happened," Nelson sounded hesitant.

"Did you and your wife, Shirley, have occasion to come back to Kingsport, and what did you do?"

"We emptied out the apartment that they were staying in."

"Where was Jeff at that time?"

"Shirley had already taken them to Greenville, South Carolina." Nelson's voice was becoming firmer, clearer.

"What did he do in South Carolina?"

"He worked for Manpower."

"Can you state what happened to the clothes that Jeff had in his apartment in Kingsport?"

"Some he took to Erie, some came back to the house, and I don't know what happened after that."

"When did you talk to Mr. Wilcox?"

"It was the Sunday evening Jeff turned himself in."

"Can you state whether or not you remember the time when Shirley was interrogated by Officer Wilcox and the other officers at the Holiday Inn?"

"I remember that night," Nelson stated quietly but definitively. "She came home very upset. Shaking, crying. I was sleeping. I usually was asleep when she came in, but she woke me up, and apparently from what she told me, they gave her a heck of a hassle."

Wells was on his feet. "Objection, Your Honor."

Again Calhoun ruled in his favor.

"Sustained. Sir, you are not to testify as to what someone told you. In that instance it is hearsay evidence."

Bixby took a new track.

"With reference to the coat, can you state if you burned it or who burned it?"

"I burned it. I burn all my garbage. The coat was garbage, and as I explained to these gentlemen, they could
come to the house and see where I burn all the garbage, the
cans and all."

"Can you state if it had any blood on it?"

Nelson's voice rang out.

"No, there was nothing on that coat. He wore that
coat around Greenville for two weeks afterwards, at least."

"When he came back to Asheville, could you say
whether or not Jeff had the coat?"

"By the time he came back, I had burned it."

"How did the coat come to be in your possession?"

"Shirley went down to Greenville and brought the
stuff back to my house."

"Did you have any discussion with anybody about any
suspicion about blood or stains on this coat?"

"No way."

"Who brought the coat to the police?"

"I did. The coat was the one important item that could
prove Jeff innocent, and that the laboratory would get it
and prove that . . ."

Kirkpatrick called out. His voice was close to a shout.

"Your Honor, we're going to object to all of this."

Calhoun adamantly cut in.

"Sustained."

Bixby rephrased.

"Well, who did you talk to about the coat?"

Kirkpatrick rose.

"Your Honor, may we approach the bench?"

Calhoun, his face flushed, said, "Take the jury out for a
moment."

He turned to Nelson.

"Now, sir, let me advise you. You cannot state your
opinion or your theories about what might prove him innocent, what might not prove him innocent. You cannot testify about matters that you did not see or observe yourself.
You cannot testify about what someone told you. Mr. Bixby,

you cannot ask questions you know the response is going to be in the nature of the responses already given. The State has a right to object, and I'm sustaining their objections."

Bixby shook his head.

"Do I understand correctly, Your Honor, that testimony as to what conversations were had with the officer, Officer Wilcox with the other officer, is not hearsay?"

Calhoun snapped:

"It is hearsay because I don't recall having Mr. Wilcox testifying about any matter regarding Mr. Dicks here, about any conversation with him. So, therefore, anything Mr. Dicks says about his conversation with Officer Wilcox is not of, would not go to Officer Wilcox's credibility and would impeach his credibility. It's just simply hearsay and not admissible. I don't recall Officer Wilcox testifying as to anything this man said or as to anything that was said in this man's presence. This witness has referred to a conversation with Officer Wilcox before Jeffrey Stuart Dicks turned himself in. This is pure hearsay at this point. I'm granting the State's motion *in limine* because I am going to be repeatedly forced to instruct the jury, Mr. Bixby. All right, bring the jury back in."

Kirkpatrick began the cross-examination:

"Mr. Dicks, you stated there was nothing wrong with the long green overcoat which Jeffrey wore on a regular basis?"

Nelson regarded him levelly with brown eyes. "Yes," he answered firmly.

"And you say that you observed that coat and it had absolutely no blemish of blood about it. Is that what you're saying?"

"Right."

"At this time, you all weren't hiding them, were you?"

"Yes."

Kirkpatrick's voice became accusing:

"How come the coat was in your possession on the 14th day of March?"

Nelson sighed, "I got the coat on a Monday."

"And after your wife came home after she had talked to Agent Wilcox, that's when this coat turned into a ball of flames and came hurtling out of the back of your house into the yard, is it not?"

Nelson was adamant: "No, it is not. That coat was burned Monday evening."

"Why did you take that coat and burn it?"

Nelson shrugged. "Because it was garbage; why did I burn the coke bottles and the milk containers and the cans?"

"Mr. Dicks," Kirkpatrick's voice was close to a shout, "the night when your wife came home is when a ball of fire came out of the back of the house, isn't that right?"

Nelson shook his head. "No," he said stiffly, "it is not right."

"You deny that?"

"Yes," Nelson said definitively.

"And you deny that you burned the coat?"

Nelson said curtly, "No, I burned the coat, but it was on a Monday, not the night my wife came home."

Kirkpatrick wasn't about to give up.

"You were willing to do anything to destroy any evidence of his guilt that you had in your possession."

Nelson's exasperation was beginning to show. "If we had anything to hide, they would never have seen the coat, and Jeff would never have turned himself in."

Kirkpatrick didn't like a witness getting the better of him; he attacked, "You were hiding him, and had transported him to Erie, preparatory to his fleeing into Canada, isn't that right?"

"No. He was setting up home in Erie."

"But that's just across the lake from Canada, isn't it?"

Nelson looked him directly in the eye.

"Yes, but it's a long swim."

Kirkpatrick flushed.

"No further questions."

Bixby began to redirect:

"Mr. Dicks, did you dig up this coat?"

"I did," Nelson said, his frustration still showing.

"And at whose suggestion did you dig it up?"

"Wilcox's."

"Did you turn it over to Mr. Wilcox?"

"I did."

"Can you state, Mr. Dicks, whether or not you had any conversation with Officer Wilcox here with respect to any tests that he wished to perform on the coat?"

"Yes, he told me the lab . . ."

Wells was up again.

"Objection."

Calhoun sighed, "Sustained, Mr. Bixby—"

Bixby shook his head. "That's all."

Calhoun said, "The jury will disregard that question and will disregard any part of the answer he started. Do you have any further questions?

Mr. Bixby repeated his last remark. "That's all."

Calhoun nodded to the witness, "You may step down."

ELEVEN

Nelson walked back out to the hallway where Shirley was sitting. He was so angry, his face was red. Clenching his teeth, he swallowed hard.

"What happened?" Shirley asked. From his face she deduced things had not gone well.

"The district attorney wouldn't let me tell how Wilcox told me to bring the coat in and the lab would analyze it to see if there were blood stains on it or not. I tried to say that, but the judge cut me off. They made the jurors believe the coat was burned the night you came home. They didn't believe it was burned a few days earlier than that."

Shirley shook her head wearily.

"Wilcox lied to us from the start. I told you that's what would happen, but you believed in them. Now it's going to put Jeff right in the electric chair. I've a good mind to run in there and tell the jurors the truth. This isn't justice!" she cried out.

Nelson saw her suddenly grow pale and wasn't sure how much more she could stand. "Now, calm down, Shirley. It won't be all that bad." A glazed look of despair began to spread over her face, and he could see tears welling up.

"Well, it's not fair that you couldn't tell the jurors about the coat and what Wilcox said to us. He said the lab could blow the picture up and see there was no blood on it. That was the picture with Jeff holding my gun. Now the jurors will think Jeff played with guns. Why didn't you just say it anyway?"

"I tried, Shirley. But Kirkpatrick kept objecting to what I was trying to say. He wouldn't let me tell them about the picture, or that Jeff was cleaning out your car that day, or that he never carried weapons, in fact, anything. I tried, really I did."

"Well, Mom," Cindy said to Shirley, "you can tell them when it's your turn on the stand. No one can stop your mouth when you start. That way at least the jurors will hear it all."

Shirley looked at Cindy for a moment, then smiled. "That's true," she murmured. "I'll just try and answer all these things when I get on the stand." She turned to see Barry Bixby along with Beeler walking toward them. Beeler's face was grim.

"When are you going to put me on the stand?" Shirley demanded of Barry.

"I'm not. I'm afraid you'd lose your temper on the stand," Bixby said. "I don't want it to look bad for Jeff. He's going to be all right. Don't worry about it." There it was again. Shirley started to answer but remained quiet. Everyone said, Don't worry about it. How was she not to worry about it?

"Then why wasn't I allowed in the courtroom all this time?" Shirley asked. "Surely you've known all along you weren't going to put me on the stand. If anything happens to Jeff . . ." She was furious by this time and didn't care who knew it. Barry had kept her out of the courtroom by lying . . . It's bad enough the prosecution lied, she thought; she didn't need to be lied to by their own attorney.

He talked faster. "I just decided. Anyway, it wouldn't have done any good for you to be in the courtroom. Your temper is well known. Hard telling what you might have said in there."

"What do you think, Mr. Beeler?" Shirley turned to

Beeler, who had been standing there silently. His face was filled with compassion. She noticed, though, how he averted his eyes. But she needed an opinion. An honest one, for a change. She pressed him, "What do you think?"

"You'll have to ask your attorney," he said quietly. Shirley sensed something a bit off in Beeler's relationship with Barry Bixby. She stared from one man to the other. Perhaps James Beeler smelled the same rat she did, she thought. More fearful images built in her mind. She was trying hard to keep her fragile control from breaking, but it wasn't easy.

She had sacrificed everything to get Barry Bixby for Jeff's attorney: her self-respect, her honor, maybe even her future. She had broken the law, involved her husband, her innocent children. And now it seemed it all was for nothing. She had known he wasn't the best, but she had counted on his ability and experience to bring the truth out to prove Jeff's innocence. Even when her instincts had told her something was wrong, she watched him and Beeler walk away, but before he was gone she heard Beeler mutter to Bixby, "This trial isn't going the way it had been expected to."

"Oh my God," Shirley said, "Oh my God."

After the lunch break Jeff took the stand. He looked incredibly young, frightened and gaunt.

Bixby was the first to question him.

"Have you ever been charged with anything other than the check charges?"

Jeff's voice trembled, "No, sir, I haven't."

"Did you ever carry a knife when you were growing up?"

"No, sir, I didn't."

"Did you ever carry any weapon?"

"No, sir, I didn't."

"Did you ever get into fist fights?"

"No, sir, I never believed in fighting."

"While you were in Kingsport, did you work?"

"I was selling Fuller Brush."

"While you were selling Fuller Brush, were you able to make do financially?"

"Yes, sir, I was."

"And was your mother helping you?"

"Yes, sir, she was. She brought me food every weekend and she would give me money, and usually she paid my rent for me."

"Are you bad to drink?"

"No, sir. I did drink beer, but not very often, like on a weekend or something, when we'd go downstairs to our neighbors. I didn't drink very often, no, sir."

"Did you ever use drugs?"

"No, sir. I have smoked marijuana, but that's all."

"And on February the 15th, you had been talking to this man named Chief, hadn't you?"

"Yes, sir."

"How did you meet Chief?"

"I had met him while I was living in Southern Hotel through another friend that I had known at the hotel there. And I had met him and Sharon Carlson in my apartment."

"Did you find him to be a likable person?"

"I liked him because I . . . you know, I felt sorry for him. He didn't have any family. He didn't have any other friends. The only person he had was Sharon. And, so, I kind of felt sorry for him, and I wanted to be his friend."

"What did he do for a living?"

"He was unemployed the whole time I knew him."

"Do you know if he had any problems with the law?"

"Not that I know of."

"What was the reason why you liked him other than that you felt sorry for him?"

"He always seemed to be a gentle person. Like when I met him just before Christmas, he didn't have any money. All he had was three or four dollars, and he spent all of it to buy his girlfriend something for Christmas. Because of that, I thought he was pretty nice to do something like that."

"Did he talk to you a great deal?"

"Yes, sir, he did. He was always telling me that . . ."

Wells rose. "Objection."

Calhoun quickly ruled, "Sustained."

"Can you state as to whether or not he bragged to you?"

"Yes, sir. He bragged all the time."

Wells signaled again, "Objection."

Calhoun murmured, "Overruled."

Barry Bixby looked up surprised and went on, "Can you state whether or not he bragged to you about being involved in criminal activities?"

"Yes, sir. He did. For that reason I never believed him because there was just too much stuff that he said he'd done in his lifetime that couldn't possibly have been done."

Wells stood up, "We object to these kinds of questions."

Calhoun was back with his usual comment, "Sustained."

Bixby sighed, "When you first met Chief, were you afraid of him?"

"Yes, sir, physically."

Kirkpatrick stood again, "Your Honor, we object."

Bixby didn't even wait for a ruling. "During the time you got to know him better, explain if you were afraid of him."

"Well, he was a very stocky fellow. I'm not the type to —the fighting type, and Chief was. He was very strong, and he was the type of person that you couldn't look in the eye because he would scare you to look at him in the eyes. He was just the type of person that would scare you."

"Now, on the day you got to know Chief, on the 15th of February, did you at anytime discuss with Chief or did you say to Chief that you would go into the Budget Shop with him and do anything that was illegal or criminal?"

"No, sir, I did not," Jeff said firmly.

"And did you—you knew when you were talking to him, what he wanted to do?"

"Like I stated, he said he was going to rob the store, and I told him . . ."

Kirkpatrick objected, "Your Honor, this is hearsay. It just continues that way."

"Well, I didn't believe he could do something like that. He was always talking . . ."

Kirkpatrick called out, "Your Honor, our objection."

Bixby, exasperated, said, "May we approach the bench, Your Honor?"

Calhoun nodded, "Yes."

Bixby said, "Your Honor, I don't see how the hell they can call it hearsay when it's all through his statement. I mean . . ."

Calhoun interjected, "I'm going to fine you fifty dollars for contempt of court for the use of that language you just used."

Bixby took a deep breath and let it out, "I'm sorry, Your Honor, but I . . ."

Calhoun cut in, "Well, you just . . . do you want to go to jail for ten days now?"

Bixby looked at the judge, "No, sir, I don't, but . . ."

Calhoun's face was filled with anger and contempt; he said, "Well, just be quiet for a minute. I'm going to excuse the jury."

Whereupon the jury retired from open court.

Afterward Bixby pleaded, "Your Honor, the statement that was placed into evidence by Officer Wilcox is replete with references to conversations and activities that occurred with regard to this man and Chief, and if Your Honor please, I would respectfully contend that if Jeff Dicks cannot testify as to what conversation he had with Chief, then, it's just, he's strapped into a position where he can't defend himself."

But Calhoun had already made up his mind he wasn't going to allow it. "I have previously ruled as to hearsay statements before. I think the conversations surrounding the transaction are relevant. The State will be allowed to cross-examine. The State has introduced admission against interest by the defendant, and the State will be allowed to cross-examine as to those statements; and matters that are generally part of the transaction, I will allow the witness to testify as to those matters."

Beeler, who had been silent, allowing Bixby to conduct the defense, felt he could be so no longer. He might not have any experience in murder cases, but he knew right from wrong, and he felt quite certain about what he was seeing here. "Mr. Dicks was not allowed to testify as to what Mr. Strouth had told him regarding what he had done, what Mr. Strouth alleged that he had done in the past. Now, I read a case, a Tennessee Supreme Court case, and I've searched the advance sheets again, and I cannot find it. It was a case involving a murder charge. The defendant pled self-defense. In that case, questions were asked like this."

Calhoun was more patient with him then he had been with Bixby, "Yes, I'm aware of that. Yes, there are cases, there's a lot of law along that line, but here we have a co-defendant that is waiting to go back to weeks before and talk about conversations with another co-defendant that are not part of this transaction."

Beeler's voice rang out loud and clear, "Your Honor, our—we're talking about a state of mind on Jeffrey Dicks' part. A state of mind which I think is going to be very important in the jury's determining whether he actively participated in this and willingly. Therefore, whether he was afraid of Mr. Strouth is of mandatory importance, and it should be up to the jury whether the events that motivated that fear were of such a magnitude that they could produce the lack of initiative on Mr. Dicks' part. And I think we should, therefore, be able to bring in these prior acts that Mr. Dicks is aware of in order that the jury should—"

The earnestness of Beeler's words even seemed to affect Calhoun, who backed down, but only a little bit, and only for a short time. "Well, you've already got a contradictory record on there, Mr. Beeler. Now, let's proceed from where we are now and see what happens at this point. Bring the jury back."

"When you drove down the second time, who drove the car?"

"I did."

"Why?"

"Because I love to drive cars, and it had been a long time since I had driven a car, and Chief asked me to drive."

"Did you know at that time, that Chief was going to rob the store?"

"He had said earlier he was, but I didn't believe him. He always talked about it; he said he was going to rob a bank, and he never did. I believed he was just talking about it for me to look up at him. But I did not believe he was capable of ever doing anything like that."

"And on that occasion did you know where you were going?"

"Not until I had gotten there and he told me to pull over, just before we got to the Budget Shop."

"And were there people around there?"

"There were a few people walking up the side street, and there was another older man in a black pickup truck across the street from where I was parked."

"Did you get out of the car?"

"No, sir, I did not."

"When Chief got out, what did he say to you?"

"He did not say anything. He got out of the car, and said nothing."

"What was on your mind at this time?"

"I was scared, and I wasn't thinking. I was basically scared of Chief, and I didn't know what he was doing or what he was up to."

"Did you go inside the store with him?"

"No, sir. I did not."

"When he came back out, what did you do?"

"He came back out, put a jacket in the car and told me to drive the car to the alley in the back. I didn't know what to do, so I moved it on back. I didn't know what else to do."

"When you got to the back and stopped the car, did you get out?"

"No, I sat in the car the whole time. Just as I stopped the car, I noticed him coming towards the car. He got in the car, and told me to leave."

"Where did you go?"

"We drove down the alleyway, and I made a right to my apartment."

At this point Laurie, Jeff's younger sister, began crying hysterically. She couldn't take them hammering at Jeff. As Brenda rose to help Laurie out of the courtroom, the judge ordered that neither of them could come back into the courtroom for the rest of the trial and banned them from the vicinity of the courthouse.

By the time Brenda reached the place where Shirley sat she was visibly shaken up. "What happened in there?" Shirley asked her sister.

"Laurie was upset so I got up to help her come out here for a few minutes, and the judge said we had to leave permanently. Leave the courthouse and not come back," Brenda said as she also started crying. "It was so bad in there. They have Jeff on the stand and he looks terrible."

When Shirley heard this, she bolted for the door, intent on getting inside to see what they were doing to Jeff. Nelson held her back, "Shirley, that won't help Jeff, it will only make the jurors think you're a crazy mother." Perhaps it was true, she thought, struggling to free herself. Her face was a glowing mask of rage. Her throat was raw with unuttered shouts.

"It isn't fair!" she finally cried out.

Nelson tried to comfort Shirley, telling her she had to calm down. "Don't keep telling me to calm down. How am I supposed to feel? My son is in there fighting for his life, and it's all my fault. I shouldn't have let him come in. It's all my fault."

Nelson didn't loosen his grip. Finally Shirley calmed down a little bit and sat back down in the hallway rocking herself to and fro, waiting.

Meanwhile Jeff continued to testify.

"Did he say anything to Cindy about what had happened?"

"I don't believe so."

"When did you first learn a man had been killed?"

"It was about 3:00 P.M. when I heard it on the T.V."

"And how did you feel at the time?"

"I was sick to my stomach, very scared, and didn't know what to do at the time. I never believed he could do anything like that. He always said he had robbed six or seven banks before, he had run a prostitution ring up in New York, and he was a bodyguard for the mafia."

"Now, when was the last time you saw Chief?"

"That evening at the motel room. He wanted us to go to Florida with him, but I didn't want anything to do with him after I found out the man had been killed, and after I found out what Chief was capable of doing. I didn't want nothing to do with him, no part of him. All I wanted to do was get away from him."

"Jeff, why did you come back from Erie?"

"Because I was not guilty, and I wanted to prove that."

"When Wilcox was taking your statement, did he bring a stenographer or court reporter or anything into the room?"

"No, sir, he did not."

"Do you know if he wrote down everything you said?"

"No. I trusted him. I always trusted in the law."

"Did Detective Page tell you what you were charged with?"

"He said I was charged with first degree murder up until the day I went to court, but that's where the charges would get reduced."

"Was the statement you gave to Mr. Wilcox accurate in every respect?"

"No, sir. I was hearing it read the other day. I noticed a lot of things I didn't say in it, and I noticed a lot of things I did say that wasn't in it. I had told Mr. Wilcox that Chief had told me he was going to rob the man, and I did not believe him. That wasn't in the statement. I told Wilcox I was afraid of Chief, and that was not in the statement. I did not tell Mr. Wilcox I saw Mr. Keegan with a wad of money."

"That's all," Bixby said.

Kirkpatrick strode to the witness box. His face grim, he began immediately to grill Jeff.

"Do you remember signing your statement when it was being done?"

"Yes."

"Do you recall signing it?" he asked icily.

"It's my signature, yes."

"And every time Agent Wilcox inserted something on the page, you initialed it, is that correct?"

"Yes, I did what he told me to do."

"Didn't you read this part of it that you were initialing?"

"No, sir. I did not pay any attention to it. Like I said, I trusted Mr. Wilcox. I just did what he said; I didn't want to make him mad. He had my mother and wife in the other room, and he told them they could be charged with the same thing if I did not cooperate. So, I didn't want to make him mad. Like I said, I trusted him. He seemed like an honest man to me." Jeff regarded the prosecutor levelly with clear gray-green eyes.

Beeler reached over to whisper to Bixby, "The basic decency of the boy has to make some impression." Bixby just shook his head sadly.

"Do you deny you've ever read this?"

"I have not read it. Like I said, I trusted Mr. Wilcox."

"Why were you running from the law over the checks if you trusted law enforcement?"

"I was guilty of writing checks. I am not guilty of murder, and that is the reason I turned myself in. If I were guilty I wouldn't have turned myself in, like on the bad check charges."

"You're telling this jury that you are a completely non-violent person, is that right?"

"Yes, sir."

"You've never had a knife or a gun in your life?"

"No, sir."

"Never had a gun or a knife in your life, that's what you just said, and that's what the defense said. Now, do you want to change that for the jury?"

"No."

"I'm asking if you ever had one?"

"My mother had a pistol, yes, sir, she does."

"I'm asking you if you've ever had a knife or a gun, would you please answer that."

"I've had my mother's gun before."

"And you've carried knives before too, haven't you?"

"No, sir, I haven't."

"Never had a knife?"

"No, sir. I have never carried a knife in my life."

"Have you ever had a knife?"

"No, sir."

"Never touched one?"

"Never had one in my life."

"But you have a gun?"

"I have not had a gun. I told you my mother had a gun."

"And you've had that gun in your possession too, haven't you?"

"I've held the gun, yes, sir."

"You've carried it too, haven't you?"

"No, sir, I have never carried the pistol."

"Mr. Dicks, are you telling these twelve people here that you were trying to talk Chief out of robbing the place?"

"Yes, sir, I was."

"You and Chief robbed Mr. James Keegan didn't you?"

"No, sir, I did not."

"And you and Chief murdered James Keegan by hitting him in the head with a rock and cutting his throat from ear to ear, did you not?"

"No, sir, I did not. I have never hurt anybody in my life. I would rather die myself than see someone else hurt. I have not hit anybody, and I have never hurt anybody in my life. I swear to God I haven't."

"And you went out that back door, the two of you, jumped over the fence and went down that alley, running?"

"No, sir."

"Here is the man you said you respected, you thought was so nice, because he was nice to his girlfriend, here is the man you associated with on a regular basis."

"Yes, sir."

"When you left Chief, why didn't you go to the police and tell them what he did?"

"I didn't know what to do at the time. I called my mother and asked her what to do."

"What you did do then, you went to Greenville, South Carolina, did you not?"

"Yes, sir."

"From there you were going to go to Canada, is that correct?"

"No, sir. We were never going to go to Canada."

"How did you know the police were not on your trail?"

"My mother called me three days before I turned myself in."

"And you told them to burn the coat, didn't you?"

"No, sir. I did not. I didn't know they had the jacket. I left it in Greenville, South Carolina when I moved to Erie. I didn't know they had the jacket. I didn't know they had anything I left."

"Well you knew they were going to pick it up, didn't you?" His voice suggested a game of cat-and-mouse.

"No, sir. I didn't know they were going back to Greenville to get the stuff."

"Well you found out, didn't you?"

"No, sir."

"You needed the money, didn't you?"

"No, sir."

"You said you didn't have any money the day of the murder."

"Yes, sir. But I didn't need any. My mother had sent some money."

"But you hadn't received it yet, had you?"

"No, but she had sent it."

"And you desperately needed it, didn't you?"

"No, sir. I did not desperately need it. I had food, my rent was paid."

"I have no further questions."

Barry Bixby got up and walked toward his client. "Jeff, is this the picture that was made before or after the 15th of February, 1978?"

"It was after because it was in Greenville, South Carolina, at my apartment."

"Who made the picture?"

"My mother did, and the reason we gave it to Mr. Wilcox was she had asked him since the jacket was burned, if he could tell if there was any blood on the jacket by the picture. He said there were ways . . ."

Kirkpatrick was up again. "Your Honor, we object to this."

Calhoun nodded, "Sustained."

"Were there any other pictures made?"

"Yes. My mother made quite a few that day, yes, sir."

"Was there any blood on your coat?"

"No, sir, there was not," Jeff said quietly.

"That's all."

Dr. David McMillian was to testify next, but the State objected. Judge Calhoun said he would listen and rule if the jurors would be allowed to hear the testimony of the doctor.

Beeler stood up and began to speak. His voice was low, emotion charged. "If it pleases the Court, what we would expect the doctor to testify to would be Jeff's capacity to actually do the acts which were alleged to have been done. The State has at least attempted to establish that Jeffrey Dicks was there and actually did participate in the act by the insinuations that the coat was burned because of blood stains on it, that he either did the act or helped hold the man, I presume while it was done. I think the doctor's testimony will relate directly to that issue whether Jeff would be capable of doing such as that. And further, we're dealing with felony murder here, the robbery itself; I would expect the doctor's testimony to relate to whether Jeff could initiate carrying through an act such as robbery. And I believe these are directly on point, not to the second phase of the trial, but to help the jury to determine a very important part of the felony murder charge, that is whether Jeff was there. The Court will, I believe, instruct that he has to be there, not in mere presence, but helping and furthering the offense of the crime or at least willing and able to participate in it. And I think the doctor's testimony will run to those lines, and therefore, I think it is abundantly pertinent to the first phase."

Calhoun seemed bored. "Well, ask him has he examined Jeff, and what you would plan to ask, what you intend to ask, so that I can rule on it."

Beeler nodded. "Dr. McMillian, did you observe Jeff Dicks, and did you conduct any tests with him?"

"Yes, I did."

"What were the findings?"

"We found that Mr. Dicks' tests indicate a bland character who has trouble coping with everyday stress, who is

. . . has problems with judgment and reasoning, has little common sense. The . . ."

Beeler knowing Kirkpatrick would soon object tried to lead McMillian to a less diffuse topic.

"Were you able to draw any conclusions about Jeff's personality?"

"Yes. The person is abnormal in the way he sees the world or the way he pursues reality. The tests indicate a weak, moody, fearful person who is highly inadequate and has much difficulty in coping with everyday stress. The person who is likely to seek out a dominant female in the male's case often to help let him take the helpless child role."

"Based on your examination, the tests, if we presume that Jeffrey Dicks became associated with a strong dominant individual—"

Kirkpatrick got up. "We object to that; there's no evidence whatsoever to substantiate a hypothetical such as that."

Calhoun said, "Well, he may ask it as a hypothetical; in the event that the question would be allowed before the jury, it's a matter for the jury to decide. Ask him assuming."

"Doctor, if we presume that Jeffrey Dicks became associated with a strong, dominant individual, would you have an opinion to a reasonable degree of scientific certainty as to whether Jeff would be able to exert his own personality, make his own decision or participate in any decision making process even to ordinary daily events such as where to go, when to go, how long to stay?"

"The patient doesn't want to take such initiative. He would be a follower. He couldn't carry such a definite act as a crime out by himself. I believe it is fact now, that Mr. Dicks wrote some bad checks. Mr. Dicks' way of dealing with his problems is to be subtle and passive, not to be direct. It would be unlikely for him by himself to directly initiate something as definite as going in with a weapon. I would find that very unlikely in his case."

Calhoun said, "Doctor, now as I understand it, you've administered these tests, and you have determined the personality of the defendant; you say he's not a dominant person. But are you aware he's a Fuller Brush salesman."

"Yes, I am."

Calhoun went on, "And could perform the duties of a salesman, and you're saying he's a follower instead of a leader, is that correct?"

"Yes. But in relation to the Fuller Brush salesman, he worked with hi—"

Calhoun interrupted, "What I'm interested in finding out, is he suffering from a mental illness?"

"Well, yes, I would say he has some kind of mental defect. Would that satisfy?"

Calhoun asked, "Can he determine right from wrong?"

The doctor nodded, "Yes, he can."

Calhoun stroked his chin. "The essence of your testimony would be he is a weak, moody, fearful person, and is a follower instead of a leader. Is that not the essence of your testimony?"

"That is a summary of what I would say."

Beeler tried to get a word in, "Your Honor, part of the motivation for this testimony is—"

But Calhoun interrupted testily, "Would it not be speculation, any question beyond that, would that not be speculation?"

Beeler said earnestly, "Your Honor, I think it would be a conclusion as to how Jeff would react under given circumstances."

Calhoun was adamant, "I'm going to sustain the State as to this witness testifying in the presence of the jury on the grounds that his testimony is not relevant to the issue at this stage of the proceeding and that it would be mere speculations. Call your next witness."

Kirkpatrick injected, "That will have to be taken up outside the presence of the jury."

Barry Bixby knew he'd lost the point. "We call Donald Wayne Strouth."

Donald Strouth, stony-faced, looking neither to the right nor left, was brought into the courtroom and took the witness stand. His attorney, J. Klyne Lauderback, stood nearby.

Calhoun advised him, "Now, Mr. Strouth, you have the right to remain silent so far as any testimony about the occurrence, alleged occurrence, in regard to killing James Keegan. Do you, after having been advised of your constitutional rights, do you wish to testify, or do you wish to invoke your right to remain silent?"

Lauderback stepped forward. "Your Honor, if I could answer that. We discussed that, and on my advice he does not wish to testify, and on his own decision he wishes not to testify and takes advantage of the Fifth Amendment rights."

Calhoun nodded, "All right. That will be all."

Bixby's exasperation had reached a breaking point. "For the record we were going to ask him one or two questions. One of the questions was: Mr. Strouth, state whether you stated to your girlfriend that you alone slit the throat of James Keegan?"

Calhoun turned toward Strouth's lawyer. "Now, Mr. Lauderback, as I understand that, the defendant wanted to exercise his Fifth Amendment right as to any statement?"

Lauderback replied, "Yes, Your Honor. He's not going to answer any questions."

Kirkpatrick interrupted, "I'm worried about a personal privilege belonging to the individual. I think Mr. Strouth ought to be in here at least giving his approval of the statements that are being made by his counsel on each one of these questions. I realize it is dangerous to have him in any more public exposure for his own safety."

Calhoun said somberly, "Under the circumstances that occurred during his trial and unconfirmed reports relative to certain people connected with the defendant in this trial, that there might be some danger, some personal danger to Mr. Strouth."

"I advised him not to answer and he asked me to answer for him," Lauderback replied.

Calhoun turned to Bixby and asked, "Do you have any other witnesses?"

"No, Your Honor," Barry Bixby said sighing. He knew when he was beaten.

TWELVE

In the front of the courtroom, those gathered at the prosecutor's table smelled victory in the air. They moved in for the kill. For the first time Shirley sat among the spectators, listening to her son's fate being decided.

"Ladies and gentlemen, we've been here now for several days," Wells began in his closing argument for the State, "and you have heard all the evidence we've told you, all of the testimony that you're going to hear regarding the guilt or innocence of Jeffrey Dicks.

"Mr. Keegan on the morning of February 15 got up and did what he normally did. From the testimony, I think it is clear that after being opened for a while, he closed the store for a few minutes and went down to the bank and got some change.

"Again from all the evidence, all the proof that you've heard, I don't think there's any question but that he went back down to his store, where within a few minutes, Donald Strouth and this man seated before you here today," he pointed to Jeff, his voice hardening, "that you're trying, came in that front door and got that seventy-year-old man and hit him upside of the head with a rock, and rendered him unconscious, knocked him on the floor, robbed him, turned his pockets inside out, and with a knife or some other sharp instrument, while the man was lying defense-less, unconscious, no threat of anything to these men, they slit his throat from ear to ear."

Shirley could stand it no longer. She jumped up. "You know this boy didn't!" she screamed. "He came back! He's innocent and you know it. You lie! You know that boy didn't do it. He wouldn't have come back if he were guilty." Shirley sobbed. She couldn't take these new lies. The district attorney was telling the jurors that Jeff went inside the store that day. She wanted them to know Chief was the one who went in. They never heard all of the testimony, only what the judge chose to let them hear. It wasn't fair. Never in her life had she felt so helpless and angry. Tears streamed down her face. She felt like she was ready to explode.

Calhoun's face whitened. He growled, "Sheriff, take the jury out."

Shirley could feel Donald's and Nelson's hands on her, trying to restrain her, but she couldn't stop. She wouldn't stop. That jury had to hear the whole story. "They lied! He didn't—" she started again.

Calhoun's voice thundered. "During the course of this trial and pre-trial hearings, and during the course of the trial of the companion case, a gun was taken from this lady who just made this outburst, in the other case while she was in the courthouse during pre-trial hearing. As I left the courtroom, this lady yelled, 'You're prejudiced,' after I had just granted a motion to change venue in the case."

Shirley was shaking all over. She pleaded, "Your Honor, I gave that gun to them. They didn't confiscate that gun from me; they lied about it to the papers." Shirley wanted this man to understand that she was trying to let the jurors know the whole story and not just half. It didn't make sense to her that a person wouldn't be allowed to prove his innocence when evidence of it existed.

Calhoun paid no attention to her. He continued to ad-dress the courtroom, "The Court has ignored all of these matters up to this point understanding that this lady is the

mother of the defendant." He looked around the courtroom and took a drink of water. Shirley felt her throat
tighten up.

"They didn't take the gun from me," she persisted, all
her feeling of frustration and pain pouring out. She
couldn't stop it. They were lying and there was nothing that
she could do about it. She knew she looked like a crazy
mother trying to defend her son, and she didn't care; she
was half crazy by this time.

"For this outburst," Calhoun said harshly, "the Court
finds this woman, Mrs. Dicks, in contempt of Court and
sentences her the maximum that is allowed of ten days in
jail and a fifty dollar fine." He turned to the sheriff. "Execute the sentence, Sheriff." His eyes flashed with anger.
Shirley knew she was finished. There wasn't anything else
she could do. She wanted to grab Jeff from these people
and get away, but she couldn't.

As she struggled with Donald and Nelson, two huge
men from the sheriff's office strode over and grabbed her.
Mike and Roger, Shirley's brothers, jumped up to assist
her. "We'll walk down to the sheriff's office with my sister,"
Mike said angrily, "just to make sure she doesn't get any
bruises on the way down there." The family was grief
stricken over how the trial was going. Watching Shirley go
to pieces compounded their agony. It was a nightmare with
no ending.

"I want a warrant made out for the two men standing
up," Judge Calhoun yelled to the sheriff. "Get them out of
this courtroom!" He stood up and banged on the gavel.

Barry Bixby rushed over to talk to Mike and Roger.
Shirley knew he was telling them to just leave the courtroom before they got into trouble also.

Shirley looked over to where Jeff was sitting helplessly
watching what was going on. Tears ran down his cheeks.

Calhoun was livid. "Any further outburst during the
course of this trial will result in punishment after the trial,
in the courthouse. Further, all parties should be advised
that it is a felony punishable by a penitentiary sentence in

the state of Tennessee to threaten a witness, court official, juror or any person involved in civil or criminal proceedings. All right, bring the jury back in."

The two officers half pushed, half walked Shirley downstairs to the sheriff's office. Then she was taken out the back door to the jail. They put her in a cell on one of the top floors of the old building. She could see the jury room from the window and watched as the jurors walked around, laughing, drinking coffee and coke. She watched as they were escorted back to the courtroom and knew the trial was drawing to a close.

"Oh God!" She grasped the bars on the window and tried to bend them with her bare hands. "What's going to happen to my son now? What are they doing in there? Why are You letting this happen to us, Lord? Please help us, help my son!"

"Let me out of here!" Shirley screamed. "Let me out of here right now!" She wanted to be with Jeff. She wanted to be in that courtroom and see what they were going to do to him. Then, as if someone punched her, she crumpled up. Her head bowed, her body slumped in despair. A moment later she jumped up again and began beating on the bars again. Loud screams filled the air and could be heard in the courtroom.

Hearing Shirley's tortured screams, her mother, Teeny, began to sob also. She couldn't help it. All she could do was sit in the courtroom, waiting for the jury to come back in. She, too, was helpless. Ernest held her hand tightly. Nelson and Donald and Cindy were the only other family members left in the courtroom. Brenda and Laurie were back at the motel, Roger and Mike had left to go back to North Carolina, and Jeff had been taken out until the jury was ready.

In her jail cell, Shirley, dizzy and faint, realized that no one was coming to let her out. She looked across the space between her cell and the jury's room and thought about the twelve people who were to decide her son's fate.

The first thing Judge Calhoun did when they returned

was to instruct the jurors to disregard any remarks they
had overheard before they were taken out of the courtroom. If they knew there was other testimony that they
hadn't heard they were not to consider it relevant. Then he
signaled the prosecution to go on.

"Ladies and gentlemen," Wells said walking forward,
"you heard the testimony of the doctor who examined Mr.
Keegan's body to determine what caused his death and it
was not the fact, the simple fact, that his throat was cut
from ear to ear. It was the fact that his heart was still beating, that he was still alive while he lie there on the floor."

He glared at Jeff. "He could have lived for fifteen minutes if anyone would have gotten through that front door
and saved his life. No, they couldn't because this man and
his companion and accomplice, Donald Strouth, fled out
the back door, ran up to the alley. This man was down
there that morning, and he was in that store and he went
there with Donald Strouth with the intentions of robbing
Jimmy Keegan, with the intention to commit a felony, and
an armed robbery. In order to find him guilty of felony
murder, you've got to find that he had intention to commit
the felony, to commit the robbery."

Wells walked back and forth in front of the jury box,
his voice gathering force. "Ladies and gentlemen, during
his opening statement Mr. Bixby told you, we will prove to
you that Jeff Dicks does not have the blood of Jimmy Keegan on his hands. Ladies and gentlemen, I submit to you
that the proof here shows that this man here had the blood
of Jimmy Keegan on the hem of his coat. The man's stepfather, who raised him, burned the coat, and I think that's
evident from the testimony and from the proof of these officers, these policemen, and Agent Wilcox, who did outstanding work on this case.

"And after they talked to this man's mother the first
time and informed her that they wanted her son on a
charge of first degree murder, they followed her home to
her house. She had been in the house only a few minutes
when a ball of flame came out the back window. Well, I

think you've seen what that ball of flame was. Was that
garbage? I burned garbage in my back yard all the time,
and that was merely garbage. Folks, it was this man's coat,
the coat he was wearing, the coat he was wearing in Greenville, South Carolina, but not the coat he wore to Erie,
Pennsylvania. Why would you throw a coat away? Because
it had blood on it, and it was the blood of Jimmy Keegan
that this man got on his coat as he stood there within one
or two feet of the body of Jimmy Keegan as his heart
pumped his blood out from the slash across his throat.

"If you believe the testimony of this man," he pointed
toward Jeff, his voice like steel, "you're going to have to
believe that on February 15, at about nine in the morning,
all this man was wanting to do was trying to talk Donald
Strouth out of robbing Jimmy Keegan, and after the robbery happened, trying to figure out how to get away from
him. And there had been no testimony at all that this man
was under any force or compulsion to go along with Donald Strouth down to the Budget Shop either the first time
or the second time or to Bristol or to the motel room or to
the place where Sharon Carlson works. There is no testimony that this man was forced to do that. He went of his
own free will because he was going with his friend whom
he liked, whom he looked at and admired, whom he
thought was a gentle person."

Wells paused briefly, then returned to the attack. "This
man tells you with his own mouth that Mr. Strouth is a
gentle person. I submit to you under the proof you've heard
that neither of these men deserve the term "gentle." It was
brutal, cold. It was calculating, it was planned. And it was
effective because Mr. Keegan is not alive here today to
point his finger at and accuse Jeffrey Dicks of robbing him
and Donald Strouth of robbing him. Mr. Keegan is never
going to get up in the morning and walk out his front door,
because he's dead at the hands of this man and his accomplice."

He shook his head emphatically. "The law is not that
we have to prove that he had the intention of killing Mr.

Keegan when they went in there. What we are required to prove is that they went with the intention of committing a felony, to wit, robbery. And during the course of that robbery, Mr. Keegan was killed.

"Folks, they told you that they were going to prove that he didn't have the blood of Jimmy Keegan on his hands, but I submit to you that we have proven that he had the blood—has the blood of Jimmy Keegan on his hands. I submit to you that under the law and under the evidence which you have taken your oath to follow, the law and the evidence, I submit to you that we have proved beyond a reasonable doubt that Jeff Dicks is guilty of first degree murder. Thank you."

Barry Bixby gave the closing argument for Jeff's defense.

"I have never in all of my life had a more sobering experience than being here in this courtroom," he began quietly. "This is one of the most important things you have ever been involved in, in your life. Because you represent somebody who has been indicted for a crime in which the state of Tennessee demands of you that you can sign his life to oblivion, send him out into eternity, that's what they are asking you to do.

"We have talked about the presumption of innocence, and we talked about the indictment being a piece of paper that formally brings the defendant into the courtroom, and about how it's really no evidence. It has no value. It's just a piece of paper that formally brings the defendant into the courtroom." He paused and looked from one juror to the next hoping to see a sympathetic response. When he didn't he went on:

"And now, how about the defendant here, Jeff Dicks, and I'm sure you know much more about him now than you did before. He didn't get a chance to go in front of the grand jury. He didn't have a lawyer.

"Let me tell you something about the powers of the State, any state. They have millions of dollars they spend. They fly witnesses into your airport here in their airplanes.

They bring FBI in from their fancy laboratories. They have
their high functioning cameras. They have all these people
trained in how to testify in front of a jury, training for every
aspect of a criminal investigation, all the technology that is
available to the government of the United States through
the Law Enforcement Aid.

"And Jeff Dicks had little ole me here, and Mr. Weddington, and Mr. Beeler, to represent him. And the only
thing that stands between him and that awesome thing
down there in Nashville that they use to consign these people to oblivion with, is us three lawyers here that don't
prosecute these felony cases all the time, and don't have
the access to all these millions of dollars in technology and
malfunctioning cameras."

He went on to discuss the footprints, proof of which
the State promised to produce but didn't.

"I see footprints because there's a plaster cast in the
courtroom. I see footprints because there's pictures of
them. I know Jeff was in the Budget Shop because some of
the clothes that you didn't see here in the courtroom were
sent to the FBI lab. An officer testified that he had five
items of clothing. But you didn't see those in the courtroom
because these gentlemen right here don't want you to see
them in the courtroom. They don't want you to see something that says Jeff Dicks is not guilty. They want you to see
all the things, all the prejudicial things that relate to Donald Strouth. That's what they want you to see.

"You come in the courtroom, and you look at witnesses, and see how they answer questions and how they
respond on the stand, and you can tell when someone is
lying. They don't look you in the eye the way Jeff did. They
don't look at Officer Wilcox and say, 'Didn't I say that, Mr.
Wilcox. Isn't that what I said?' And did you see him, did
you see Officer Wilcox look down when Jeffrey Dicks
looked him in the eye and said, 'Isn't that what I said, Mr.
Wilcox?' Did you see him look down, look away from the
eyes of that young boy there, those green eyes that looked

of honesty to every one of you and told you what happened, what he did, what his involvement was.

"I tell you, it would make me sick if he had a mother who didn't cry. And this boy here, Jeff Dicks, came to the light. He did. He turned himself in. He came back and he said, 'I wrote bad checks, and I ran from the law because I wrote those checks because I was guilty of it, but I came back because I'm not guilty of murder.'

"The law is not perfect, but it is the best that we know. And if there's anything that approaches perfection, it is. Because it recognizes that this man, Jeff Dicks here, this young boy who is impressionable and yet can sit there in that chair and tell you specific clear instances of times that he sold Fuller Brush. And I thought he was eloquent. He was fighting for his life. He was fighting for what he deserved and what he wanted. And he wants to live.

"I've seen many a mealy mouthed witness get up on the stand and make a fool of themselves because they were lying. But he trusted Officer Wilcox. He trusted these people that told him when he came and gave himself up that he'd be charged with first degree murder, but then, when he got over here, it would be reduced. But Jeff Dicks trusted everyone. He trusted his mother, he trusted—he even trusted a psychopathic killer; couldn't go into a place and rob it and do what was done in there.

"And I think that you will agree with me when I say that there was a picture taken there—a lot of this evidence, by the way, was turned over to these people by the family. There was no testimony that the burned coat was obtained pursuant to a search warrant except that it was turned over to them by the family.

"But I submit to you that Jeff Dicks trusted too many people. He was in the wrong place at the wrong time with the wrong person, and that's bad. Take a young boy that's got family, that acts meek the way he does, that has the mannerisms that he has, that can look you in the eye and talk to you about the way things really happened, and looks Mr. Wilcox right in the eye and says, 'I trusted you.'

"And you talk about somebody that's got some character. He may be foolish and stupid, and hang around with a
bad man. He may give himself the vulnerability of being
impeached in the courtroom by living with a woman without the benefit of clergy, and having to be subsidized by his
mother for his groceries and having to go down to the welfare office every once in a while. But it was Donald Strouth
that came into his house that morning, the 15th, with a
hawkbill knife. It wasn't Jeff Dicks.

"That coat that so much has been made of was photo-
graphed in Greenville, South Carolina. I don't think there
was any blood on it. Because any blood that was on any
garment could have been washed off. I don't know if he
burned the coat on that particular night or not, that this so
called fire came out of the window. But I do know this:
That if it was evidence being destroyed or if these—these
officers were there, two cars having this house under sur-
veillance, and something went flying out that was on fire. It
seems to me like they would have wanted to go and get it
right quick and see what it was. Or at least to avoid tres-
passing on somebody's property, go back and get some
kind of process or go down and knock on the door and
whoever comes to the door and just say, what was that you
just threw out the back door, and what was that just
thrown in your back yard, to determine what it was. Not
just come to court and say we saw a ball of fire and therefore it had to be this coat there that was burned.

"I submit to you, ladies and gentlemen, that the coat
was brought back to these officers voluntarily by his family,
that when a jury is called upon to make a determination of
guilt beyond a reasonable doubt in a capital case. Now I'm
sorry that James Keegan is dead. And I'm sure that Jeff
Dicks is sorry that he is dead. But if you find him liable by
putting him in the shoes of Donald Strouth on that kind of
evidence that you've heard here, I don't think you'd do it.

"I ask all of you when you go back to your room to
deliberate the fate of this man, Jeff Dicks, that you ask for
divine guidance, that you sum up all the energies of your

mind, and look Jeff Dicks here in the eye, and look Officer Wilcox here in the eye and walk down there to the scene where Mr. Keegan was murdered. He said, whenever he got a question that needed no, he said, 'No, sir.' And he said that he respected officers, and trusted Officer Wilcox when he understood that he was charged with murder in the first degree, and it was time for him to come back and face up to it, and reveal what part he had in it. And they told him that he had a right to an extradition proceeding he went ahead and signed the extradition papers, and came on back to Tennessee.

"I feel that the State has failed to overcome that awesome burden that it has to enable the State to take this man's life. Not maybe. Not probably. And not even almost certain, but beyond a reasonable doubt. Thank you."

Barry Bixby sat down.

Upstairs in the jail, Shirley waited. After what seemed like an eternity, she heard footsteps in the hall. Her heart pounded with fear. She walked over to the door and saw Barry standing there. "What's happening?" she asked anxiously. Shirley watched his face to see if he had bad news for her.

"The jury is out," he said giving her a tight lipped smile. "Everything is going to be all right. I'm sure Jeff'll get a light sentence out of this. I have some papers for you to sign." He pushed the papers in through the bars and she signed them without asking any questions. Then he turned and walked away. Later she found out the papers he had given her signed over her home.

The jury was sequestered in their room. Shirley watched from the window. She had quieted down, but tears stained her face. She saw them walking around, drinking more coffee. Sometimes loud voices could be heard. She wanted to plead with them to save her son, to believe that he wasn't guilty, but their windows were closed. She prayed their hearts weren't.

More time passed. Then she saw Mr. Beeler. He had Donald with him. Slowly she walked to the cell door and waited. As they drew close, the pity in Mr. Beeler's eyes made her gasp. She felt her knees give way. She grabbed the door and heard his voice as if through a long tunnel.

"I'm sorry, Shirley," Mr. Beeler said.

Shirley put her hands to her ears, covering them so she wouldn't have to hear the words she knew he was going to say. "No!" she screamed backing away . . . "No! I don't want to hear. Get out of here, both of you. Get out!" Knowing they could not help her they walked sadly, silently away. "This can't be happening."

Running back to the window, she looked out. "This is a dream," she tried to convince herself. "I'll wake up soon. It's not really happening." She couldn't stop the tears that started again, and soon loud sobs racked her body.

"Oh, God," she prayed hoarsely, "please don't let them kill my son. I'll do anything you want. Take me, but don't take my son. He has not done anything and he has so much to live for and if you take him from me, I'll have nothing. I've made a lot of mistakes in life and done a lot of wrong things, but please, don't take it out on Jeff. Please!"

The walls were closing in on her, and she wanted to run and get away, but there was nowhere to run. Outside the sun still shone; the birds were still singing. Couldn't they see the heartbreak that was going on? "Oh, God, please," she whimpered over and over again.

A few hours later one of the trustees came back and handed a newspaper to her through the opening of the cell. Wordlessly she took it and began to read. "Jeff Dicks, the father of a baby girl, stood expressionless as the verdict was announced. But those of his family members who remained in the courtroom could not hold back their disappointment. Donald Creteur stood with his arm around Dicks' grandmother, Tina Mathews as she gently wept. Jeff's wife, Cindy, who had successfully restrained herself through highly emotional final arguments, also broke out into quiet sobs. Shirley Creteur, however, was not in the courtroom to hear the damaging verdict. She had been sentenced to ten days in jail and a fine for losing control of her emotions during an argument presented. Throughout the trial, the defense had maintained Dicks had nothing to do with the killing of Keegan. Their defense was that Dicks only drove the car, and he did that only because he was afraid of Strouth and did not believe that Strouth was actually going to commit the robbery. Before the final statements were given, the defense attempted to call three witnesses to the stand. All testified or refused to testify, but not in front of the jury."

Shirley stopped reading and sat down. She closed her eyes reliving the pain of that scene. She could not speak; she could not cry. She was drained.

"Only one witness was called for the sentencing phase of the trial. Dr. David McMillian, the psychologist who was not allowed to testify during the trial, was called by the defense. He said largely what he had told the jurorless courtroom before: that Jeff had a sort of mental defect, but that Jeff knew the difference between right and wrong. But under cross-examination, Dr. McMillian said it was possible that Jeff could manipulate other people into carrying out his will. It was this point which the prosecution attacked in their closing statement.

"The prosecution said that Jeff was the only person to gain from killing Mr. Keegan. Wells said that Jeff hit Keegan on the head with a rock first, then Strouth cut his throat. The jurors never heard testimony from Sharon Carlson and Livingston that Chief admitted to hitting Keegan on the head; admitted to killing him alone. Kirkpatrick said a death sentence was necessary to show criminals they wouldn't get away with killing eye witnesses to their crimes in Tennessee. 'If you say life in your verdict,' he told the jury, 'you're saying it made good sense to kill Keegan.'

James Beeler and Barry Bixby both spoke in Jeff's defense. Beeler had only one thought now, to try to save Jeff's life. He pointed out that Strouth was the one who had

wielded the knife. He reminded them of the nickname
Strouth had given himself—"Chief." "Why was Keegan's
scalp cut?" Beeler asked. "It makes no sense unless with
his deranged mind he thought he was an Indian and
thought he wanted a scalp."

Bixby pointed out that Jeff had no history of violent
crimes and asked the jury not to let justice fail. "Don't let
justice die because of all the gory details that have been
paraded before you in this trial," he said.

Then the jury was taken out to decide whether Jeff
would receive a sentence of life in prison or death in the
electric chair.

Later, as their sentencing of death was being read,
James Beeler fought back tears. Cindy cried, but the rest of
the family in the courtroom seemed to be drained of their
emotions. Jeff did not even rise for the reading.

When Shirley saw the back door of the courtroom
open, saw her older daughter, Tina, coming slowly out in
the yard, her head bent low, her long brown hair covering
her face, Shirley yelled down to her, "Tina, what happened?" Tina looked up, and Shirley saw the answer in her
face.

Shirley knew in that instant they had chosen death.

"No!" she screamed. "No. You can't do that. Please,
God, no!" Her throat was raw, but she couldn't stop.

"Shirley, please stop," her mother's voice drifted
faintly up to her from below. "We'll fight this. Just please
stop." She looked up at the window, and Shirley could see
the tears and pain on her mother's face. Her father, his
snow white hair shining, stood off to one side. Tears rolled
down his face. He seemed to be a broken man. He made no
attempt to wipe the tears off, just stood there looking up at
his daughter, helplessly.

Just then Detective Wilcox came out the back door of
the courthouse. He stood watching the scene, a half-smile
on his face. "You people go on home now. Don't be talking
to the prisoner," he said. His voice had a steel edge to it.

The two old people, their faces filled with despair,

their shoulders slumped, slowly turned and walked back to their car.

Shirley backed away from the window. She could not erase the pain. Fear such as she had never known before consumed her. Her face was pale and pinched as deep sobs tore her. Her whole body was engulfed by tides of pain. She wanted to lash out at something, anything. She wanted to get her son and run away, far away where they would never find him. At that moment, for Shirley, time seemed to stop. Darkness began to cover everything. She couldn't catch her breath. The cell seemed to spin around and around.

She limped over to the cot and fell upon it. Later, how much later she could not be sure, a nurse came in. Gently the nurse wiped a place on Shirley's arm with alcohol and began to give her a needle.

From a distance Shirley heard her mother. "Please, Shirley, don't do anymore yelling and screaming. The judge said you can go home with us soon," Teeny said. She and Donald had been allowed in to see Shirley. They bent over the cot now, their faces anguished. Shirley nodded. Of course she didn't believe what they'd been told. They'd been lied to so many times before.

"Try to rest," Donald said gently.

"How can I be quiet when they just tore my heart out and broke it into little pieces?" Shirley cried. "I'd rather they kill me than to take one of my children." She watched as the nurse finished medicating her and went back outside.

Donald stroked Shirley's face and pushed her hair back from over her eyes where it had fallen. "We have to go now. I love you. Please just do as they say," Donald said. He stood looking at this woman he loved. He wanted to take her pain away, but he also was helpless. Shirley could feel the shot starting to take effect.

THIRTEEN

Slits of sunlight hit her closed eyes. Awakening, Shirley didn't know where she was, only that morning had come. Slowly she sat up, looked around and saw the cell bars. Then she heard the jingle of keys and footsteps slapping on concrete as a burly guard appeared carrying the breakfast trays.

Then she remembered. Picture after agonizing picture of the past twenty-four hours flooded her mind. She wanted to cry out, but said nothing. Silently she took the proffered tray and sat down again on the hard cot. She stared at the gray, lumpy cereal, touched the lukewarm coffee with her finger and idly stirred it. She wanted nothing to eat. She wanted nothing to drink. Looking around at the sterile surroundings, she wondered how long she would be there.

She was careful not to make a sound in hopes that she would not anger her jailers further. It was a surprise, though, when not long after breakfast, a guard came. "Get your things," the petite brunette guard announced, "and come with me." Shirley stared at her for a moment. Then she got up and followed her to the sheriff's office. When she got there, Donald and Cindy were waiting. Their eyes were red, swollen, and their faces weary. She knew it hadn't been any easier on them than on her.

"You can leave now," the sheriff, a morose-appearing bulky man said in a thin southern accent. Shirley watched quietly as he got her pocketbook out of the drawer and handed it back to her. "We're giving you an escort to the border of this county. I don't want to see you back in this town again," he scowled. For once Shirley knew better than to argue. She didn't want to come back to this town that had given them so much pain and heartache.

Their escort consisted of one police car with two officers in it. They got out and approached Shirley as she headed for Donald's car. "I'm sorry about all that's happened," the younger blond one said. There was pity in his blue eyes. "I was in the courtroom most of the time, and I don't believe your son got a fair trial. I hope you have good luck on the appeals." Shirley merely nodded. At this time, she didn't feel very congenial toward anyone in a uniform. She knew it wasn't those men's fault, but all the same, she felt hatred for the system and all who were involved in it.

As they drove, the police car ever-present behind them, Shirley, in a kind of daze, mutely watched through the window as the stately green evergreens so filled with life blended one into another like an impressionist painting. She didn't think of the beauty around her. She remembered what Barry Bixby had promised: that Jeff would walk away with them. Suddenly anger toward him surged through her. Surely he must have known that wasn't going to happen, she thought as they drove along. She figured he had just wanted their money. As her emotions awakened, the realities of Jeff's trial hit her. "Where's Jeff? I want to see him." She looked at Cindy in the back seat. Cindy turned away. Then Shirley turned to Donald at the wheel and waited for his answer, afraid that Jeff had been taken to Nashville already.

"He's being held in Brushy Mountain, over in Knoxville," he answered, reaching over to touch her hand.

"He'll stay there until they take him on to the prison in Nashville."

"When is—" Shirley's eyes flooded with tears, but she went on, "When is it supposed to happen?"

Donald tried to change the subject, but Shirley was not to be put off. "Tell me, I have to know." Her voice was low, emotion charged.

"The execution date is September 26," he said quietly. "The lawyers have thirty days to file a motion for a new trial, which they're already preparing to do."

He told Shirley how Jim Beeler and Barry Bixby had gotten into an argument right after the trial on the way it had been handled. "Beeler almost took a swing at Bixby," Donald said.

"I wish he had," Shirley said, a trace of her usual spiritedness returning. "It would have made me feel better."

The police escort left them at the county line. Donald drove without a break until they reached the prison in Knoxville. As they entered the complex of Brushy Mountain, the huge, dingy, gray stone buildings, the dark towers, and the dreariness seemed ominous.

"I feel like we're entering hell," Shirley said. Her mouth was dry, her eyes hollow. "I can't go in there," she cried. "I just can't go in there and face him. I can't let Jeff know how I've failed him. I love him so much and I can't bear to see the pain and fear on his face." She sobbed until there wasn't anything left. Donald held her tight.

"It's okay, Mom," Cindy said as she started to step from the car. "You stay right here." Donald got out and was going inside with Cindy to visit Jeff and make sure he was all right.

"Just tell him that I'll see him next week." Shirley was hoping she could control herself by then and not let Jeff see her in such an emotional state.

"Okay, Mom."

"And tell him that it'll be all right." Now she sounded like everyone else, Shirley thought. They were always saying that to her, and she had hated it. Now she was repeating the same thing to Jeff.

"Okay," Cindy turned again to go.

"And tell him," Cindy turned back yet again, "tell him that I love him. So much."

Shirley watched as Cindy and Donald walked up the cement steps of the prison. "How could you do this to Jeff?" she asked God. "If you're really up there, how could you hurt my son like this when he's innocent. You know he's never hurt anyone in his life. Why? Why?" She knew she shouldn't be questioning the ways of God, but she couldn't seem to stop. She had become a Seventh Day Adventist a few years back. At that time, she thought herself a true believer. Now her faith was wavering and she couldn't stop it.

In a short while Cindy and Donald returned. Donald said that Jeff looked as well as could be expected under the circumstances. Shirley nodded. At least they hadn't tried to fool her by saying he was doing "great" or "fantastic" or some other candy-coated description.

The ride back to Asheville was long and tiring. They weren't far into North Carolina when Donald saw Shirley's car with Tina in it pulled on the side of the road of Interstate 40. She spotted her mother and waved them down.

Shirley's first thoughts were that something had happened to her father. She knew the trial had been enormously straining for him. She was afraid he had had another heart attack. "Something's happened to Pop!" Shirley cried out as Tina ran toward them, tears streaming down her face. Shirley knew it had to be something awful.

"No. Pop is all right," Tina said through the car window. "It's the police. They have a warrant for your arrest, Mom. They're looking for you. You can't go back." She was crying hard now. Shirley's heart constricted. She knew it was her fault Tina was in this pain. She hated herself for all she had done to the kids and hoped they'd understand. She had done it all for Jeff.

"They're going to put you in jail too," Tina said hiccuping from crying. "First Jeff, and now I'm going to lose you, too." Getting out of the car, Shirley held her daughter tightly.

Donald, who had also gotten out by this time, implored them all to calm down and think rationally. "Maria and Trevor are at my sister's house. Let's get a motel room for the night. Then I'll rent us two trucks," he said. "Teeny and Ernest can bring the kids and some of our stuff to us in the morning."

Shirley nodded. "We'll have to leave until we can pay off the charges against us. Then we'll be able to come back home."

When Shirley's parents brought the children and some clothes the next morning, Shirley and Donald were ready to go. Shirley would drive a truck pulling a U-Haul, and Donald would be driving another truck pulling a travel trailer.

Teeny gave Shirley the numbers of different telephone booths around Asheville. They set up a day and a time each week that she would call. Saying goodbye to her mother and father was hard. Pop came over to hug Shirley, and she saw tears in his eyes. "Please try to take care of yourself," he said. "You have to start eating or you'll get sick." As he kissed her she wondered how she would stand not seeing him for a long time knowing how frail he was.

"Don't worry about us, Pop," she said, tears streaming down her face. "We'll be fine. I'll eat, don't worry. You just stay well. She hugged her father and clung to him for a few minutes like a little girl again. She felt comfort in his arms and didn't want to leave. But she had to; she couldn't go back now, not until the credit cards had been paid. Now not only had the law taken her innocent son, she had become a fugitive trying to save him. The horror of it all was too much to think about.

Cindy had decided to move to Nashville to be near Jeff. Shirley and Donald put her on a bus and gave her some money to get started on. She said goodbye, and Shirley begged her to see Jeff as often as she could.

With Maria in her truck and Trevor in Donald's, they started out not knowing where they would end up. Shirley was crying harder now as she waved to her mother and father. As they pulled away, it struck Shirley that now when her need for her family was greatest she couldn't be with them. A feeling of utter desolation swept through her.

As they drove south, Shirley started making plans. She realized she could not send Trevor to school, as they could be easily traced from the school's records. She made plans to tutor him herself at home. She knew he would not be receiving the same quality of education as he could get at school, but at least for now, she thought it was the best she could do.

Then Donald decided to head west. Texas seemed far enough away for them to be safe. Since they couldn't afford a home, they would live in a trailer. In two days they were in a small town in Texas, not far from Dallas. Donald found a trailer they could rent, and they moved in. Donald even began building a greenhouse to make it more homelike.

Shirley tried to be upbeat for the children's sake. She tried to make their new home seem like an adventure. Everyone tried to relax and settle in.

A few days later Donald was working on the electricity so Shirley decided to serve dinner outside like a picnic. It was wonderful to be able to give the children a home cooked dinner. The meal of fried chicken was a pleasant one and they all enjoyed it, even Maria, as young as she was, licked her fingers as she gnawed on a drumstick.

After dinner Shirley started to carry Maria back to the trailer to put her to bed. As Shirley ambled toward the steps she stumbled in a hole, and an intense jolt of pain shot up her foot. She screamed, "Donald, help me!"

Donald came quickly and took Maria from her arms. Shirley could see her foot hanging straight down and limp. The pain was unbearable, but she held herself together in front of Trevor and Maria, sensing their fright at the accident. Donald saw her face grimacing from pain. "Trevor, you watch Maria," he said quietly. He carried Shirley to the car and sped to the hospital.

The hospital was not more than a mile away, but every bump on the road was torture. Once inside, the nurse on duty in the emergency room took one look at Shirley's foot and yelled for a doctor.

They gave her an injection. The pain stopped. Shirley entered a dream world while they cut her jeans and shoe off. The next day she underwent surgery. Several bones and tendons were broken: two pins were put on either side. She remained in the hospital for ten days. A cast covered her leg, her foot held high in the air.

Until she was put in a walking cast a few months later, Trevor did most of the house cleaning, cooking, and caring for Maria. Shirley didn't know how she'd have managed Maria without him. The medicine they gave her for pain made her drowsy most of the time. They told her she would be in different casts for over a year and a half. That ended Shirley's plans to begin working right away so she could repay the things she'd charged on her grandmother's credit card. Everything was going wrong. Even after she healed, the doctor said her foot would never be the same. She'd always walk with a limp.

Teeny and Pop called them every week from a pay phone; so their phone number would not be on her bill at the end of the month. Shirley felt homesick just hearing their voices, but knew she couldn't go home even for a visit; it would be too dangerous. Teeny sent her mail from Jeff and sometimes a cassette tape from him, but even that didn't assuage her guilt.

Shirley cried each time she listened to Jeff's tapes. Hearing his voice and not being able to see him was tortuous. Jeff wrote that the FBI was questioning him frequently about her whereabouts. He begged his mother over and over to be careful.

Teeny became increasingly fearful, too. One night she called to say that she was being watched closely by the police, obviously in their search for her daughter. Teeny felt they should leave the country altogether and go up to Canada.

Not long after her mother's call, the trailer park was hit by a tornado. Donald had built a small greenhouse on their lot to raise plants to sell, and as the wind swept through in its fury, it destroyed the greenhouse and all the plants they had toiled over for so many months.

The tornado shook them all up, but none of them were hurt. They were lucky. Many people were killed and damages were extensive. Donald thought back to Teeny's suggestion of moving, and after some deliberation they decided to pack up and move yet again.

This time their destination was Toronto. Their life in Canada did not last long. Donald got hired right away at a company, but he could not accept the job because he had to have a visa in order to work and live there. They pulled up stakes and once again took to the road.

Their next stop was a trailer in New York State. Trevor visited with his father, Nelson, who lived nearby; and Laurie, who had been staying with Nelson, decided to stay with her mother. Shirley didn't tell Nelson exactly where they lived, as he was still drinking, and she knew from his indiscretion to the police regarding Jeff's coat that he could unintentionally, while drunk, give them away.

Fear was always with them now. They decided to move yet again, this time to the south. They drove until they found a small town in South Carolina, about six hours from Asheville. It felt good to be near family again. Donald rented a trailer and found a job as mechanic. Shirley was out of the cast and walking with crutches and a cane, but she was still in pain. Scars ran across the length of her foot, and she was subject to many a joke from Trevor about being a victim in the film *Jaws*.

At Shirley's request, Teeny found a new attorney for Jeff. She hired Bart Durham, a lawyer in Nashville, whom they paid $250 a month to take Jeff through the appeals court. Occasionally Shirley would speak to Bart by phone to hear how Jeff was doing.

Then a surprising but fortunate piece of luck came. Tina made an arrangement with the bank to pay off the credit card charges that her mother had incurred on her grandmother's card. The bank agreed not to press charges against Shirley as long as the payments were made each month until all the money was paid back. Now the only thing the authorities had against Shirley was her failure to appear before the grand jury earlier.

At least that problem seemed solved. Laurie was back with them, and it was wonderful having her. But Shirley still missed the others terribly. Moreover, she hadn't seen Jeff in over a year. One day she decided she couldn't stand it any longer. She decided to go back.

"I've decided to turn myself in," she told Teeny on the phone. "I can't stay away any longer without seeing Jeff. I want you to contact the FBI and ask them if I come in on my own, would I be able to see Jeff before they sentence me."

"I'm afraid for you to turn yourself in," Teeny answered worriedly. "Look what happened to Jeff—and he was innocent. I'm afraid that you'll get a long time, and what will happen to Maria? I can't watch her with Ernest so sick."

"One of our relatives will take her. We always help each other," Shirley said. "I don't want to go to jail, but I never thought I'd be running from the law. I'm not a crook. I have to come back, Mom. I have to see Jeff." Teeny still didn't like the idea but said she would get back to Shirley after talking to the FBI.

In the interim, Shirley decided to take the kids down to Florida before she went in to the FBI. She had no idea of how much time in jail she would be given, and she wanted to give the children something happy to look back on later.

Donald had to stay in North Carolina and work, but she piled the children into the trailer. They drove along the highway singing nonsense songs. When they reached Georgia the gas gauge was sliding toward empty. Looking at it, Shirley suddenly realized she had never filled the trailer with gas before. Donald had always done it. It required driving in reverse, a feat Shirley wasn't sure she could execute. Still she had no choice.

She pulled into an Avex station and informed the teen-aged attendant of her plight. He gave her directions. Shirley was apprehensive, but she began to pull backwards. Then, as the man waved her on, she heard a sudden crash. Through her rear view mirror Shirley saw she had ripped the pump out of the ground. The white-haired manager came flying out of the building. "Hey, are you crazy!" he yelled.

Shirley offered to pay the damages so she could get out of there. She didn't want them to call a policeman. Shirley didn't want to get caught now, not when she had decided on turning herself in as soon as she had spent this time with the children.

"It'd be more than you could afford," the manager said grumpily. "At least a few thousand dollars." He glared at Shirley and she knew this was the end of the line. The kids had begun to cry, and she tried to quiet them down.

"But your man waved me to come on," she argued. "I don't think it's entirely my fault." Shirley watched as he and his helper exchanged looks.

"I'm sorry, ma'am," he said. "I'm going to have to call the police and report it."

Tears sprang to her eyes. Just when she was going to come in on her own she would be arrested. There was no running now. The trailer alone would make her conspicuous.

It didn't take long for two cruisers to pull into the small garage. "They know who I am," she thought to herself. Shirley sat there in the truck, waiting for them to come over and arrest her.

One of the officers started taking down the tag number on the trailer. Shirley was hardly breathing. Then he came over. His tone was friendly. The officer told her that this happened all the time at this station. "I think they do it on purpose," he laughed. "What insurance do you have?" he asked her. She didn't know what to say, so she said the first thing that came into her mind.

"Blue Cross. I have Blue Cross insurance," Shirley said.

"I'll have to have the number on your policy. I didn't know they carried car insurance," he said looking quizically at Shirley. She couldn't decide if he knew she was lying, but she played along.

She reached into her purse, dug out an old policy card, and handed him the card. She was beginning to sweat now, certain that he was going to tell her it was all over. He took the card, wrote the number down and smiled. "You can go," he said softly. Shirley wasn't sure she had heard right, but she drove out of there as quickly as she could.

They went to a campground in Orlando where they spent a marvelous week of swimming, picnicking and sunbathing. On the way back home Shirley had to stop for gas again. She got off the freeway and inadvertently began pulling into the same station where she had destroyed the pump.

"Mom," Laurie said, "this is that same gas station. Don't go back there. They might have realized their mistake by now." She looked worriedly at her mother. "Darn right," Shirley said. "Good thinking." She quickly turned the trailer around and headed back onto the interstate.

Once back in South Carolina, Shirley prepared for the trip to North Carolina to turn herself in to the authorities. Her mother told her the authorities had said Shirley would be allowed to visit Jeff no matter what the sentencing was. That was good enough for Shirley. She decided to go back immediately. Shirley ached because Donald couldn't come in with her, but he had written far too many checks for them to pay back at that time.

"I don't want to lose you," Donald said as she got ready to go. "You don't know how long you'll have to spend in jail. And it won't do Jeff any good. Please stay here with me. I love you so much." Shirley watched as the tears fell from his face onto his faded blue shirt. She ran to him and they clung together, tears mixing.

"I have to go, Donald. Please understand, I have to be with my son and I can't stay on the run forever. I love you and I'm sorry that I've ruined your life. We'll be able to pay off your charges soon, and you'll be able to come back too. Please say you understand."

Donald closed his eyes and held her. Shirley was ashamed but she felt that she had no choice. She had to go.

"Just remember, Shirley, I'll always love you, and if there's any way that we can get this mess cleared up, I'll be waiting for you." Again the tears slid down his face, and she wiped them away putting her face close to his. Why was everything so painful. "I think I'll get a job as a truck driver and just travel all over the country. I can't bare to lose you, but maybe it's best if we never see each other again. I don't want to spend my life in prison, and I don't want you to blame yourself for what I did. I did it because I love you."

Shirley got into her car. Tears streamed down her face. Somehow she knew she'd never see this man again. He had done so much to help her and Jeff, and now they were going to lose each other. Donald waved until she was out of sight. The look on his face would haunt her forever.

Shirley met her mother back at Asheville. Together they went to the FBI. She spent the day giving handwriting samples and answering all questions truthfully. Court would be held the next morning.

One of the FBI officers, George Connell, went before the judge on her behalf. He said she had cooperated fully with his office. Connell agreed to let Shirley go home in her parents' custody.

The next morning an officer told Shirley if she pleaded guilty she would receive a year's probation and a fine of $500. It was more lenient than she had dreamed of, and she readily agreed.

At the final hearing the judge said Shirley would be granted a pass to visit Jeff. It was the first time in all these

months a member of the judiciary had shown himself to be
human. She began to cry. "I don't know how to thank
you," she said. "This means so much to Jeff and me. You're
so kind."

However, when she met her probation officer, a short
bald man with beetle brows, Shirley's favorable impression
of the law ended. With her mother at her side, nervous and
hesitant, Shirley greeted him with a wan smile. It was returned with a cold, hard stare. In a curt voice he informed
Shirley, "You are to report to me once a month."

"I will need a pass to see Jeff this weekend," she said
softly.

"You can't go every weekend," he said as though he'd
just been insulted. "I think once a month should be
enough."

"I don't want to see him once a month," she protested.
"I want to see him every week. That's the only reason I
came in, to be able to see my son."

"You'll do as I say! In fact," he snapped, "otherwise
you can just serve your year in jail. Now, just sit in that
chair," he pointed, "while I go and talk to the judge. It
seems as if you don't want to do as you're told; we'll just
see what the judge has to say about that."

Shirley's upper lip began to quiver. She held in the
tears threatening to come. "I didn't say I wouldn't do as
you tell me, but I was told I could visit with Jeff and I'm
going to go." He stormed out of the room, his face red, his
brows drawn in a thick line.

"Shirley, you should have kept quiet," Teeny said, her
face pale. "Now what's going to happen. That man could
put you back in jail and you won't get to see Jeff at all."

Shirley was already wishing she had kept quiet, but
the man had been so rude. He had talked to her as if she
was nothing but scum. She could even have taken that if he
hadn't threatened her with not seeing Jeff at all.

In a few minutes, a different man, big boned and
ruddy with brown eyes and a pleasant, direct look introduced himself. "Mrs. Dicks, I'm Mark Stuthers, your new

probation officer." She wondered what had happened but knew better than to ask. After they exchanged a few polite words, he patiently went over the rules she was to follow and handed her a pass that allowed her to see Jeff each and every weekend.

"Thank you," she said, clasping his hand. "I won't let you down."

He nodded. "I know you won't."

It was a six-hour drive to Nashville. It felt longer. This would be the first time Shirley had seen Jeff in over a year.

Shirley decided not to take Maria this first time as she knew it would be very emotional. She and Teeny went alone. They rented a motel room for Saturday night so they could see Jeff both Saturday and Sunday.

They drove onto the grounds of the Tennessee State Prison. The large, yellow building was built like a castle complete with towers and turrets. From a distance it almost reminded you of Disneyland at first glance. As you drew closer the atmosphere was silent, sinister. You knew you weren't in for a day of fun when you got there.

They had to sign their names at a desk in the front building. Then they were searched thoroughly by a burly woman guard.

Death row was a small building in the middle of the prison compound. A barbed wire fence surrounded the whole place; guards with rifles drawn stood on the towers on every end of the walk.

Shirley and Teeny slowly walked into the building where Jeff was housed and took their place in a small visiting room. A thick wood table and some plastic chairs were the only furniture in it. The steel door locked behind them as they entered. They knew their every move was watched through a glass paneled door at the rear of the room.

Jeff was brought in. Shirley ran to hug him. Tears ran down her cheeks even though she had told herself that no matter what, she wouldn't cry.

But it was so good to see her son again. He held his mother tight for a long time. She could see tears in his eyes as he looked at her. She was astonished and happy to see he had gained a lot of weight in the past year. Later she learned his weight gain wasn't due so much to the diet he was receiving, but more to the activity he wasn't receiving. Prisoners on death row stayed in their cells twenty-three hours a day with one hour each day used for optional exercise.

Standing back from his embrace, she searched his face. The circles under his eyes weren't as bad as she had remembered, but his lids were dark as if someone had put sable eye shadow on them and his eyes had a new look of resignation. She wondered how else he had changed. But then he smiled and she knew he was still her gentle son—a boy in a tough man's environment.

His time there had given him a stoic attitude that allowed him to cope under conditions men twice his age could not cope with. His positive attitude let him fit in, or at least get along with everyone there. As they talked Shirley realized that Jeff had come to accept his imprisonment as she never could.

Jeff didn't seem surprised to see Shirley. "I had a feeling you were going to come soon," he said as he hugged her again. "I could tell from your letters that you wanted to come home."

They were lucky because Henry Kogan was on guard duty that day, and they were able to stay for a long visit. The guards only had to give prisoners one hour, but depending on the sympathy of the particular guard that day, you could receive two or even three hours to visit.

Soon afterward Shirley brought Maria to see her father at the prison. At first she looked upon Jeff as a stranger, though she had seen his photograph often enough. Before long, though, she learned to love him. She would sit on his lap and try to talk to him, but most of her gratification came from her sloppy kisses on Jeff's face.

Shirley went to see Jeff's new attorney, Bart Durham, not long after she had come back to face her charges. Bart was a tall, thin man in his late forties with a friendly face and a disposition to match.

Unlike Barry Bixby, who had always brushed off her questions, he spent a long afternoon patiently explaining what was going on at that point in the appeals. "The State," he said, "sets an execution date for Jeff periodically, but since he has appeals left they will be stayed. Please don't panic every time a date is announced."

She felt better after meeting Bart, who seemed both competent and committed. When she got up to leave he walked her to the door. "It may," he said looking directly into her eyes, "take five years or longer, but in the end I'm sure Jeff will get a new trial. I'll do all I can for him," he said, "because I think he's innocent."

Shirley felt reassured after their consultation, and she left his office that day a little braver and more ready to face what she knew would be the long, difficult fight ahead.

FOURTEEN

A few months later Shirley decided to move to Tennessee with Trevor and Maria to be near Jeff. Cindy had divorced Jeff by this time, and although Shirley didn't like the idea of moving so far away from the rest of the family, if she were to see Jeff, who was terribly lonely, on any sort of regular basis it was the most practical thing to do. It would be cheaper in the long run than staying in motels every weekend, and the rest of the family could stay at her place when they visited him. Wanting to spend as little money as possible, she found a trailer to live in and settled as close to the prison as she could. Shirley's brother-in-law, Dick, moved in with Maria, Trevor and Shirley to help out with the finances. He was close to her age and they all got along real well.

Cindy continued to live in Nashville. At first, after Shirley had been forced to leave, Cindy visited Jeff fairly often, but after a while the visits dwindled and then stopped. During all the time Shirley was gone Cindy hadn't seen him, nor did she write. It was all the more important, Shirley sensed, that she see Jeff as much as possible. By moving to Tennessee, she and Maria would be able to visit twice a week.

Jeff's execution was scheduled again, this time for

June 2, 1982. His execution was stayed by a motion for a new trial. Jeff's post-conviction hearing was to be held in April of that year in Greenville, where his trial had taken place.

Bart Durham called her. "I want to go to the Kingsport area to see the site of the Keegan murder. I want to talk to the witnesses and James Beeler, who lives in Kingsport."

"Ma and I want to go along with you," Shirley pleaded. "We'll help any way we can, just tell us what to do."

Bart seemed to sense their need to be involved. He told them he'd welcome their help, and although Shirley had been told by the authorities after Jeff's trial not to come back to that area, Bart Durham assured her it would be all right under the circumstances.

They met James Beeler outside the Budget Shop in Kingsport. A cold, stinging rain had begun to fall. The surroundings of the Budget Shop were filled with ghosts for her. The shop had been closed since the murder of its owner, and the absence of people around there made it seem more desolate. Shirley shivered in silence as she waited outside the shop for the two attorneys to make their investigation. Shirley looked to her left. There Jeff had sat in Chief's girlfriend's care four years earlier. That was the place where he had waited in uncertain terror for Strouth to come out of the store. She shuddered, her eyes followed the path the car took on that day, when Strouth came out and ordered Jeff to go around to the alley. It was not a far distance for Jeff to drive, she thought to herself, but it was a drive that took him right to a cell on death row. She felt a spasm go up her arms and her teeth began to chatter. It was like a bad dream being where it all began. She was afraid she was going to start screaming and began to shake, unable to stop herself.

"Take it easy, Shirley," her mother said. "I hate being here too, but we have to. It's for Jeff. We have to hope for a miracle."

"I hate this place more than anything," Shirley said in an anguished voice. "I wish I'd moved Jeff somewhere else before all this happened." Shirley stared at the rain falling; the dreariness of it was almost hypnotic. Mr. Beeler was showing Bart the rear of the store, where the prosecution had said the footprints of both Jeff and Strouth had been; again Shirley thought of the pictures the officer claimed to have taken of those footprints. Yet none had come out.

It was remarkable how all of their high-class equipment failed suddenly when the "pictures" of those footprints were taken, yet their equipment worked extremely well for the photos of Keegan's body. They came out in excellent color, with all of their gore developed to a high degree of professionalism.

No pictures of the footprints; no plaster casts. Nothing physical to prove there were two sets of footprints. Yet the jury believed they did indeed exist. They could take the word of the law officers at face value—the law officers who lied on several different occasions alone to herself and others. But they could not take the word of her son when he truthfully told of his part in the crime.

When Bart felt satisfied he had seen enough, the two lawyers walked back to where Shirley and Teeny were. Then they drove to the motel.

"Let's stop in the coffee shop and have some coffee," Bart said. Shirley was grateful that unlike Barry Bixby, Bart always seemed to have time to talk. She noticed Beeler, whose honesty she had faith in, seemed to like Bart too. Shirley breathed a sigh of relief.

Sitting down at a small table Bart told them he was confident that if they carefully and assiduously looked for evidence, they would come up with something and in the morning start their search for the witnesses that never got a chance to testify at Jeff's trial. Shirley felt assured. That night she slept better than she had for a long time.

Mr. Carlton, the Fuller Brush manager, gave them a statement to the fact that Jeff had been a good employee and worked for him selling Fuller Brush products.

Shirley next called Chris Livingston. He was still living in the same house. Bart, Teeny and Shirley went there to see him. Chris had gotten married and had a child now.

"I haven't changed my mind, Mrs. Dicks. I told you at Chief's trial that I would come, but I never heard back from anyone. Why didn't your attorney call me?"

"I don't know," Shirley said. "Barry Bixby said he was going to call you, and a lot of others, but he never did."

"I don't have a job right now," Chris said. For the first time Shirley looked at him more closely. Something seemed the matter with him. "So I would need for you to pay my way over to testify. I don't have the money for that," he added.

"I wouldn't expect you to pay your way over. Like I told you at Chief's trial, I'll pay your way over and your week's wages that you'll lose because of it."

As they drove away from the Livingston house, Bart told Shirley what was wrong. "Too much dope. It messed up his head. I've seen it happen so often. These kids think they can mess with that stuff and nothing will ever happen."

"I thought something was the matter. He acted differently than the last time I talked to him," Shirley said shaking her head. "I've never seen anyone who was into drugs before. It's a shame for anyone to ruin their lives that way." Then a frightening thought crossed her mind. "He can still testify, though, can't he, Bart?"

Bart frowned. "It's a little more complex than that, Shirley," Bart said as he drove in the dark night. "Hard telling what kind of a witness he'll make. The prosecution will make plenty out of the fact that he can hardly relate in a normal manner, and you can be sure they'll bring up the drugs to show he doesn't know what he's saying."

Shirley's agitation was growing. Bart saw it and tried to be optimistic. "Look, this is America. Somehow, in the end, the system won't let us down. Justice will prevail. People who sit out in a car, who have no knowledge of a murder being committed by their passenger, don't get sent to the electric chair." But Shirley still couldn't shake her feeling of dread. Perhaps it was a sign, she thought, an omen of things to come. She tried to shut the thought out of her mind, but it hung on. The rest of the drive the three of them retreated into silence, each lost in his own thoughts.

Once back in Tennessee, Shirley began getting ready for the post-conviction hearing. She was scared at having to face the judge and Wilcox again. All too soon, it was time to leave. Her mother drove the car to Greenville while Shirley sat in the back seat with Nelson. He had flown down for the post-conviction hearing. For a change he was sober, and Shirley felt comforted that he was with her.

"I hope they don't beat on him," she said to Nelson, her voice trembling. He had lit a cigarette, and blowing the smoke out turned to look at her.

"They wouldn't dare do that to Jeff. Don't worry. They didn't beat on him the last time he was here." Nelson didn't feel as confident as he sounded. All the times he had told Shirley not to worry, and Jeff was still on death row. He never dreamed that was possible. Now he didn't know anymore. Anything could happen, but he wanted to spare his ex-wife as long as he could.

"I've got Jeff's cigarettes and clothes in the trunk for him," Nelson said trying to be upbeat. "I think I'll stop and get a couple of magazines for him to read. They don't have a television or anything in the cell here." Shirley nodded, but she was getting more nervous as they neared the town. She sat on the edge of the seat and her teeth began to chatter. She didn't know what to expect anymore and remembered the last time she had been in this part of the state.

Nelson kept on talking, hoping it would relax her. "I'll leave him some money too so in case they let him buy drinks or anything he'll have it," Nelson said. He reached back with one hand and patted her. "Don't worry, Shirl, I love you, and I still think God will save our son."

As they drove to the back of the jail, the captain strode out. Shirley had just stepped out of the car and was turning to shut the car door. She was heavier than a few years back but was dressed smartly in her dark blue suit.

"Mrs. Dicks, you get back in the car! You cannot come inside this jail." The captain looked stern, his mouth set in a straight line. Shirley wasn't sure she had heard right and didn't move right off. Ernest stopped and asked why his daughter wasn't allowed out of the car.

"I said to get back in the car!" This time the captain's voice was louder and Shirley stared at him. Two more officers stood with their hands on their guns behind the captain. She was suddenly afraid. She couldn't see what she had done wrong.

"I'm just bringing my son some cigarettes and clothes," Shirley pleaded. She felt like saying more, but knew it wouldn't help. She didn't want the authorities to be angry and then take it out on Jeff later on.

"I don't care what you have. You get in that car and get out of here. Your mother can bring the things in, but you don't move from there." He gave her such a look of hatred that Shirley wondered what she had ever done to him. It didn't make sense.

"Can I just see my son for a minute?" Shirley asked softly, near tears this time.

"No! You can't see him. And you can't talk to him either." He turned around and headed back inside, followed by the other two officers. They stared hard at Shirley also; not one smile came from either man. Teeny shrugged and said she'd take the things inside for Jeff and see if she could find out what was going on.

Nelson helped Shirley back inside the car, where her tears started. She had tried so hard to hold them in, but this was too much. Nelson held her tightly and didn't say anything. He didn't know what was going on either, but he didn't like the sounds of it.

Teeny and Ernest followed the officer into the building. They had gotten some magazines and newspapers to

leave so Jeff would have something to read. They didn't
know Jeff would never get any of the items they had
brought for him. Shirley sat in the car with Nelson, not
saying anything, just crying. She could picture how hag-
gard Jeff had looked the last time she'd seen him. Now she
wondered if they were hurting him and that's why they
didn't want her to see him.

Later when they checked in the hotel, they found Bart
Durham and asked him what the problem was at the jail.

His face reddened. "They say they're afraid of you,
Shirley. All that publicity at the other trial, when they took
the gun from you, and your acting out in the courtroom has
made them skittish. They remember reading about the attempted jail break and don't want you to case this place
out."

"I can't believe that they think I'm dangerous." Her
voice rose, "I was only trying to give Jeff some cigarettes."

"Try to calm down," Bart said noticing Shirley's face
beginning to get red. He knew she was terribly upset and
worried about Jeff. "Don't give them anything more to use
on you. I know it's hard, but it'll be harder on Jeff if you
don't." He paused and patted her hand. "Shirley, you
know this is just a first step. We have more chance of getting the verdict appealed later in another court. But we
have to do this first, and we need to be together in how we
approach it." Shirley knew Bart was right. Everything she
had done so far had only made things worse for Jeff. Shirley didn't want to cause him any more pain, but she felt so
damned frustrated and helpless not being able to do anything to help him. "Another thing," Bart continued, "and I
know this is going to be hard, but I want you to apologize
to the judge and district attorney for the letter you sent
them after the trial." Bart looked intently at Shirley.

She started to protest. "I don't remember sending him
a threatening letter," Shirley said hesitantly.

"Look, Shirley I don't know if you sent the letter or
not, and to tell you the truth I don't care; but we have to
appease him."

"If I sent it," Shirley said thinking out loud, hardly hearing Bart, "I must have been out of my mind. I could have sent it, I was in such turmoil the weeks after the trial."

"Well, whether you admit to sending it or not, I want you to say you're sorry. Can you do that for Jeff? You can't blame the judge and district attorney for doing their job, and you can't go around threatening people. You're lucky that they didn't bring charges on you for that."

Shirley nodded slowly, "Okay, I'll say I'm sorry. For Jeff's sake. But I have to tell you I don't think they did their jobs the right way. They're supposed to uphold justice. I think they should have let us take a lie detector test like we asked. Jeff asked if he could take truth serum so they'd know he was telling the truth. They could have made Wilcox take the test and they'd know he lied about the coat. What the hell good is our legal system if it doesn't help protect the innocent as well as punish the guilty?" Shirley ranted, her voice filled with emotion. She didn't wait for an answer. "In fact, it's no good if it's justice sending an innocent person to death."

The next day they all sat in the hallway outside the courtroom waiting for the hearing to begin. Shirley spotted Wilcox walking up the corridor toward them. He had his usual mocking smile on his face. He spoke to her, still smiling.

"So nice to see you, Shirley," Wilcox said, his eyes meeting hers. "How have you been doing? I hear you're doing just fine. Didn't think you'd come back here," he shook his head.

She was about to answer something smart back, but Nelson caught her arm. "That's all he wants," Nelson said. "He's just baiting you to open your mouth. Don't do it. For once, keep your mouth shut." She knew he was right, but she was livid. Shirley stared as Wilcox started walking up and down the hall right in front of her. He glanced her way every time he drew near, smiling that smile that wasn't a smile. Each time it was becoming tougher and tougher to hold her anger. Shirley was relieved when the hearing was called to begin.

"Look, there's Cindy!" Nelson said to Shirley. "I wonder why she's sitting over there on the other side of the room and not here with us." Shirley glanced over. Cindy had lost a lot of weight and looked pale, but other than that, she looked like she had the last time they had seen her.

"I have some pictures of Maria I'll take to her," Shirley said. Shirley got up with the pictures in her hand and headed over to where Cindy was sitting. Suddenly two heavy set guards stepped in front of her.

"Where do you think you're going?" one of them snarled at Shirley. His eyes were glaring, and he looked ready to strike out at her.

"Well, I'm taking these pictures over to Cindy so she can see Maria," Shirley answered. She felt her face get hot as other people were beginning to look their way. Teeny started over but the other guard motioned her to stay where she was.

"I don't care what you have there, you are not going to bother Mrs. Dicks. Go back and sit down, and don't give me any trouble."

Shirley started to say something, but stopped. Puzzled, she walked back to where Nelson and Teeny were sitting and sat down. Shirley didn't want to start any trouble, but these men were angry at something. Shirley wished she knew what was going on. Teeny got up and walked over to where the officers were sitting. They looked like they were guarding Cindy, and Teeny was determined to find out the whole story.

"Hello," she said to the officer who had yelled at Shirley. "I would like to talk to you for a minute."

"What do you want?" the officer snapped.

"I want to know why you were so rude to my daughter a few minutes ago? She has done nothing to you, and I heard you order her to get back in her seat."

"Well, she don't need to be going over there and bothering Mrs. Dicks after the things she did to her."

"And just what is it she is supposed to have done to Cindy?" Teeny was getting angry and the officer seemed to know it. His tone was softer this time, but he kept looking over at Shirley.

"She stole her child away from her. Then she put her in a mental institution. I'm sure you know what your daughter did to her. I can't believe anyone doing something like that. Imagine taking a baby away from her mother."

"Listen here, my daughter did not take the baby away from Cindy. I don't know why she tells such lies, but I'm going to set the record straight. My daughter adopted Maria after Cindy physically abused her. She wanted to sign the baby away to an orphanage in Knoxville. As far as putting Cindy into a mental institution, she'd have to be crazy to think that story up. My daughter left her in Nashville after the trial with everything she needed to set up housekeeping. I think you had better get your story right before lighting into my daughter." Teeny's face was flushed; she was very angry now. She pointed her finger at the man as she talked.

He just looked at her for a few minutes, then stammered, "I'm sorry if I upset you, but I'm only going by what the young lady said to me. She told me how your daughter stole her child and said she was afraid of her. Asked me to protect her if she tried to come around to her side of the room. I'm sorry, really."

"Well, next time you had better get both sides of the story. My daughter loves that baby and she was good to Cindy too. Cindy didn't want the baby, but she didn't want Shirley to have her either. She is just a chronic liar. Always was, but Jeff loves her, so we make the best of it. But I will not let these stories be told against Shirley. All she was doing was taking some pictures of the baby over to show Cindy. She didn't have to do that. She thought she was being nice."

"Tell your daughter I'm sorry. I have my orders, though, about her talking to Mrs. Dicks." Teeny walked back to Shirley and told her and Nelson what had been said. Shirley shook her head sadly but said nothing. There was nothing to say.

T hey walked into the courtroom. Shirley was surprised and not happy to see Judge Edgar Calhoun, the same judge who took part in the trial, presiding over the hearing. There was no jury.

Calhoun's strident voice began the proceedings: "Before we start with the testimony, would you state just what issues you expect to rely on in these proceedings, Mr. Durham."

Durham's reply was polite but firm. He knew this was only the beginning of a long battle and he wanted to be on record. "Thank you, Your Honor. May it please the Court, I've raised two issues: number one, the effective assistance of counsel, and I am particularly directing that at Attorney Barry Bixby of North Carolina; and number two, I have alleged that the representatives of the State had knowledge that Mr. Livingston had such information, had given them such information that they knew that Strouth had exonerated Mr. Dicks, and it is a Brady type violation if they had covered that up, or not revealed it, not covered it up, but they failed to disclose that."

Calhoun gazed at the defense counsel. His tone was more brisk and formal now. "Are there any other issues that can be raised in this proceeding?"

Durham's own style was low key. "No, I can't think of any."

Gregory Wilcox was called to the stand.

For a few moments Durham and Wilcox stood perfectly still taking each other's measure. Then Durham said, "What is your name?"

"Gregory F. Wilcox," he enunciated the words as if he was teaching school.

"Did you have occasion to investigate a case involving Jeffrey Dicks?"

"Yes, I did."

Durham wanted to be sure Wilcox understood exactly where he was going. He paused and then asked, his voice hardening, "You took a statement from Chris Livingston in High Point, North Carolina?"

"Yes."

"Do you recall what he told you about the participation of Mr. Strouth in that crime?"

"He only made one statement that was material, I think. He stated he committed a crime in Hickory, North Carolina."

"Did he state whether or not he had a partner in that crime?"

"He did not have a partner."

"He was never able to give you any information about any participation by Dicks in that crime?"

"On that specific crime, he did not give me any information that pertained to Dicks or Strouth."

"Did he say to you anything about Mr. Dicks or another person involved with Strouth?"

"I didn't know Mr. Livingston knew anything."

"That's all," Durham said succinctly. For a moment he fastened his gaze intently on Wilcox and then turned away.

Next the deposition of Keith Goodman was heard. Jeff worked for him in South Carolina a short time after James Keegan's murder. Goodman was another one of the witnesses who was supposed to be called for Jeff's defense by Barry Bixby, but was not.

"Mr. Goodman, did you know Mr. Jeff Dicks?"

"Yes."

"Have you made a written statement in any form to Mrs. Dicks?"

"Yes, I did."

"I'd like to ask you if you observed the army type coat Jeff wore?"

"Yes."

"Did you notice anything about the condition of that coat?"

"No."

"Did you ever observe what you have a reason to believe were blood stains on there?"

"No."

"And since the statement you gave Mrs. Dicks, has any attorney ever contacted you except myself?"

"No."

Greely Wells cross-examined him.

"When you were contacted and gave your statement on March the 28th, 1978, was Shirley Dicks the one that contacted you, and you wrote out that statement for her?"

"Yes."

"Now at that time, did she offer to pay you any money for your testimony, sir?"

"No, she did not."

"Are you aware of the fact that she has publicly agreed to pay up to a thousand dollars to anyone who would testify for her son in this matter?"

"No, I'm not."

"Has she ever offered you any money at all to testify?"

"No."

"What about his wife, has she ever offered you any money?"

"No. I don't even know his wife."

"Did you talk to Mrs. Dicks today?"

"Yes."

"What did you talk about?"

"We just spoke in this office."

"What did you speak about?"

"We just said hello and she said she appreciated my coming in."

"That's all."

The redirect was handled by Mr. Pascal.

"I have one question for you. If an attorney had contacted you back at the date of that statement, would you have given him any information more than that statement?"

"I don't believe so."

"Would you have given him any less information?"

"No."

"That's all."

Liz Ventura, a co-worker of Cindy's at the restaurant where Cindy worked when she lived in Greenville, South Carolina, testified also. She had seen Jeff's coat when Cindy had worn it after the Keegan murder. Ms. Ventura had written a statement in 1978. Shirley had given it to Barry Bixby so he could call the woman at the trial, but he hadn't. Liz said she had not seen stains on the coat that Jeff, and sometimes Cindy, wore.

Again, the prosecutor undermined her testimony by saying that the coat could have been a different one. He suggested that she just didn't remember any stains, not that there were none. As with all the other witness Durham called, Wells asked Ventura if Shirley had offered any money for her testimony. Ms. Ventura said no.

Chris Livingston appeared. Shirley's heart pounded as he was sworn. Then Durham asked him about the conversation Livingston had with Strouth shortly after the Keegan murder.

"He said that him and some other guy was in on a robbery in Tennessee. He said that his partner froze up on him in the car. And that he went in and he robbed the old man. He said he beat him in the back of the head with a rock. And said, before he left, he cut the man's throat."

"Did he say who did rob him and cut the man's throat?"

"Well, the way he talked, it had to have been him because he said his partner froze up on him in the car."

"Did he name his partner?"

"No."

"Did you give this information to any police officers?"

Livingston nodded and indicated he had. "Yeah, the two detectives that come down from Tennessee."

The prosecutor argued that when Livingston testified at Chief's trial, he didn't say anything about Chief's partner "freezing up."

"That's mainly because all you was worried about was him, man. You wasn't saying much about his partner. I remember it well."

"Did anyone contact you to come and testify at the Dicks' trial?"

"Somebody did call and asked me about coming out there. And I said, you know, I'll come out there, and you're going to pay for it . . . I mean, you know . . . I'll come out there. But they never did call back. I just let that ride."

Wells came forward to begin the cross-examination. He looked distastefully at Livingston. "Let me ask you if you recall your testimony in the trial, if you weren't asked the question regarding seeing Donald Strouth and your conversation with him. Nowhere in that statement did you say anything about Strouth telling you that his partner froze up on him in the car."

"I think I did, buddy," Livingston said responding in the same tone Wells had used.

"Well, look and see," Wells said cryptically.

Livingston inclined his head, "Well, maybe it might not bc, but that's what the man told me. That's what I told that guy from Tennessee. I don't see it."

"Now at Strouth's trial you were at the same motel as Dicks' wife and mother?"

"Yeah."

"I'm sure you're aware that Mrs. Dicks is publicly offering a thousand dollars to anyone who may have seen Jeff in the car in front of the store. How much money has she offered you?" he said. His tone had become icily rude.

Livingston was not intimidated, "They offered me two hundred dollars to come and testify. I can only tell you what Chief told me at the bridge. And he said his partner froze up in the car. I don't give a damn whether she sent me money or not," he said forthrightly. "I just want to get this stuff over with. Don't make it sound like I'm trying to make no bucks or anything."

"I'm just asking you what they said to you."

"No man is going to turn down a thousand bucks for telling the truth," Livingston looked him directly in the eyes.

Livingston, like the previous witnesses, said he had never been contacted by Jeff's lawyer before. However, he also admitted he had consumed six or eight beers before the hearing. That didn't help matters.

The statement Livingston had given to Wilcox in 1978 was read into the record. Part of it was chilling. "The first time I had ever seen Chief was when he got out of a cab at the crossroads. He said he left a lot of empty cash registers and dead bodies over the territory he had traveled. He said he was a hit man, that he had killed about 360 people. He said he had cut some of them, drowned some of them, and shot some of them."

After Livingston was excused, he added his own statement to the testimony he had given. "All right, now. Let me tell you one thing. When I seen Chief down at the bridge and he told me about killing this guy, he said his partner froze up in the car. And when he said froze up, that means the guy stayed where he was. So obviously, this Dicks guy stayed in the car. I don't know. Chief lied to me so many times, you know, it's plum pathetic the whole deal come out like it did. But that's what the man told me, and that's what I am telling you all."

Shirley wondered why they couldn't see Livingston was telling the truth. Sharon Carlson had told the court the very same thing at Strouth's trial, that Jeff froze up on Chief.

Next Jeff was called to testify. He was in handcuffs and shackled. He had sat very quietly throughout the proceedings, much as he had during the trial before. Shirley watched as he got on the stand and looked around. His gaze lighted on Wilcox, who had lied about him. She

looked intently at his expression; it was one more of sadness than anger.

Jeff said that Barry Bixby, his first attorney, did not
interview him or even discuss his testimony before he testified at his trial. He was put on the stand cold. Jeff said that
he had wanted James Beeler to be in charge of his case, but
after his mother hired Bixby, he took over. Jeff hadn't told
anyone other than Shirley that he was unhappy with Bixby.

Bart Durham tried to elicit exactly what had occurred.
Again he was building a record, "Who was your principle
attorney at trial?"

"Barry Bixby."

"Did you have anything to do with his employment?"

"No, my mother hired him."

"Did he go over your statement with you?"

"No, he did not."

"When you were questioned by Carl Kirkpatrick, had
you seen your statement?"

"The first time I heard my statement was when they
read it at the trial."

"That's all, Your Honor."

Wells, his stance hovering-like, moved in. "You are
saying your attorney, Barry Bixby, did not at any time interview you and did not discuss with you your possible testimony at your trial?"

"That's exactly right."

"You say that Mr. Bixby was supposed to have put
certain witnesses on the stand before you testified?"

"Yes."

"None of the people testified at your trial that you
wanted? Did you complain to Mr. Bixby?"

"I figured he was the lawyer; he knew what was best. I
did ask him why he didn't call my mother."

"Did he respond to you?"

"No. Once Barry Bixby was hired, he took over, and
did not let my other lawyer do anything. I was wanting Mr.
Beeler to take over."

"Were there any other witnesses you wanted to testify

that Mr. Bixby did not put on the stand other than your mother, your wife, and Mr. Carlton?"

"There was a lady in Kingsport that I had sold Fuller Brushes to. There were character witnesses that were supposed to have come: a state patrolman in North Carolina, two police officers, and a police officer from the Buncombe Sheriff's department."

Wells had heard more than he wanted to. "That's all the questions I have."

Gertrude Mathews, Shirley's mother, whom everyone called Teeny, was next to testify. Durham asked, "Are you still living in the same place as you did in 1979 when you testified in this trial?"

"Yes, sir."

"Can you state what the circumstances are, and what part you played in hiring of Mr. Bixby?"

"My daughter Shirley, Jeffrey's mother, hired Barry Bixby to represent him. At the times I went to Barry's office, I paid him, I believe twice, towards the case. I also called him, and asked him how things were going. I took him in papers, statements that I had, people that would testify to Jeff's character and everything."

"What statements did you take to Mr. Bixby?"

"I took him statements that we had received from Greenville, South Carolina."

"Did you ask him to subpoena those people, or what did you ask him to do, if anything with those statements?"

"He said he would use them as witnesses; they would be good witnesses for Jeff because they had seen him."

"What else did you give him?"

"I gave him names of witnesses. One officer's name to be called was Officer Casey. I don't recall the other names, but I have the list at home."

"Now you said on two separate occasions you brought Mr. Bixby money. What was the amount of money?"

"One time it was two hundred dollars, and the other time it was four hundred."

"Did you attempt to talk to Mr. Bixby at the trial?"

Teeny inclined her head and sighed heavily, "He didn't have the time for us. He said he was busy. He assured me that Jeff would walk out of the courtroom with me."

When Durham finished his questioning, Wells began the cross-examination. "You say nobody talked to you before you took the witness stand?"

"That's correct."

"You say you have a list of people including Officer Casey, who would have come here and testified as character witnesses for Jeff, but you don't have that list with you?"

"No. I have them in a safety deposit box."

"You mean the original statements you claim that you have of Ms. Ventura and Mr. Larsen you retained. You don't have those statements here today?"

"No, I was not told to bring them."

"I suppose you told Mr. Beeler all of that. You told him about the witnesses?"

"Yes, I did."

"What about the motel room where the attorneys were staying, did you talk to them?"

"I said for a minute."

"Was Mr. Beeler there also?"

"No."

"That's all."

Shirley knew she was next. Nervously she walked to the front of the courtroom. Please, please, she said a silent prayer. Let me say the right thing. Let me help Jeff. Durham smiled reassuringly. "You're Mrs. Shirley Dicks?"

"Yes."

"And you are the mother of Jeff Dicks?"

"Yes, sir."

"And before we get into the testimony, you and I have had some discussion about your previous behavior, have we not?"

"Yes, sir."

"And I told you I thought you owed Judge Calhoun and Mr. Kirkpatrick and Mr. Wells an apology."

"Yes, sir."

"Do you wish to make that apology?"

Shirley took a deep breath and let it out slowly. She looked over at Calhoun. "I apologize, Judge."

"And you know a threatening, hostile letter threatening to kill these gentlemen, these fine people who work for you and me, was sent, don't you?"

"Yes, sir."

"Do you have anything to say with respect to regret about that letter?"

"I'm sorry about the letter," she said, her voice quivering, "but my son is innocent."

"Well, let's . . ." Durham searched for the right words. He knew they were in a hostile courtroom and that Shirley was going to have to trust him. His voice was firm. "Let me control you, and don't you start anything else now, you understand?"

"Yes, sir."

"You know that it is wrong to take the life of Mr. Keegan, don't you, whoever took his life?"

"Yes, sir."

"And you know you didn't mean it when you wrote those letters, or you had them written, or they got sent threatening the lives of these men, don't you?"

"Yes."

"And you know that's wrong don't you?"

"Yes."

"And you know there was a gun involved in this courthouse; whether or not you had it, or they took it away from you, or you gave it to someone, it doesn't make any difference, does it?"

"No."

"And Mrs. Dicks, other than these bad checks you wrote, and when you ran away, you have never been in trouble in your life have you?"

"Never," she said fervently.

"And you've lived, and your whole family has been law abiding, have they not?"

"Yes," she said quietly but firmly.

"Now I read the deposition to you, and you are familiar with the testimony of Chris Livingston about offering money. I want you to explain to the Court the circumstances under which an offer of money was made."

Shirley sighed heavily, "Well, the State pays your way and wages when they have you come, and after his testimony I said I would do the same if he would testify for my son."

"I want you to go through the details and tell us how you hired Barry Bixby." Bart's tone was supportive but decisive as he asked the questions. Shirley tried not to look at the district attorney, of whom she was afraid.

"Well," she began, "I went to Mr. Bixby, and I gave him $5,000 and told him that was all I had at the time, but I could get more if I wrote checks or used my grandmother's credit cards. He said, 'Use your own name if you use checks.' I told him where I'd be in Florida and said I'd send him a money order each week. I bought merchandise, and I went down there and sold it and sent the money back to Barry every Monday."

"How long after Jeff was arrested did you have the idea to hire Barry Bixby?"

"After I had tried every legal way to hire an attorney for Jeff."

"Did he express an opinion as to the ultimate result that would be obtained?"

Shirley's eyes filled with tears. She tried to hold them in. "He told me that Jeff would walk away with me. He said that no jury in the world would convict him."

Bart walked over to the defense table and glanced down at his notes. "During those times after the first visit, did Mr. Bixby know how you were obtaining the money, and who else was present at the time?"

"Yes. My husband and my ex-husband were present when I discussed what I was doing."

"Now at that time, was there a payment made?"

"I gave him $5,000," Shirley said bitterly.

"And where did you get that money from?" Bart walked from the table back to Shirley. She felt her heart beating faster, and she looked over at Jeff sitting at the table. His face was gloomy. She knew he didn't approve of what she had done.

"Check writing. I made close to $18,000 in cash that I mailed to Bixby, including the initial $5,000."

"After you told him that you obtained this money from writing bad checks, and selling at the flea market, did he give you any advice as to what to do?" Bart's voice was quietly firm, and he nodded at Shirley reassuringly.

"I told him that I was going to take my grandmother's credit card and use that too. He said, 'Don't tell me about that one.' "

"Did he give you advice about criminal prosecution for writing these bad checks?"

"He said it would be a misdemeanor if you kept them under $100 and used your own name."

"And did there come a time when there was a warrant out for you?"

Bart looked kindly at Shirley; his calmness was soothing. She looked around the room. The district attorney was staring hard at her, whispering to Wilcox, who was sitting with him. He made her nervous, but she had to go on.

"Yes, and he warned me ahead of time. It was at the trial, and he said, 'Don't go back to North Carolina.' "

"Mrs. Dicks, did you testify at the trial? Were you interviewed by Mr. Bixby?"

"No, I didn't testify. I wasn't interviewed. He told me that I couldn't sit in the courtroom because I would have to go on the stand, and then he made me sit there for nothing. I asked him about the other witnesses. Every time I did he said, 'Leave it to me. I'm the boss.' "

"Did you mail him money on a regular basis from Florida?"

"Every Monday after the flea market I would send between eight hundred and a thousand dollars."

"And this went on for how long?"

"Until I came back for the trial."

"And when you first gave Mr. Bixby money, did you tell him where it came from?"

"Yes, I told him I got it from check writing."

"Mrs. Dicks, were there others present when you had these conversations on later dates with Mr. Bixby?"

"My husband, and I believe my ex-husband was there one time."

Wells strode forward. He leaned toward her, over her.

"You had written checks before you ever met Barry Bixby, hadn't you?" he said sharply.

"Yes."

"And you had been involved in that, your husband and your ex-husband; was anybody else involved in that?"

"No."

"Did you send the money by check or money order from Florida?"

"I got money orders from the ice service store."

"And I expect you have the receipts for that?"

"No. I didn't have any reason to keep them."

"So you threw them away?"

She took a deep breath. "Yes."

"Were you the only one in the family to send him money?"

"Yes."

"You never used your mother as an intermediary to take money to him?"

"Yes. I got the money."

"How many times did you send your mother?"

"Two or three times."

"How much did you send with her?"

"I think a couple of hundred."

"So you never gave her the eight hundred or thousand to take to him?"

"No."

"You had been helping your son flee from the law?"

"Yes."

"And you obtained false identification for him?"

"Yes."

"During the course of the trial, weren't you also talked to by a federal marshall or an FBI agent?"

"Yes."

"Wasn't it because of that, he told you not to go back to North Carolina?"

"Yes. He came with a paper and had me sign my home over; he had Donald sign his trailer and land over, and said, 'I'll sell it, get the money and send it to you.' Donald wasn't served with anything, but Barry told him there were warrants out for him too."

"Did you offer to pay Chris Livingston to get him to testify that Donald Strouth told him that your son froze up on him and stayed out in the car?"

"I offered to pay his hotel, food and wages."

Wells cut in rudely, "My question is, did you offer to pay him two hundred dollars to testify what I asked you?"

Shirley's voice shook. "I don't think I put a price on it. I said I'd pay him what the State paid."

"You have publicly offered to pay a thousand dollars to anyone who may have seen your son in the car in front of the store where Mr. Keegan was killed?"

"Yes, because there were people who walked by that day."

"Did your son ever tell you he was dissatisfied with Mr. Bixby?"

"He told me he like Beeler better, but I don't remember his asking me to take Barry off."

"That will be all."

James Beeler testified after Shirley. He told how he first met Jeff and what he had done on the case before Barry Bixby was hired. "I sent a letter to the elementary schools where he went to school, to ask about any problems he may have experienced. I went to the scene where it all occurred. I talked to the widow of the man that was killed, talked with the people in the stores on both sides of the street, and I attended the trial of Donald Strouth."

According to Beeler, after Barry Bixby was hired Beeler and Weddington, Jeff's other lawyer, did "basically whatever he wanted us to do." Bixby was the lead counsel then; he was in charge. All of the information about possible witnesses for Jeff was turned over to Barry Bixby, and it was up to him to decide who would be called on to testify.

Shirley was surprised to hear Beeler say that, "There never was in this case a situation in which all three attorneys sat down together at the table and hammered out a uniform approach to this trial." Bixby never informed Beeler of his working with prospective witnesses independently.

Besides Chris Livingston and others, one of the witnesses Beeler said he would have called had he been in charge of Jeff's case was Lisa, the woman for whom Jeff had written the bad checks which had initially gotten him into trouble and the reason he had been living under an assumed name.

"If for no other reason, to explain the second phase of the trial, the reason for the bad checks that Mr. Dicks had written," he paused and passed his hand across his brow thoughtfully, "hopefully to place a whole different motive on the checks rather than his just wanting money, an effort to assist her and her family from starving to death."

Beeler went on to say there was a lack of communication between himself and Barry Bixby. "I sent him a letter on one occasion asking him to call me so that we could set a time for a meeting, so that we could work out an approach." He shook his head. "I contacted him I believe by telephone at one time, telling him that if he was going to subpoena these witnesses from North Carolina that it needed to be done because time was running short. I never got a response."

Less than a month before the trial, Beeler said he wrote Bixby a letter, again requesting a meeting so the three attorneys could meet. Beeler wrote that the attorneys were going in three different directions with each other not

knowing exactly what the other was doing. He got no response to the letter.

"Did the time come when the case was set for trial,
and did you become worried about the context of the preparation?"

"I was concerned because I really wasn't sure where
everything was. I knew from checking with the clerk's office that certain witnesses that we had considered subpoenaing in North Carolina had not been subpoenaed, and I
called to enquire as to why they were not. He never answered." Obviously that perplexed Beeler, who went on. "I
believe that our approach to this trial is to present the case
as though Jeff had no intent to participate in the robbery,
and, therefore, attempt to insulate him from the felony
murder rule."

"Who was it you thought should be subpoenaed by Mr.
Bixby?"

His voice rose. "I would have called, without any
question in my mind, Chris Livingston."

"Would you have called him had you known he was
paid to change his testimony?"

"To my knowledge, I was not aware that he had been
paid to change his testimony."

"Was your conversation with him consistent with his
testimony on the witness stand in the Strouth case?"

"My particular inquiries to Mr. Livingston would have
been whether or not Strouth said anything to him about
Jeff freezing up. He told me that Strouth told him that Jeff
froze up on him, and used the words, 'I killed the old
man.' "

"You are telling the Court here today that Chris Livingston made that statement to you and you did not cause a
subpoena for him to testify at Jeff's trial?"

Beeler nodded. "I felt that Mr. Bixby was preparing
the case as he wanted to. I felt he didn't need any help or
he would have asked for it. And after the trial, the first
phase or the second phase, Mr. Weddington, myself and
Mr. Bixby were at the restaurant. There was a little ex-

change of temper. I guess we all had frayed nerves from the long trial. But I did question at that time exactly what his trial strategy was, and at that time, I was told by Mr. Bixby that I was jealous because he had come up here and taken over my case.

"I did not feel at the time that Mr. Dicks was not getting an adequate trial. I will say, however, that looking back on everything, that if had I to do everything all over again, I would have filed a motion asking that I be allowed to withdraw because of the lack of cooperation between the three attorneys, and because I didn't feel like that circumstance permitted me to contribute whatever I may have had to offer or contribute to the case."

Durham wanted Beeler's problems with how the case was to be handled and his lack of input to be absolutely clear, so he emphasized them, "Are you telling the Court that Chris Livingston made that statement to you and you did not cause a subpoena for him to be issued to come and testify at the Dicks' trial?"

Beeler said emphatically, "I did not cause a subpoena to be issued for the very simple reason that I don't think three attorneys can try a case, that if I am subpoenaing witnesses to appear down there that conflicted with Mr. Bixby's presentation of the case, I felt it would inherently convey to the jury that we were not coordinated and, I felt, hinder the case. In addition, Mr. Bixby had informed us that he would prepare the case and the witnesses he wanted to have there, and the family had told us Mr. Bixby would make the decisions in this case, and prepare it. I could have subpoenaed the witnesses to the trial, and then would have ended up with a disjointed, disconnected presentation of the case which I felt would cause more harm, and I left the preparation and presentation to Mr. Bixby, whom I considered to be lead attorney."

Durham went on, "When you found out Mr. Livingston was not here for the trial, did you attempt to get process issued for him?"

"I talked with Mr. Bixby, and he said his feelings were

Livingston wouldn't be any help to us; he had chosen to leave him out as a witness."

"Now I think you've already testified you heard the testimony of Chris Livingston at the Strouth trial. And you say he told you outside the courthouse that Strouth told him that Jeff froze up on him, and stayed out in the car?"

"He said, 'Jeff froze up on me.' I think the statement was 'I hurt the old man, or I killed the man.' He said 'I.' I thought that was important. What I was looking for was the distinction between I and we. He used the pronoun 'I.' "

"If you had subpoenaed him, it would have been for the purpose of saying or attempting to prove that Strouth was the one who actually cut the man's throat, not to prove that Dicks was outside the store?"

"I would have been wanting to use that by implication that Jeff was outside the store; but I couldn't have had a direct statement that Jeff stayed outside, no."

"And you as an officer of the Court and as an attorney for this defendant, Jeff Dicks, on the day of the trial, did not ask the Court for a continuance in order to obtain these witnesses that you felt would be material in proving his innocence, or mitigating the circumstances regarding his guilt?"

"I did not ask for a continuance, the reason being that at that point in time, it was Mr. Bixby's case, and the preparation and planning . . . that's what I had been told by Jeff and his family. I got a letter from Mr. Bixby on December 22, a copy of a letter sent to Jeff's stepfather, saying he was making arrangements to subpoena all the witnesses that he would be calling from North Carolina, and if he had any names of any other witnesses, please advise him. I don't see how you can present two cases at one time. Mr. Bixby had told me that he would be interviewing all these witnesses in North Carolina and that he would be organizing the case, and . . ." he hesitated, "I did not subpoena any witnesses because he said that he did not feel that Livingston would be helpful to us—told me that during the

trial. And while I might have tried the case differently from
him, we can't try two cases at one time. I did personally
consider a couple of these witnesses that I would have
called. I had trouble with that after it was over, and after
looking back over the record. I will say, looking back, I
would have filed a motion asking to be allowed to withdraw from the case, and in fact, insisting that I be allowed
to withdraw from the case because of the lack of cooperation between the three attorneys, and because I did not feel
like the circumstances permitted me to contribute whatever I may have to offer."

"That's all."

Barry Bixby was called next. Shirley watched him intently. She knew now she had made a mistake in hiring
Bixby, who seemed to care only for money and not proving
Jeff's innocence. Almost immediately Bixby was asked if
there was any indication made by Shirley as to how she
obtained the money she gave him.

"Well, not directly. I just understood that she was involved in an enterprise where she was using somebody's
credit card, and I think it was her grandmother's."

"At the time you got that initial money did you give
Mrs. Dicks any legal advice or any advice as to how she
might obtain more money in order to pay you?"

"Absolutely not, not advice about anything illegal, no,
sir."

Bixby denied that he ever told Shirley Jeff would be
freed after the trial. He also denied that he had warned her
about the warrant for her arrest and advised her to leave
the state. "I know better than to advise a client or the
mother of my client to flee the jurisdiction of the Court," he
said.

Durham said wryly, "Did you, ever tell Mrs. Shirley
Dicks that Jeff would walk out of the courthouse with them
a free man, or get probation and walk out of the courthouse
following the trial?"

"I never guaranteed that. I was optimistic that we
could, but never guaranteed it."

"Did you ever specifically during the course of Jeffrey Dicks' trial warn Shirley Dicks that there was a warrant outstanding for her in the state of North Carolina, and that she would be well advised not to go back there because it would be served on her?"

"No, not in those words."

"What did you advise her of?"

"I advised her that an officer from the U.S. marshall over there was looking for her, but never warned her what to do."

"Did you personally try to locate any witnesses?"

"Yes."

"Did you contact Livingston?"

"Yes. I talked to him on several occasions. He said Shirley said to say that Jeff froze up on him."

"Were you notified of any witnesses from Greenville, South Carolina?"

"No."

"Let me show you Exhibit Number 5, the deposition of Liz Ventura, and the deposition of Larry Fisher. To the best of your knowledge, have you ever seen that statement before?"

"I don't think so. Well, I don't think so. I may have . . . I may have been told about this; but after I checked it out, I decided that was not . . . I don't remember seeing these statements."

"What about G. R. Carlton, were you ever given his name by either Shirley Dicks or her mother and asked to have him present?"

"No."

"Were you ever asked to put on any witnesses relating to Mr. Dicks' employment, working for the Fuller Brush?"

"No."

"Were you ever asked during the course of the trial by Jeffrey Dicks to call his mother to the witness stand?"

"Probably."

"You did not do so?"

"Well, because she just . . . she would not in my

opinion have been a very good witness; and I have participated in many trials, and many different courts, and she, in
my opinion would not have made a good witness. There
were too many things that she would have said . . . that
she could have said either on direct or cross-examination
that I thought would have been damaging. No matter how
much she loved her son, I believe, I mean, I would like to
correct . . . clarify the fact that I think she loves her son
very much; nonetheless, I don't think she would have made
a good witness."

When Bart Durham asked Bixby about the money
Shirley had paid him, he repeatedly said he didn't know
how much, he couldn't remember. He admitted he took a
trailer and some property that belonged to Donald. He also
had taken a deed of trust on property of hers, which she
legally stopped shortly afterwards. Donald and Shirley had
signed many papers in Greenville, South Carolina, and
Bixby had them notarized by his secretary in Asheville,
North Carolina, which was illegal. Under oath Bixby
claimed he didn't know that it was illegal. It was in fact, a
felony.

"Did Shirley Dicks pay you anything on the first
visit?"

"She could have, but I don't think she did. She may
have. I don't . . . I think she didn't pay the money until
sometime later."

"That sometime later, was that some five thousand
dollars?"

"That sounds right."

"And on one occasion, did her mother, pay you two or
three hundred dollars, and then on another occasion four
or five hundred?"

"That sounds right."

"You testified in response to Mr. Wells . . ."

Bixby backtracked, first going in one direction then
another. "I mean, I'm not saying . . . I may be wrong but
it sounds . . ."

Durham was not about to let him wheedle out of the

contradictions in his previous testimony. "I understood your testimony to be, if you didn't answer the question fully, but on occasion she did send you money orders from the state of Florida, or elsewhere?"

"She sent some money orders, maybe one, or two, or three, in that approximate amount."

"All right, and in addition to that, when you got to Greenville, were you given some more money?"

"Possibly, I don't know. I don't remember."

"Now on the house, one of these instruments was executed at the jail while Shirley was locked up, was it not?"

"That's possible because Mr. Creteur signed the two of the instruments."

"And you took them back to Asheville, and had your secretary notarize them back there, and record them, did you not?"

"Yes."

"Donald Creteur or Shirley Creteur signed that instrument, and it was sworn to in the state of North Carolina, and the truth of the fact is, it was done in the state of Tennessee, is that correct?"

"Yes."

"And they were notarized in the state of North Carolina?"

"Yes."

"Barry, as a lawyer, you know that is improper, do you not?"

"Well . . ."

"In fact that is a felony, is it not?"

"No."

"Did you know that Richard Nixon's campaign manager was disbarred for that?"

"No."

Durham shook his head disgustedly. "Now we'll move on. You mentioned the net fee you received, what was the amount?"

"Somewhere between six and ten thousand. I turned

some of the money over to other people like Mr. Rogers, and the psychologist who came down to testify."

"You stated he was paid one or two thousand dollars. The truth of the fact is, he was paid nine hundred dollars, and there is three hundred dollars still owed him. Isn't that correct?"

"He is claiming that."

"Mr. Bixby, is it true that you wrote a letter to the Creteurs in which you told them you were making arrangements at this time to subpoena all the witnesses that were to be coming from North Carolina?"

"Yes."

"Just read that top sentence, and tell us what you meant by that?"

"This is to acknowledge receipt from you in trust the sum of nine hundred dollars for the benefit of the psychological evaluation of Jeff. I am making arrangements at this time to subpoena all the witnesses that we will be calling from North Carolina."

"What witnesses were you making arrangements to subpoena?"

"I was making arrangements to discuss with the witnesses their possible testimony."

After Bixby stepped down, Greely Wells made a statement that he wanted on the record. "Mr. Bixby had said on more than one occasion that the district attorney's office had instructed various witnesses not to talk with him or other defense counsel.

"I would like this record to reflect that I have never made such statements to any witness not in this case, and I certainly do not think that anyone else in the district attorney's office would have made such statements to any witnesses."

Calhoun nodded, "Does either side have anything further?"

Wells said, "Not from the State, Your Honor."

Durham concurred, "Nothing from the defendant."

Calhoun's voice was brisk and formal, "All right. The

defendant should be transported back to the Tennessee
State Prison, and I will expect to decide the matter very
shortly after you file the transcripts. That will be all."

After the hearing Shirley and the rest of Jeff's family
along with Bart Durham went back to the motel until they
could leave the next morning.

"How could they say I tried to get Livingston to
change his testimony," Shirley asked Bart. "After all, he
said that same thing to Mr. Beeler about Jeff freezing up on
Chief. Those aren't my words, they are Chief's. He said
them to Sharon, and she said them at Chief's trial long
before I met Livingston, and then Livingston said the same
thing to Beeler, even before I met him."

"Shirley, I know these things are hard to take," he
rose to leave, but you made a mistake in offering to pay
Livingston for testifying. It doesn't matter about the State
paying their witnesses; you can't do it."

Shirley nodded. "I know that now but I didn't then. I
thought we were supposed to give him the same thing they
did."

Shirley and Nelson sat in silence for a while. Then
Nelson said, "Do you want me to get the newspapers? The
hearing will probably be in them."

"Please," Shirley said. A little while later he came
back and began reading the papers out loud to Teeny and
Shirley.

"The sixth attorney to represent Jeff Dicks charged a
previous attorney was ineffective and asked for a new trial.
Dicks of North Carolina, was convicted and sentenced to
death in 1979 for the slaying of James Keegan. Dicks' new
attorney, Bart Durham of Nashville, Tennessee, based the
new trial motions entirely on allegations that Bixby, as lead
attorney, did not provide adequate counsel.

"Dicks, sporting a beard and about fifty pounds
heavier than four years earlier, sat quietly in the heavily

guarded courtroom. His mother, however, came close to displaying the temper and emotions that led to a contempt charge against her at the start of her son's trial. Shirley Dicks apologized to Calhoun for her previous behavior and threats against the judge and district attorneys. Her son's attorney, however, often had to calm her down during her apology and testimony.

"Allegations against Bixby include that he accepted payments from Mrs. Dicks knowing that the money was obtained in a check writing scheme, and warned her about outstanding warrants against her, guaranteed that Dicks would be found innocent, failed to adequately prepare the case, failed to plan trial strategy with the other attorneys and failed to interview witnesses. Voicing dissatisfaction with Bixby was Dicks, who wanted Beeler to handle the case, and Beeler who said he disagreed with Bixby's approach. Dicks, shackled and handcuffed, was returned to the state penitentiary pending Calhoun's ruling. Judge Calhoun ordered Dicks' mother to be searched upon entering the courthouse because of threats made against him."

"Well, I can see things haven't changed much. I don't see how Jeff can get a fair hearing here," Shirley said despondently. "As for me, I think I handled myself pretty good today. I may have been a little hostile, but nothing like I was at the trial."

The next morning, Shirley, Teeny and Nelson headed to Asheville, where Nelson would fly back to New York. Shirley would drive back to Tennessee and await the verdict.

FIFTEEN

Jeff's request for a new trial was denied. They half expected it, as Bart Durham had told them before the hearing that this hearing was only a first step and because it was before the trial judge. Jeff had a better chance of receiving a new trial at the federal level, but Shirley was terribly disappointed nevertheless. She had hoped against hope that Jeff would be freed.

Meeting with them right afterwards, Bart Durham explained that, "The appeals process for a person on death row is extremely long. After the conviction at the trial, there is what is called an 'automatic appeal' which goes directly to the Supreme Court of the particular state that person was convicted in. If the conviction is affirmed at that level, the case goes to the United States Supreme Court, and they are asked to hear it. If denied there, it comes back to the trial court level again. After that comes the Criminal Court of Appeals and then to the State Supreme Court. If no relief is had there, the case goes to the United States Supreme Court. If no relief is had there, the case goes back down to the Federal District Court on a writ of habeas corpus. If no relief is granted at this level, then the appeals are directed to the circuit court, which for Tennessee is the Sixth Circuit Court in Cincinnati, Ohio. After

263

that the case goes to the United States Supreme Court for a third, and final, time. When all else fails the defense can apply for clemency by the governor in a last attempt to stop the execution. If that is denied, the execution is carried out.

"The appeals process is long and costly. It may take years to get from one of the steps to another and as many as twelve years before all of the steps are carried out. But, Shirley, we are going to get him out, you have to believe that no matter how long it takes."

During the next few years Shirley learned all she could about the death penalty issue, joined organizations that fight against it, got to know the men on Tennessee's death row and helped them in small ways. She tried to get churches involved in donating packages to the men at Christmas, corresponded with those who were lonely, got to know people who make the death penalty issue their life's work, and wrote hundreds of letters to anyone she thought could even remotely help on her son's case.

One reply she received was from Mrs. Lillian Carter, the mother of former President Jimmy Carter, written in April of 1979. She wrote:

"Dear Mrs. Dicks, Although my heart bleeds for you, there is no way I can help you. I am not allowed to interfere with the Justice Department, although my son is the president. I do hope you can get help. Sincerely with regret, Lillian Carter."

One day Teeny called to tell Shirley about a program she had just watched on television. It was called *Lie Test*, and F. Lee Bailey was the host. In the show, he put people on who wanted to prove something and had them take a lie detector test in front of the viewers. Teeny suggested that Shirley write to them. "Perhaps you and Nelson can get on the show. You might be able to answer the questions about the coat or find someone else who saw Jeff in it," Teeny said to Shirley. She knew Shirley was trying everything she could do to prove that there was no blood on the coat. "I think he will let you be on the show if you explain all about the case to him."

"That's a good idea. I'll write to him tonight. But I won't get my hopes up that he'll even answer me."

"Well, don't give up. We have to keep fighting," Teeny said.

Shirley immediately got a letter off, and it wasn't long before she received a reply. They wanted Nelson and her to be the first ones on the show when it resumed in the fall.

During the summer Durham kept filing appeals. Then Shirley got a call from the station telling her the show had been canceled. She was devastated. This had been their chance to tell everyone that they had not been lying, to beg for further witnesses and evidence that Jeff had not participated in the crime. It just seemed that everywhere she turned, doors closed. Yet each time she thought she couldn't go on any longer, she found the strength. Jeff needed her, and that thought alone kept her going.

It was lonely for Shirley and Maria in Tennessee. She missed her family, and it was hard to make new friends at the trailer park they were living in. As soon as people heard about Jeff being on death row, she was quickly avoided. She felt like a leper. Some of the children were not allowed to play with Maria and would taunt her with cruel names. She began to have headaches that would keep her out of school a lot.

Eventually Shirley met and became friends with other people who had a family member on death row. She attended countless meetings throughout the years. Once she went to Washington, joining a group of people who were in favor of abolishing the death penalty. At one gathering, she met Mike Farrell of television's *M*A*S*H* and spoke to him about her son's case. Like many others, he was sympathetic but powerless.

In August of 1984, Teeny and Pop had come to visit them from North Carolina. They made the trip every five or six weeks to see Jeff and be with Shirley and Maria. It was near the end of their visit that Pop complained of his back hurting.

"Are you sure you're all right?" Shirley asked. Her father was lying on the bed watching television and grimacing. She worried it was his heart again. "Is the pain in your chest?"

"I'm all right. Don't worry so much. The pain is in my back anyway, not my heart. What's the matter, afraid I'll die?" He laughed at the expression on Shirley's face, and she felt better just seeing him laugh. Still he was so white.

"Why don't you let me take you to a doctor?" she asked as he began watching television again. He picked up his ice water taking a drink before answering.

"No," he said slowly, "I'll just wait until we go home and see my own doctor." He winced again.

"Do you think I should go over to North Carolina with you tomorrow?" Shirley asked. "It may be something serious. I can take Maria out of school for a few days."

"No. I think he'll be all right," Teeny injected. "I'll call and let you know what happens." Shirley looked over at Teeny and saw the concern on her mother's face. She felt her own tears starting. With all that had happened to them even small things upset her, and this, she was afraid, could be serious.

The next morning Teeny and Ernest left for North Carolina.

"Don't worry, Shirley. I'll let you know what happens right away. Tomorrow I'm going to take your father to the doctor's and have him thoroughly checked over."

"Are you sure I shouldn't go over with you? Maybe it's his heart." Again, Shirley felt her throat tighten up; tears began falling. She hugged her father and he smiled weakly.

"Don't worry. I'm tough. No need of you driving all the way over there just to find out I have some sort of flu bug or something." He smiled and took his daughter's hand. Shirley waved until the car was long gone, a gnawing feeling in the pit of her stomach.

The following morning Teeny called and said Pop was

in the hospital but would be coming home in a few days. She said there was no need for Shirley to come; the doctor felt it was an infection. She said Maria didn't need to be missing school. Shirley hung up, still worried, and told her mother to call if anything else happened.

The next afternoon, when she came home from marketing, Shirley found a note on her front door. Her hand shook as she opened it. The note said her father had taken a turn for the worse and for her to come immediately. When Teeny hadn't been able to reach Shirley by phone, she had called Shirley's next door neighbor, who had come over and left the note.

Quickly Shirley went inside. The color had drained from her face, and she felt a terrible uneasiness come over her.

Just then her brother-in-law came in. She told him about the note. "Don't worry," he said. "Pop will be all right, just take your time driving and get there in one piece. Remember Maria. What would she do if anything were to happen to you?" Shirley could see his worried look and knew he was right, but all she could think of at that moment was her father. She had to get to him.

She left Dick to take care of Maria and ran to her car. She could not stop the tears. "Please, God, don't take my Pop. I love him so much. Don't take him, please!" Shirley prayed over and over.

Five hours later, she pulled up in front of the hospital. She could see her sister, Brenda, leaning against the front door, head in hands. Jumping out Shirley ran to her sister. As she got close she saw Brenda sobbing and knew the news was bad. Brenda hadn't noticed Shirley driving up and looked up startled as her sister reached out to touch her shoulder.

"He's going to live, isn't he?" Shirley cried. "Please tell me Pop is going to live!"

Shirley saw her sister's face crumple. "They don't have much hope for him," Brenda said. Sobbing, Shirley ran inside the hospital.

"Please, where is my father?" Shirley cried to the
blond nurse standing behind the front desk. She saw the
puzzled look on the nurse's face and Shirley knew she
hadn't been making sense.

"I'm sorry," the nurse said. "I don't know who your
father is."

"Mr. Mathews," Shirley cried through hiccups. "My
father is here in the hospital and I have to see him."

"He's behind the doors over there. Just walk in and
you'll find him in one of the cubicles," the nurse said. Shirley could see pity on the nurse's face, and it scared her.

"She knows he's going to die," Shirley thought to herself. Shirley ran through the doors and saw a man lying on
the bed. He was hooked up to a machine. She ran over to
the bed and stared down at the man lying there. It wasn't
her father. She ran to the next room and looked in. There
was Pop lying on the bed, still and white. A hissing sound
came from the machine he was hooked up to. Picking up
his hand Shirley held it tight. His other arm was tied down,
and he kept trying to get at the respirator that was taped to
his mouth. It was evident he didn't want that thing in there.

Shirley couldn't stop crying, and Ernest squeezed her
hand as if to comfort her. He tried to talk to her, but the
respirator made it impossible. She held his hand and listened to the beep, beep of the heart monitor. She felt powerless, just the way she had with Jeff.

"I'll be back in a little while," she whispered to her
father. She had to get out of there. She couldn't bear to
watch him suffer at each breath the machine took for him.
Turning, she ran out and leaned up against the wall in the
corridor. Brenda, who had seen Shirley come out of the
room, walked over and put her arms around Shirley, and
they cried together.

None of them left that day or the next. They took turns
going into their father's room. Pop was getting weaker and
weaker, but still he clung to life. Teeny called David, her
other son who still lived in Concord, New Hampshire. He
said he would come down the next day.

Early the next morning the nurse walked over to where the family was sitting in the chairs. Some were sleeping, some lost in thought. Shirley, who looked up and saw her, knew in that instant the time had come.

"Mrs. Mathews, please come with me," she said to Teeny. Shirley couldn't catch her breath, tears began and she watched helplessly as her mother slowly got out of the chair. She looked over at her daughters, her son, her grandchildren and straightened her shoulders. Then she followed the nurse.

Brenda and Mike got up, walked over to Shirley and put their arms around her. They all began crying.

A doctor walked toward them. Shirley was afraid of what he was going to say. "I'm sorry," he began. Shirley felt her knees begin to buckle. "We've done all we can for him, but his heart is just too badly damaged. I'm surprised that he made it this long."

"No! You have to save him. Don't let my father die, please . . ." Shirley screamed. She couldn't breathe and was crying hysterically by then. "You have to save him, you have to. I can't lose him too."

"I'm really sorry, Shirley. We did all we could. It's in the hands of God now," he paused for a few moments and then he continued. "You may all go in and see him now," he said.

The family gathered around Pop's bed. He was almost unconscious, and Shirley bent down to kiss him. "I love you, Pop," she cried. The tears came tumbling down. Teeny was crying hard, holding on to the hand of her husband of forty-five years.

"Please live, Pop," Shirley begged. "I love you, I love you." Suddenly the monitor went straight. There was no heartbeat. Shirley screamed. The nurses and doctors were applying electric paddles. Nothing helped. He was gone. Shirley ran past the doctor and threw herself down on the bed over Pop. "Please hook him up to the respirator. You have to bring him back," she shouted at the nurse. The nurse just looked at her, not knowing what to say. The rest

of the family stood around the bed crying. Shirley stroked
her father's hair and kissed his cheek one last time.

"Come on, Shirley, we have to go now," Mike said;
tears ran down his face too.

"No! I don't want to go. I want to stay here with Pop."
She hugged Pop close to her body as if willing him to
breathe. His chest was still, but she couldn't believe he was
gone.

The nurse ushered the family out to the waiting room.
Mike helped his mother. They handed her a paper bag with
Ernest's clothes in there.

Teeny looked down, her voice a whisper. "I came here
with a husband, and I'm leaving with this bag of clothes,"
she cried.

Now the once happy family who had suffered through
Jeff's agonizing trial came together to share yet another
sorrow—the death of the father whose love and faith had
sustained them in that crisis. Shirley felt it was more than
she could bear. "Why, God, why are you taking from me
everyone I love?" she asked in utter desolation.

At the funeral everyone wrote notes to Pop, read them
and laid each in the casket. Mike placed his first Bible in
his father's hand. When it was Shirley's turn, her voice was
too hoarse from crying to speak, so she handed the song
she had written to Mike, who read it for her:

"I was not ready. I still recall my daddy, as I watched
him grow old. His hair was silver-grey, and his heart was
purest gold. And now my daddy's gone, but we'll never be
apart. My daddy is a picture that I carry in my heart. I
loved my daddy so as we passed down through the years.
He was always there to help me dry my tears. There were
so many times when I'd do something wrong, but daddy
would forgive me, and then he'd lead me on. I was not
ready, to let my daddy go. I was not ready for I loved him
so. No I can't let go. Daddy, wait for me, and we'll both be

together, for all eternity. All of us were there, as my daddy's time drew near. I could feel his pain, I knew of his fear. But Daddy was so brave, and hoped I could not see. But I knew deep inside, that soon he would be free. Then he smiled at me as he reached out for my hand. I knew he was ready, to see the promised land. Then I bowed my head, held his hand as I prayed. And at that moment, I felt him slip away. Please, Jesus, take me home, a place where I'll be free. Where there's no more sorrow, that's where I want to be. I'm coming to you, Daddy, that's where I want to be. I'm coming to you, Daddy, I see your dear sweet face. So take me home today, to a better, kinder place."

Mike put his arm around his sister and placed her note in the casket with Pop. They stood looking at him. He looked like he was sleeping, so peaceful. Sounds of crying could be heard, and the smell of flowers filtered through. Ma was crying and looked so forlorn. Ernest had been her whole life. For forty-five years they were together, and now he was gone.

Shirley left the next day to go to Tennessee. She wanted to comfort Jeff, who hadn't been allowed to go to the funeral. Jeff had loved her father very deeply, and she knew how difficult not being able to say good-bye must have been for him. They sat and cried together most of their first visit.

For the next couple of months, Shirley seemed to sink further into depression. She knew she would have to snap out of it, for Jeff, for Maria. But it was very difficult. This further loss seemed another proof to Shirley of the injustice of life. Her father had done nothing but good. Now he, like Jeff, had been taken from her. It was another seemingly senseless, tragic event. Only her struggle to save Jeff's life and her family kept her going.

SIXTEEN

"Without question, Tennessee has the worst death row." This statement was made by Dr. Dorothy Lewis during testimony given in a 1984 lawsuit which urged the Department of Corrections to improve conditions there. Dr. Lewis went on to compare Tennessee's death row to cages in a zoo and to Dickens' England.

Outside, Tennessee's death row looks fairly inconspicuous among the rest of the prison complex at the Tennessee State Penitentiary. It is merely a one-story brick building.

Inside this meager structure are four walkways. Three have thirteen one-person cells with walls on three sides and bars on the fourth. No cell faces another. The fourth row contains seven cells, two holding cells and the death chamber where "Old Sparky" stands waiting with open arms.

Each cell contains a man who waits to die. Jeff lives in one of these cells. His cell is two doors away from the electric chair.

The inmates live in cells six-by-eight-feet in size. This minuscule space contains their bed and every item they own and are allowed to have. "Just imagine putting all of your possessions in your bathroom and living in it," one inmate has said when describing his living conditions.

Standing in the middle of the cell with arms outstretched, the hands can touch opposite sides of the wall. Here the men live for twenty-three hours out of each day.

One hour per day they are allowed out in the exercise yard, a small cage for each inmate. Socializing is limited to the time in the exercise area in groups of three and six.

Noise is constant and loud, radios and televisions blaring, each trying to outdo the other. Shouting goes back and forth between the inmates and the guards. There always seem to be many people around, yet each man is lonely.

There is no real processing procedure. Jeff went right from the county jail to his cell on death row. Physical and dental checkups come later, if at all. Personal belongings which are allowed are given back to the inmate three to ten hours after they are thoroughly shaken down.

At one point Jeff needed his teeth fixed, but the dentist decided to pull all of them. During the procedure he accidentally cut Jeff's tongue. Jeff's tongue began to swell, and the day Shirley went to visit, he couldn't talk. His mouth was almost closed shut, and he kept gasping for breath. Shirley had to leave, she was crying and so upset. Zel Morris, another of Shirley's friends, was visiting her husband that day, and when they got outside, she called the warden and told him that Jeff needed to be seen by a doctor quickly before he died.

Jeff was taken up to the prison hospital, where the nurse's aide gave him some aspirin. With his tongue so enlarged, he couldn't swallow anything, much less a pill. The aspirin wouldn't have done any good anyway; he needed penicillin. Later that night, he was rushed to an outside hospital because he couldn't breathe. He almost died.

The cells are icily cold in winter and suffocatingly hot in summer. Small fans are allowed, but they do little to alleviate the oppressive heat. Many new boys who come to the row cannot afford fans, or anything else. Shirley started a ministry, and between the Catholic Church and her own

Seventh Day Adventists was able to give a fan to all who
needed one.

Before the inmates can leave their cell for anything,
such as an occasional visit with family, they are strip
searched. They must strip naked, hand their clothes to the
guard, open their mouths, and turn around with their
hands raised above their heads. Some visitors who are suspected of bringing in contraband are also subject to strip
searches. It depends on the guard who is on duty. Some of
them abuse this procedure and do it just to harass the visi-
tor.

Mail, visits and phone conversations take precedence
over anything else in the inmates' lives. The telephone
comes around twice a day for an hour. That hour telephone
time is to be divided by the number of men living on each
wing. Generally they try to work it out so each man can
talk for an hour once or twice a week.

Many inmates have emotional problems. Always there
is a high degree of stress on death row. The men are troubled by loneliness, fear and almost total powerlessness.
Their prolonged isolation contributes to the pressures.
Their hope mixes with despair as each appeal comes and is
lost. The conditions are prime for insanity.

Jeff spends most of his time listening to cassette tapes
of music. "My music is my last link to the outside," he told
his mother. "Through it I can go back in time and enjoy the
good times over and over." When he isn't listening to his
tapes, he reads a lot.

Shirley has visited many of the inmates on death row;
some who have no family or friends, some whose family
live too far away to come often. Every one of them has only
good things to say about Jeff.

"He has an outstanding personality with a knack for
association with people regardless of sex, religion, or national origin," one inmate told her. "He is one of the few
who can maintain his dignity and self-control in this high-
tension setting."

"I have never met anyone more likeable or easier to

get along with than Jeff. If he has something it belongs to anyone who wants to borrow it from him."

"Whenever someone is in need of any assistance, Jeff would inevitably be the one to come to the rescue," wrote Gary Cone, a death row inmate who had known Jeff for years. "If someone needed shopping done on the streets and he had no family to do it, Jeff volunteered to get his mom to do the errands."

Gary shared a particular story about Jeff's attitude toward others. "One night an inmate started a fire on our walk, and the guards rushed all of us to the enclosed yard in varied states of dress. It was winter and cold, and I only had a shirt and trousers on. I got colder as time dragged on and couldn't stop shivering. Jeff, who had a coat on, offered it to me. If there ever was any truth to the adage of giving the shirt off your back, it applies to Jeff."

During Christmas the inmates are allowed to receive two Christmas packages containing food items. Christmas is the only time of the year that foods are allowed into the prison. Shirley has heard that Jeff divides his gifts among the inmates, giving especially big shares to those who have no one to send them packages.

Shirley started sending in packages to those Jeff told her were not getting anything. She went to churches and asked for donations so that she could send small gifts to inmates who had been forgotten.

She hears people say, "How can you feel sorry for those on death row?" She does and believes it's because she has met so many tragic people. Some of these boys killed during a robbery while high on drugs or alcohol. Others seem to have been railroaded for crimes others committed. All are poor and couldn't afford decent representation. Most of the time it's not the mass murderers or perpetrators in torture rape cases who sit on death row. Too often it's those who can't plea bargain or get a good lawyer.

Families of the death row inmates suffer as much, if not more, than the inmate himself. The pain and suffering of the family is perhaps even worse than that of those related to terminally ill patients. They are humiliated. They are helpless. They are ostracized by members of their community when it's learned that a member of their family has been sentenced to death.

Shirley feels the most tragic thing about the death penalty is that innocent people can be sentenced to death—people who it cannot be officially proved were not guilty of the crimes that sent them to death row. Shirley knows Jeff is one of them. She knows and wishes someone would listen, someone would care.

SEVENTEEN

During the past few years Shirley has searched for Joe Murray, Jeff's father, as well as working for Jeff's release. She thought it was important for Joe to know what had happened to Jeff and hoped that the two would meet. Finally she was able to get in touch with Joe's mother and ask where Joe was now living. His mother said she wouldn't tell her son about Jeff for fear of breaking up his present marriage. He had never told his children or anyone that he had been married before and had two children. He now had four other children and didn't want to be reminded of the past. She did say she would start writing Jeff, as he was her grandson. She wrote for a little while and then stopped.

Shirley can't count the many calls she placed—calls to information in all different states trying to track Joe down.

She appealed to newspapers where she and Joe had lived, and they ran a front page story on Jeff and her. Their pictures appeared on the front page of the paper, and the article told of her search for Joe Murray and gave a factual account of the Keegan murder trial as well. The article brought results. Joe saw it and wrote to Jeff and Tina. It was the first Jeff had heard from his father since he was a small child. But Jeff had no bitterness; he was happy they were finally in touch.

Having seen the same newspaper article, one of Joe's sons by his present wife came to visit with Jeff. Paul Murray and his wife stayed with Shirley when he visited. He looked a lot like Jeff and was so happy to find he had a half brother and sister. Unfortunately, the rest of Jeff's half brothers and sister did not want anything to do with Jeff or Tina.

For a year Joe corresponded with Jeff and Tina, then he said his daughter didn't want him to have anything more to do with his first two children and stopped writing to them. It was then, for the first time, Shirley felt hatred toward her ex-husband. She couldn't understand his cruelty. Paul, on the other hand, continued to visit with Jeff and Tina, so it wasn't all in vain.

From the very beginning Shirley took Maria everywhere with her. Each time she looked at the child's soft brown hair, vivid blue eyes and nose peppered with a sprinkling of freckles, she saw herself and especially Jeff. Maria and her other children have brought Shirley the only happiness she has known in those difficult years. Unfortunately, Maria is frail. She seems to get ill a lot. Always there are colds and strep throats. One day Maria complained of pain in her legs, and in the days that followed Shirley took her to several doctors, but they couldn't find anything wrong. However, the pain became so bad that Maria couldn't walk or even stand up. Shirley was terrified and took the child to the hospital.

They admitted her and after running test after test, they diagnosed Maria as having rheumatoid arthritis. Finally, Maria came home and was in a wheelchair for six months. She had severe, unremitting pain that no medicine seemed to alleviate. It was a hard six months for them all. Every week Maria had to have her blood tested so the doctors could adjust the huge amounts of aspirins and other drugs they gave her for the arthritis. The doctors told Shirley that Maria would always have the disease; it might go into remission, but it would cripple her eventually. Shirley was crushed, but for Maria and the other children's sake, she tried to act optimistic. Inside though, she was devastated at this new blow. During this period Maria was taught at home by a home bound teacher.

On Sunday of each week, Shirley took Maria in her wheelchair to the prison to visit with her father. The visits seemed to comfort them both. Finally, Maria's disease went into remission.

Several months later, however, a new problem surfaced. Maria began having pain in her stomach and again Shirley found herself at doctors' offices and the hospital. They found Maria had an ulcer because of the amount of aspirin she had taken and prescribed a new regime of medicine for her. It was a difficult existence for a child, but Maria kept her spirits up and tried to be brave even though she again was in pain.

Maria knows everything about Jeff. She knows the true story behind the crime that sent him to prison. She even knows that the State wants to kill him. Maria has seen pictures of Chief and knows who he is. She knows that this man could save her daddy if he only told the truth, and she cannot help asking, "Why does he keep lying?"

Despite all this, at thirteen Maria is a lovely, loving girl who has been Shirley and Jeff's only bright spot through the years, but sometimes even her high spirits falter.

Some days as they leave the prison, Maria will start crying. When Shirley asks her why she says, "Why do they want to kill my daddy? I know he could never hurt no one. Will he come home to us one day?" Shirley chokes back her own tears as she tries to answer Maria and tells her that they have to trust that God will save him.

Shirley has returned to her religion. She and Maria were both baptized at the Seventh Day Adventist Church in town. For eight years Shirley had blamed God for their problems, then she took a long look at herself and decided they needed God in their lives. She took Maria to church and realized that God didn't make the decisions which destroyed Jeff's life, human beings did.

Because of this realization, Shirley decided she had to

do something to change the system. Shirley's initial reaction to her son's conviction was outrage and incredulity. "I couldn't believe that this could happen in the United States." But as she began researching the death penalty she found that her son's predicament was by no means atypical of our justice system. "Many innocent people who are poor have been tried, convicted and sentenced to death, not because they have committed a crime but because they cannot afford a competent defense. Like Jeff, they are the losers in an arbitrary lottery in which only the rich have the right numbers. You won't," she says, "find a wealthy person on death row. A system like this does not enhance respect for human life; it cheapens and degrades it."

After learning more about the justice system and the plight of many innocent people convicted of crimes, Shirley decided to write and inform the public about the injustices that the poor are subjected to. Her first book, called *Death Row*, was published in January of 1990. Her second, *Congregation of the Condemned*, was released in 1991.

In addition, Shirley has joined the Death Penalty Resistance Project in Tennessee and has become an avid spokesperson against the death penalty.

Still, the major cause for which she fights is the overturn of Jeff's conviction. Over the years Shirley has written to some famous attorneys in hopes that they could help Jeff. Shirley believes if just one of them would read his trial transcript, he would be convinced of Jeff's innocence and might be able to find where mistakes were made in Jeff's bungled defense. But most have never answered. The ones who did said they couldn't take a charity case. Never giving up, Shirley has done all she can to prove Jeff innocent. Now she's put his fate in the hands of God.

Jeff has only one last appeal left. Time is running out.